The Social and Political Potential of Cash Transfers

T0331437

Cash Transfers, for all their notable successes, have been criticised for their limited ability to move poor households to provide sustainable routes out of poverty. This book draws on original qualitative research by leading scholars and development policy experts from a range of disciplines to examine whether cash transfers can have transformative spillover effects on individuals, households and communities. With chapters on Psycho-Social Wellbeing, Social Accountability and Social Capital, this book casts new light on the ongoing debates over the significance of the Cash Transfer 'revolution'.

This book was originally published as a special issue of *The Journal of Development Studies*.

Maxine Molyneux is Professor of Sociology at University College London, UK.

Nicola Jones is a political scientist and Principal Research Fellow at the Overseas Development Institute, UK, where she also directs the Gender and Adolescence: Global Evidence (GAGE) programme.

Fiona Samuels is a social anthropologist and Senior Research Fellow in the Social Development Programme at the Overseas Development Institute, UK.

The Social and Political Potential of Cash Transfers

Edited by
Maxine Molyneux

With
Nicola Jones and Fiona Samuels

Routledge
Taylor & Francis Group

LONDON AND NEW YORK

First published 2017 by Routledge

2 Park Square, Milton Park, Abingdon, Oxfordshire OX14 4RN
52 Vanderbilt Avenue, New York, NY 10017

Routledge is an imprint of the Taylor & Francis Group, an informa business

First issued in paperback 2018

British Library Cataloguing in Publication Data
A catalogue record for this book is available from the British Library

ISBN 13: 978-0-415-41508-8 (hbk)
ISBN 13: 978-0-367-14253-7 (pbk)

Typeset in Times New Roman
by RefineCatch Limited, Bungay, Suffolk

Publisher's Note
The publisher accepts responsibility for any inconsistencies that may have
arisen during the conversion of this book from journal articles to book chapters,
namely the possible inclusion of journal terminology.

Disclaimer
Every effort has been made to contact copyright holders for their permission to
reprint material in this book. The publishers would be grateful to hear from any
copyright holder who is not here acknowledged and will undertake to rectify
any errors or omissions in future editions of this book.

Contents

Citation Information

The chapters in this book were originally published in *The Journal of Development Studies*, volume 52, issue 8 (August 2016). When citing this material, please use the original page numbering for each article, as follows:

Chapter 1
Can Cash Transfer Programmes Have 'Transformative' Effects?
Maxine Molyneux, with Nicola Jones & Fiona Samuels
The Journal of Development Studies, volume 52, issue 8 (August 2016), pp. 1087–1098

Chapter 2
'Being Able to Breathe Again': The Effects of Cash Transfer Programmes on Psychosocial Wellbeing
Fiona Samuels & Maria Stavropoulou
The Journal of Development Studies, volume 52, issue 8 (August 2016), pp. 1099–1114

Chapter 3
Can Social Protection Affect Psychosocial Wellbeing and Why Does This Matter? Lessons from Cash Transfers in Sub-Saharan Africa
Ramlatu Attah, Valentina Barca, Andrew Kardan, Ian MacAuslan, Fred Merttens & Luca Pellerano
The Journal of Development Studies, volume 52, issue 8 (August 2016), pp. 1115–1131

Chapter 4
Accessing the 'Right' Kinds of Material and Symbolic Capital: the Role of Cash Transfers in Reducing Adolescent School Absence and Risky Behaviour in South Africa
Michelle Adato, Stephen Devereux & Rachel Sabates-Wheeler
The Journal of Development Studies, volume 52, issue 8 (August 2016), pp. 1132–1146

Chapter 5
Effects of Cash Transfers on Community Interactions: Emerging Evidence
Sara Pavanello, Carol Watson, W. Onyango-Ouma & Paul Bukuluki
The Journal of Development Studies, volume 52, issue 8 (August 2016), pp. 1147–1161

Chapter 6
From Social Accountability to a New Social Contract? The Role of NGOs in Protecting and Empowering PLHIV in Uganda
Badru Bukenya
The Journal of Development Studies, volume 52, issue 8 (August 2016), pp. 1162–1176

CITATION INFORMATION

Chapter 7

Programming for Citizenship: The Conditional Cash Transfer Programme in El Salvador
Michelle Adato, Oscar Morales Barahona & Terence Roopnaraine
The Journal of Development Studies, volume 52, issue 8 (August 2016), pp. 1177–1191

Chapter 8

Pathways to Citizen Accountability: Brazil's Bolsa Família
Natasha Borges Sugiyama
The Journal of Development Studies, volume 52, issue 8 (August 2016), pp. 1192–1206

Chapter 9

Transforming Cash Transfers: Citizens' Perspectives on the Politics of Programme Implementation
Nicola Jones, Bassam Abu-Hamad, Paola Pereznieto & Kerry Sylvester
The Journal of Development Studies, volume 52, issue 8 (August 2016), pp. 1207–1224

Chapter 10

Understanding Social Accountability: Politics, Power and Building New Social Contracts
Sam Hickey & Sophie King
The Journal of Development Studies, volume 52, issue 8 (August 2016), pp. 1225–1240

For any permission-related enquiries please visit:
http://www.tandfonline.com/page/help/permissions

Notes on Contributors

Bassam Abu-Hamad is an Associate Professor based at the Department of Public Health, Al Quds University, Gaza City, State of Palestine.

Michelle Adato is the Senior Operations Advisor for Gender and Social Inclusion and Sector Operations at the Millennium Challenge Corporation in Washington DC, USA. At the time the research was conducted, she was a Senior Research Fellow in the Poverty, Health and Nutrition Division of the International Food Policy Research Institute in Washington, DC, USA.

Ramlatu Attah is a consultant in the Poverty and Social Protection portfolio, OPM (Oxford Policy Management Ltd, Oxford, UK).

Oscar Morales Barahona is Professor of Economics at Universidad Centroamericana José Simeón Cañas (UCA), San Salvador, El Salvador. At the time the research was conducted, he was part of the staff of Fundación Salvadoreña para el Desarrollo Económico y Social (FUSADES).

Valentina Barca is a consultant in the Poverty and Social Protection portfolio, OPM (Oxford Policy Management Ltd, Oxford, UK).

Badru Bukenya is a Lecturer in the School of Social Sciences, Makerere University, Kampala, Uganda.

Paul Bukuluki is a Lecturer and Researcher at the Department of Social Work and Social Administration, Makerere University, Kampala, Uganda.

Stephen Devereux is a Research Fellow at the Centre for Social Protection, Institute for Development Studies, Brighton, UK.

Sam Hickey is Professor of Politics and Development at the School of Environment, Education and Development, University of Manchester, Manchester, UK.

Nicola Jones is a political scientist and Principal Research Fellow at the Overseas Development Institute, UK, where she also directs the Gender and Adolescence: Global Evidence (GAGE) programme.

Andrew Kardan is a senior consultant within the Social Policy Programme at OPM (Oxford Policy Management Ltd, Oxford, UK).

Sophie King is a Research Fellow for the Realising Just Cities Programme at the Urban Institute at the University of Sheffield, Sheffield, UK.

Ian MacAuslan leads the OPM (Oxford Policy Management Ltd, Oxford, UK) global education portfolio, based in New Delhi and working across Central Asia, South Asia and sub-Saharan Africa.

Fred Merttens is a senior consultant at OPM (Oxford Policy Management Ltd, Oxford, UK) who works on the economics and politics of social policy sectors such as health, education and social protection.

Maxine Molyneux is Professor of Sociology at University College London, UK.

W. Onyango-Ouma is an Associate Professor at the Institute of Anthropology, Gender and African Studies, University of Nairobi, Nairobi, Kenya.

Sara Pavanello is an independent Researcher, based in Malaga, Spain.

Luca Pellerano is the Chief Technical Advisor on Social Security at International Labour Organization.

Paola Pereznieto is an independent consultant based in Mexico City, Mexico.

Terence Roopnaraine is a senior consultant in Social Development at OPM (Oxford Policy Management, Oxford, UK).

Rachel Sabates-Wheeler is a Professorial Research Fellow, at the Institute of Development Studies, University of Sussex, UK.

Fiona Samuels is a social anthropologist and Senior Research Fellow in the Social Development Programme at the Overseas Development Institute, UK.

Maria Stavropoulou is an independent scholar, based in London, UK.

Natasha Borges Sugiyama is an Associate Professor at the Department of Political Science, University of Wisconsin-Milwaukee, USA.

Kerry Sylvester is based at the Associação de Nutrição e Segurança Alimentar, Maputo, Mozambique.

Carol Watson is an independent Researcher, based in Nice, France.

Can Cash Transfer Programmes Have 'Transformative' Effects?

MAXINE MOLYNEUX*, WITH NICOLA JONES** & FIONA SAMUELS**

*UCL Institute of the Americas, London, UK, **Overseas Development Institute (ODI), London, UK

ABSTRACT   *Cash transfers (CTs), for all their evident success in relieving poverty, have been criticised for failing to incorporate transformative elements into their programme design. In recent years changes have been introduced into the design of CT programmes that go some way towards addressing this concern. This article critically engages the meaning of transformative social protection and introduces a collection of papers that examine whether and under what conditions cash transfers can be 'transformative'. Among the issues addressed are whether CTs can be catalysts leading to positive changes, material, subjective and relational in the lives of poor people; what are the social effects of CTs for beneficiaries, their households and communities; and can they foster horizontal relationships within communities and vertical relationship with the state through developing forms of social accountability and citizenship engagement?*

Introduction

With the eradication of extreme poverty as a priority Millennium Development Goal, cash transfer programmes (CTPs) spread rapidly across the world to reach more than 750 million people in low and middle-income countries in the global south by 2010 (Arnold, Conway, & Greenslade, 2011). As new programmes multiplied, older ones expanded their coverage to reach significant numbers of targeted populations in the lowest decile. Driving the expansion of CTs was their widely acclaimed record of positive results. Evidence from across the world confirmed that well targeted, well designed social transfer programmes were an effective and affordable instrument for reducing the incidence and intensity of household poverty with measureable improvements in child health and educational attendance (Arnold et al., 2011; Cecchini & Madariaga, 2011; Fiszbein et al., 2009; Soares, Soares, Medeiros, & Guerreiro Osório, 2006). One commentator, echoing a commonly expressed view, went as far as to state that they were 'as close as you can come to a magic bullet in development'.[1]

Cash transfers, however, had their critics.[2] Some focused on the various implementation shortcomings, including inaccurate targeting and leakage, and poor quality and clientelist and/or corrupt service provision. While these issues could be overcome with closer attention to CT programme management, other critics went further in questioning the underlying rationale of CT programmes and doubted whether cash transfers were as effective as claimed in tackling poverty. The small size of the transfers, and the lack of linkages to training and livelihood skills for adult household members represented little advance on the minimal safety net or 'risk management' approaches to poverty relief[3] associated with earlier World Bank policies (Holzmann and Jörgensen, 2000; Slater, 2011).

These latter criticisms of the cash transfer model were accompanied by calls for more far-reaching or 'transformative' social protection interventions that would bring about positive, lasting changes in the lives of poor and destitute people. This would involve measures designed to help people move out

1

of poverty by providing training and income generation schemes, and designing programmes that addressed the contextual specificity and multi-dimensional nature of poverty and vulnerability. In other words, a key aspect of any transformative programme, would be the measures it took to tackle the causes of poverty. For some authors this also necessarily involved empowering the poor to tackle oppressive social relations, and treating poor people as citizens with rights, with a voice in programme design and implementation (Devereux & Sabates-Wheeler, 2004; Kabeer, 1999; Koehler, 2011; Molyneux, 2006; Morgan & Yablonski, 2011; Sen, 1999; Slater & Farrington, 2006; Stewart, 2002).

Recent years have brought changes in the design of CT programmes that go some way towards meeting the above criticisms. Centralised data management systems pioneered in Latin America for example, have done much to reduce corruption and improve the inclusivity and reach of programmes (Cecchini & Madariaga, 2011). In addition, despite initial resistance on the part of donors and governments to expanding the objectives of CTs beyond income support, some of the ideas associated with transformative social protection programming appear to have entered the mainstream of international development policy planning. Discussion over the post-2015 development goals has seen repeated calls for a transformative and sustainable development agenda that brings 'tangible results in fighting poverty',[4] while the World Bank and donor governments have responded by supporting changes in the objectives and design of social protection programmes. At the same time, no longer content to rely only on quantitative indicators of anti-poverty programme successes, there has been increased interest in the on-the-ground findings of qualitative research in order to assess the social impacts of CTs and to increase their effectiveness by making them more closely attuned to local conditions (Adato, Roopnaraine, & Becker, 2011; Holmes & Jones, 2013).

This special issue of JDS considers the conditions under which cash transfers can have transformative effects – whether as the result of deliberate policy design or as spill over effects. Among the issues addressed are whether CTs are associated with positive social consequences for beneficiaries, their households and communities, and if so what are these, and how meaningful and how sustainable might they be? And in what ways can CTs contribute to broader goals of transparency and accountability and enhance citizenship awareness? In other words, can CTPs be catalysts leading to positive changes, material, subjective and relational, in the lives of poor people, and can they foster horizontal relationships within communities and vertical relationships with the state?

Much depends of course on what is meant by the term 'transformative'. Like its cognate 'empowerment', the term transformative has joined the lexicon of current development policy without any consensus over how to define it. This fuzziness may account for its ubiquity, with 'transformative' appearing in different guises in scholarly journals and in 'theories of change' manuals that require development practitioners to forecast what the pathways towards specified transformational goals will be. 'Transformative' despite its analytic hazards, has become the idiom of choice to distinguish between different orders of policy intervention, between those which are deemed to lack a positive change dynamic and leave basic conditions much as before; and those which introduce changes that are expected to result in positive effects because they tackle some of the factors that prevent change.[5]

In terms of social protection the common distinction between transformative and non-transformative interventions can be summed up as between those providing palliative measures that smooth over the effects of poverty (for example simple cash transfers or food aid programmes); and those that aim to enhance the potential of poor people to move out of poverty (for example by investing in their capabilities, changing their behaviour, and helping them to overcome disabling/oppressive social relations). Whether the expected changes occur, and if they do, whether they are the result of these programmes, and whether they have lasting effects, are dependent on analytic assumptions, but they are also empirical questions on which only longitudinal data would be able to settle.[6] In the meantime, a body of research is emerging which has begun to cast some tentative light on how change dynamics might occur and in what measure.

Innovations in CT Design

As CT programmes have evolved over time there have been some positive changes to their design. Some are explicit in aiming to go beyond the basic safety net approach and have begun to incorporate elements aiming to develop beneficiaries' skills and knowledge through training and awareness-raising.[7] More attention too has been paid to treating the causes of poverty and vulnerability as multidimensional which has led in some cases to more gender-aware programming (Barrientos, Gideon, & Molyneux, 2008; Holmes & Jones, 2013). Latin America's cash transfers were the first to include human development conditionalities that required children to attend school and health checks. These (or the simple fact of having the cash) have resulted in improvements in children's nutritional levels and child attendance at school and health clinics (Fiszbein et al., 2009), although success in meeting their objectives can be undermined by poor quality schooling and health provision (Morley & Coady, 2003; Reiners, Da Silva, & Trevino, 2005), while fulfilling the conditionalities has imposed sometimes onerous burdens on the beneficiary mothers (Benderly, 2011; Gammage, 2011; Molyneux, 2006). However in some initiatives, such as Mexico's Prospera (formerly Oportunidades), beneficiaries are offered employment training and income-generating opportunities, as well as being provided with subsidised childcare through the *Estancias* subsidised crèche scheme (Holmes & Jones, 2013). Similar complementary services exist in Brazil's Bolsa Familia programme (Fultz & Francis, 2013).

Participation and Citizenship in Social Protection

A different order of innovation in CT programme design involves measures that promote beneficiary rights, citizenship and participation. While the first generation of CTs were, as some saw it, merely managing poverty or even depoliticising the condition of poverty, the more recent programmes have increasingly also been designed to 'empower' poor people by promoting citizen voice and participation through social accountability and social audits.

In contrast to other areas of development practice (such as environmental management and rural development projects) social protection programmes were slow to include participatory elements of any kind. However, the last decade has seen a growing momentum in the inclusion of participatory processes in social protection programmes. This has been in large part spurred by pressures to make their administration more efficient as programmes designed for the poor have often been prone to poor delivery and corruption, with service personnel overloaded, poorly trained, underpaid and lacking in motivation because of the limits placed on their own capacities to bring about system change (Pellissery, 2010; Rose-Ackerman, 2005; Shah & Schacter, 2004). Social accountability as an idea and set of practices involving the direct participation of beneficiaries and stakeholders was first officially endorsed for social protection programmes in the 2004 World Development Report, *Making Services Work for Poor People* (World Bank, 2004). This identified the lack of accountability mechanisms as the primary cause of service delivery failures. Noting that the 'long route' to accountability through public officials and elections did not serve the poor, it advocated 'shorter routes' or 'chains of accountability' to be put in place at meso and micro levels, enabling direct accountability between users and providers. By increasing stakeholders voice, and introducing principles of transparency, communities could not only regularly monitor service provision but were also entitled to expect responses to suggestions, complaints and abuses.

CTs have recently begun to include social accountability elements and some of these align with the 'transformation' agenda. In addition to tackling oppressive social relations and forms of exclusion, mechanisms designed to promote voice, rights and justice values are being embedded in programming. In giving more voice to programme beneficiaries, and more rights to participate, claim and complain, a change dynamic is incorporated into CT programme design which some argue may empower the poor and foster collective identity and action (Corbridge, Williams, Srivastava, & Veron, 2005).

At the most basic level, social accountability involves establishing grievance channels and creating greater transparency in programme management; but it also extends to using techniques of community or participatory monitoring and evaluation (PM&E), along with newer tools such as community scorecards. When these work well they serve to gain valuable feedback from beneficiaries and other stakeholders about the quality and regularity of service delivery. Such mechanisms have been shown to have a number of benefits beyond increasing programme efficiency, from strengthening social capital to creating some of the embryonic forms of citizenship that can emerge when recipients of welfare begin not only to 'see the state' (Corbridge et al., 2005) but also engage with it and challenge it where it falls short of expectations (Hickey and King, this issue; Ringold, Holla, Koziol, & Srinivasan, 2012). Beyond project and programme levels, however, more institutionalised forms of social accountability that are linked to citizen and social rights are also being established in a number of countries for example in Brazil (Borges Sugiyama, this issue) and in large scale social audit processes such as India's Mahatma Gandhi National Rural Employment Guarantee scheme (MGNREGA).

While these forms of social accountability draw on decades of development theory and practice that has advocated incorporating participation and voice into programming, they differ in one important respect: by promoting civic engagement and citizenship, social accountability approaches mark a shift in development thinking from seeing participatory practices as confined to local project level activities towards viewing them as a key element of the processes deployed by organisations, agencies, and governments to ensure responsiveness to citizens' concerns. These initiatives resonate with civil society demands for greater accountability and good governance that have been highlighted in debates around the future of the post-2015 Sustainable Development Goals (United Nations Development Programme, 2013).

The articles that make up this Special Issue address the theme of transformative social protection by exploring some of the ways in which CTPs have introduced change dynamics into the low-income communities that they serve. They are divided into sections corresponding to three socio-spatial levels or scales with several articles also highlighting linkages across them. The articles grouped in Part 1 deal with the micro-level subjective changes that are reported by programme beneficiaries to have occurred as a result of receiving the transfer. The second part of the Special Issue examines those changes that can occur at meso or community level either as a result of programme activities or as effects of the dynamics between programme participants and implementers. The final section, Part 3, is concerned with exploring social accountability measures that have implications for citizenship and citizen action at macro or governance levels. Together they span a range of disciplinary perspectives, and present new research from diverse country contexts in Africa, Latin America and the Middle East, including the findings from a five-country DFID-funded qualitative research study on unconditional cash transfers in fragile or post-conflict environments.[8] In what follows, a brief context and introduction to the articles in each section is provided.

Part 1: Micro-Level Subjective Transformations

What are here referred to as the 'micro-level' effects of CTPs concern the individual experiences and subjective changes that appear to follow from participation in cash transfer programmes. With a few notable exceptions (Adato, 2000, this issue; Gonzalez De La Rocha, 2006) much of the evidence of CTPs' social effects draws on the more easily quantified data on their physical benefits. However, in response to a growing literature on the importance of subjective and relational dimensions of human wellbeing (Ferguson, 2015; MacAuslan & Riemenschneider, 2011; Pouw & McGregor, 2014; White, Gaines, & Jha, 2013), analysts have begun to examine the psychosocial effects of cash transfers. These include improvements in individuals' feelings of dignity, respect, self-confidence and self-esteem; and reductions in feelings of shame and hopelessness, and relief from worry and stress. Some studies have also drawn on quantitative datasets that include measures of mental health (Baird, De Hoop, & Özler, 2011; Haushofer & Shapiro, 2013); however these tend to rely on a narrow range of indicators and do not adequately capture the complexity of psychosocial wellbeing.

The articles in the first section of the Special Issue find that CTPs have largely positive outcomes including enhanced self esteem at the individual level, as well as enabling greater participation in social interaction. However in some cases there can be negative side effects of being part of the programme such as feelings of humiliation, stigma and shame due to reliance on the transfer for support. The article by Samuels and Stavropoulou discusses findings from the Transforming Cash Transfers project in sub-Saharan Africa and the Middle East; that by Attah et al. draws on evaluations of CTPs in east, west and southern Africa, while Adato et al. focus on a South African case study. There is evidence in all three articles of the effects of cash transfer programmes on psychosocial health and behaviour. Both Attah et al. and Samuels and Stavropoulou look at how psychosocial wellbeing affects both individuals and their relation to others. Attah et al. present findings from a mixed method evaluation of a cash transfer in Kenya, and from cross-country qualitative research from Ghana, Zimbabwe and Lesotho. They pay particular attention to the intrinsic and instrumental dimensions of psychosocial wellbeing showing that cash transfers can have positive impacts on psychosocial well-being leading to further positive impacts on educational performance, participation in social life and empowerment for decision-making.

Samuels and Stavropoulou draw on sociological frameworks to highlight the limits of a one-sized fits all approach to understanding psychosocial wellbeing arguing that each vulnerable group is targeted by different social protection programmes and is likely to face different types of psychosocial stressors. Older people for example may find social isolation the main problem whereas for young people the mismatch between future aspirations and available opportunities may lie at the root of their psychosocial ill-being. Similarly, different vulnerable groups may have access to different sorts of coping strategies, depending on their immediate and broader contexts. This makes it necessary to take into account not only the specific psychosocial vulnerabilities of different vulnerable groups, but also the contexts in which they find themselves, and the range of formal and informal coping strategies that may be available to them.

Adato et al. examine the extent to which the Child Support Grant (CSG) in South Africa responds to the material and symbolic needs of adolescents, and particularly its effects on school participation and involvement in risky behaviours. Cash transfers are typically seen to promote change through the economic benefits they confer but Adato et al. argue that this theory of change fails to account for the complexity of poor people's lives. They examine hidden behavioural drivers such as shame to account for expenditure preferences and higher drop out rates from school. Drawing on Bourdieu's (1986) conceptualisation of 'capitals' they identify three levels of need: basic subsistence, basic symbolic and consumptive symbolic, arguing that the CSG contributes most in the first sense, moderately in the second, and very little in the third. Therefore, like Samuels and Stavropoulous, Adato et al. emphasise that CTs should not be expected to address all developmental vulnerabilities, and in fact it may be necessary to look at different types of complementary interventions that can more effectively address drivers of psychosocial ill-being, such as shame and loss of dignity.

Part 2: Community Impacts: Social Capital and Social Inclusion Effects

A critical component of wellbeing, even survival, is its relational dimension, that is, the way in which individuals relate to others both in their immediate (for example family/household) and broader (for example community/neighbourhood) environs. As Ferguson has expressed it: 'cash in the pocket [...] is related [...] to multiple socialities and mutualities that are all (quite literally) a matter of life and death' (Ferguson, 2015, p. 137). The second section of the Special Issue focuses on the meso-level community effects of CTs. CT programmes can enhance participants' social capital and social inclusion as is found in Adato et al.'s article on El Salvador, Bukenya's on Uganda and Pavanello et al.'s article on the social capital effects of CTs in post-conflict settings. As these authors emphasise, any effects that occur at the meso-level will be shaped to some degree by the nature of the communities concerned, and how they are governed, whether for example, by village elders whose authority is sanctioned by appeals to customs and norms, or those in which the decentralisation of power and resources has been brought about by legislative processes effected through local government and administrative institutions.

Social transfers can provide vulnerable and stigmatised groups with the means to become participants in their communities through, for example, being able to engage in relations of reciprocity. Pavanello et al.'s article, drawing on concepts of social cohesion and social inclusion, shows that even small amounts of regular cash can allow participation in traditional and family ceremonies (for example marriage, birthdays, funerals) by enabling the purchase of gifts, clothing or even soap to improve hygiene practices that are necessary for taking part in community/family events.

However, bonding social capital, (Putnam, 2000) the horizontal linkages that can exist between community members, does not always result from cash transfer programmes. In a number of contexts recipients of transfers report experiencing stigma or are the object of envious gossip by non-beneficiary neighbours who feel entitled to transfers and other benefits that the programme may confer, but do not qualify (MacAuslan & Riemenschneider, 2011; White & Ellison, 2006). Even so, such concerns about unfairness do not always arise: Pavanello et al. find in their review of five cash transfer programmes in Africa and the Middle East, that grants targeted to children and the elderly seem quite uncontentious as these groups are seen as the deserving poor. They note, however, that accusations of unfairness arise where there is little understanding of the rationale of the programme and where inclusion errors are also high. This supports findings elsewhere and underscores the need for CT programmes to ensure that the principles of targeting are adequately publicised and that there are mechanisms in place to allow abuses to be effectively dealt with (Arnold et al., 2011; Ringold et al., 2012).

The extent to which any re-entry into society by previously excluded groups is transformative or merely palliative depends on the degree to which individuals gain some capacity to tackle the social relations that produce or reinforce their vulnerability and exclusion. Pavanello et al. argue that this may result from an increase in confidence and dignity or from gaining access to other services, rights and forms of collective endeavour. By and large, however, their findings indicate that there is less evidence of bridging social capital, as vertical linkages between citizens and authorities remained weak or non-existent.

Bukenya's study of the Ugandan *Aids Support Organisation (TASO)*, an NGO-led social assistance package targeted at HIV-positive communities highlights the significant role of outside actors in fostering the confidence of beneficiaries and helping to develop vulnerable groups' collective capacity for agency. Bukenya documents the aggregate outcomes of what Hossain (2009) calls 'rude account-ability' or informal contentious actions. When twinned with a complementary emphasis on empower-ing excluded and stigmatised individuals to speak out against poor service provision, programme participation did help to promote a collective dynamic. Moreover, part of the TASO approach was to reorient HIV-affected communities towards accessing – and thereby increasing demand for – public health services rather than focusing solely on the provision of alternative private sector services. Bukenya concludes that NGO-led social assistance is not necessarily depoliticising as some have maintained, especially if it is proactively mediated through a set of interventions, including awareness-raising and confidence-building initiatives. Programme participants can be encouraged to engage in citizenship practices and demand-making and can effect positive changes in service delivery, some-times reaching beyond community level to local government.

Adato et al.'s research on El Salvador's Red Solidaria CT programme reports on an unusual case of 'citizen promotion' through a social protection programme. Using data from two rounds of fieldwork in El Salvador, Adato et al. are able to capture what can happen in a CT programme when there is an increase in political commitment to citizenship agendas as part of a broader poverty reduction strategy. This occurred during a particular political moment in El Salvador that favoured rights and citizenship promotion following the new left Farabundo Martí para la Liberación Nacional (FMLN) government's election in 2009. Participation increased in community committees and NGOs were given an important role in promoting linkages between CT beneficiaries and municipal committees. Nevertheless, the authors conclude that even with a long history of civic organisation and strong government backing, community-level programme committees struggled to convert greater opportunities for beneficiary voices into wider citizen engagement with political authorities. As such, due to the committees' limited capacities and lack of formal authority with respect to programme management, broader transforma-tions in state-citizen relations were not realised.

Part 3: Governance, Citizenship and Social Accountability

The articles in the third section of the Special Issue explore the conditions under which CT programmes can have a transformative effect on state-citizen relations and the social contract. While the earlier generation of CT programmes arguably focused primarily on individuals and households, thus limiting the potential for broader spill over effects on state-citizen relations, CT programmes have increasingly adopted a range of social accountability and citizen engagement mechanisms, repositioning participants as active citizens rather than as passive beneficiaries of these interventions. Such initiatives range from light-touch mechanisms to more high-intensity approaches. The lighter-touch end of the spectrum includes information provision to citizens and the establishment of grievance mechanisms, while those at the other end of the spectrum encourage more sustained engagement between citizens and service providers, for example through social audits, participatory monitoring, and community score cards.

The core principles of social accountability are those of good governance, and as Malena, Forster, and Singh (2004) have noted, social accountability is seen as having potentially four positive effects – strengthening policy effectiveness, improving the quality of governance, empowering poor people within the policy process and ensuring government responsiveness.[9] But how far are these optimistic expectations of CTs realised? Do the new social accountability mechanisms contribute to the process whereby poor people acquire the resources, financial, subjective and social, to engage more fully in their communities and societies? Does this in turn enable them to acquire more voice and self-confidence to participate in the practices of citizenship and render policies and governments more responsive to their needs? Or are these new developments just 'old wine in new bottles' and doomed to fail?[10]

Natasha Borges Sugiyama examines these issues at the subnational level in north-east Brazil among participants in the Bolsa Família CT programme. The Brazilian Constitution of 1988 established a statutory obligation to create mechanisms of citizen accountability, and social protection programme participants have representation on people's municipal level councils or *Conselhos*. Focusing on the ways in which built-in institutional guarantees for democratic representation operate at the local level, Borges Sugiyama examines whether citizen-driven bottom-up demands or state-managed administrative mechanisms have been more effective in promoting accountability in the Bolsa Família programme. Bolsa Família has incorporated a number of social accountability mechanisms in addition to the *Conselhos* that are responsible for regular monitoring and evaluation. These include measures designed to promote good management practices, fiscal transparency mechanisms and seemingly robust complaints procedures. Crucially, Brazil also has a civic culture that has, over 20 years, developed both the institutions and experience of participatory governance. Citizens, including the poorest, are aware that they can make political demands and that they have a right to hold power-holders to account.

Borges Sugiyama finds, however, that while participatory spaces exist, community level engagement is hampered both by a lack of *appropriate* institutional arenas in which Bolsa Família beneficiaries are represented, and by their belief that the councils and collaborative spaces that exist, are not truly available to them for participation, monitoring, and accountability. Nevertheless, the programme did benefit from, and was responsive to, certain monitoring mechanisms such as fiscal transparency, which along with other government- instigated accountability procedures, allowed the media and interest groups to investigate and report poor management and suspected wrongdoing. Social accountability was therefore assured in this case by top-down measures that were incorporated into the administration of the programme, rather than by the active participation by beneficiaries.

These findings underscore a widely acknowledged view that programmes which rely solely on beneficiary participation to ensure accountability risk failure particularly in the very deprived social contexts that are precisely the ones served by anti poverty programmes (Engberg-Pedersen & Webster, 2002, pp. 255–271; Fox, 2015; Mansuri & Rao, 2013; McGee & Norton, 2000). Where extreme poverty and social exclusion prevail, the scope for active and independent engagement is often limited as the most vulnerable are not always able or willing to provide feedback on programmes, let alone complain to higher authorities, often fearing reprisals. In these circumstances, closer attention to administrative forms of accountability to secure transparency and ensure the proper procedures and conduct of officials is especially necessary.

Jones et al. explore some of these social accountability mechanisms within three programmes with considerable longevity and scale in conflict-affected contexts: Mozambique's Basic Social Subsidy Programme (PSSB), Palestine's National Cash Transfer Programme and Yemen's Social Welfare Fund. Their findings highlight that even in very challenging conflict-affected contexts, there is demand for greater voice and spaces for involvement from beneficiaries in programme governance. This said, there is a range of design and implementation problems that more technocratic approaches on the part of donors in particular are failing to address. Even if poor people engage in accountability mechanisms, the authors question the degree to which their complaints or suggestions receive a positive response from social programme authorities. The Palestinian National Cash Transfer programme for instance has invested in recent years, with World Bank and EU support, in a state-of-the-art proxy means test poverty targeting system and a computerised single registry database, but by contrast the processing of beneficiary complaints from local to national level remains un-computerised and significantly under-resourced. It is also unclear whether efforts to embed social accountability approaches and tools within contexts where consolidating good governance and understandings of citizenship rights remain longer-term endeavours ever achieve much success. The authors' findings indicate that programme participants (often among the most vulnerable and excluded in society) are frequently unable to take advantage of social accountability opportunities because they remain ensnared in a clientelistic worldview whereby programme benefits are attributed to governmental (or even God's) beneficence.

A further issue raised by Jones et al. is that programme designers and implementers fail to adequately take into account the effects that the political context can have on programme governance. In particular there are limited incentives for frontline providers and government officials to provide meaningful spaces for the articulation of citizen voices. The findings from the Yemen research indicate that where local communities are highly politicized any over-reliance on local leaders to arbitrate complaints about programme exclusion errors is likely to undermine citizen trust. These problems tend to arise in contexts of limited institutional infrastructure, including weak data collection and monitoring systems, under-investment in staff capacities, broken feedback loops and lack of institutionalisation.

Recent research by Hickey and King has engaged the broader issue of how welfare programmes might affect state-citizen relations in those programmes that encourage more sustained engagement between citizens and service providers, for instance through large scale social audits.[11] Hickey and King's article for this issue reviews over 90 studies in the social accountability field and aims to identify the underpinnings of 'citizenship empowerment'. Like Borges Sugiyama, they find that there has been a misplaced technocratic over-emphasis on bottom-up accountability mechanisms, and point to a common failure in ignoring how contextual factors, power dynamics and incentive structures affect outcomes. These problems tend to be greatest in contexts of limited political will, or weak institutional infrastructure, including poor data collection and monitoring systems, under-investment in staff capacities, and lack of reliable citizen's channels.

They emphasise the importance of creating synergies between upward and downward forms of accountability, but above all call for greater attention to be paid by policymakers to the specific characteristics of civil society, political society and state-society relations, and the interplay between them. These together determine the likely efficacy of social accountability programme interventions. Social protection in aid dependent countries also tends to be driven by external agencies which limits the opportunities for strengthening the social contract between the state and its citizens and inhibits the emergence of coalitions across different social groups who collectively may be better placed to hold the state to account.

Hickey and King see the success of social accountability as dependent on the ways that programmes are implemented, with attention to proactively engendering social belonging and political voice. But while there have been some recent if still fledgling attempts to strengthen opportunities for voice and engagement between citizens and service providers in cash transfer programmes, they argue that so far cash transfer debates have side-lined the broader issues of politics and power. Analysts and policy makers alike need to pay more attention to factors such as whether or not there is political will to actively support these initiatives, whether institutionalised political parties exist, whether human resources and bureaucratic capacity are adequate to the task, and whether civil society has the capacity to mobilise and form strategic alliances. All these shape the possibilities for fostering active citizenship and the ability to hold power holders to account.

A realistic appreciation of the highly contingent and political character of social accountability therefore suggests that for all the benefits that it can bring to beneficiaries, there are still formidable obstacles in the way of 'empowering' the poor including inadequate political, administrative and financial support. Positive outcomes also depend on efficient administration and attention to under-lying structural conditions such as entrenched power relations that may limit the ability of social protection interventions to serve as conduits to citizenship (Hickey & Mohan, 2008).

Conclusions

The shifting of social protection programming parameters away from a narrow focus on tackling income poverty towards promoting broader positive changes has begun to deliver some positive, if as yet inconclusive and mixed results. The articles in this Special Issue show that CTPs have the potential to generate a variety of change processes, from small shifts in people's subjective dispositions to collective engagement with public policymaking. While beneficiaries of these programmes view cash transfers as an essential component of their coping repertoires, there is evidence that they also tend to increase their sense of self-worth, dignity, and their assertiveness. As a result of gaining some economic security CT recipients report that this has afforded them a degree of more financial independence and control over their lives. An awareness of rights and entitlements can also embolden beneficiaries to challenge unacceptable behaviour by officials and make collective demands. At the community (meso-) level, a positive impact on social relations was evidenced where transfers enabled poor households' engagement in religious, family and social events. This formation of bonding social capital could in some contexts and with NGO support, also lead to horizontal solidarity between beneficiaries over issues that concerned them.

However, in regard to the more ambitious objectives of social protection – ensuring that pro-poor policies are responsive to a broader definition of poor people's needs, are accountable to them and foster active citizenship – the evidence suggests more modest achievements. Three points stand out: first, any improvements in wellbeing and self confidence as may accompany CT programmes have no necessary consequences for citizenship action and hence for politics; second, the circuits that connect programme level activities and the wider spheres of politics and policy appear to be weakly articulated and are not systematically embedded in social protection; third, without robust regulatory mechanisms to ensure representation and transparency, even a culture of grassroots activity and citizen awareness can be ineffective in securing accountability. Nonetheless in some contexts social accountability mechanisms do appear to have helped reduce corruption, improve service quality and empower people (Claasen & Alpin-Largies, 2010; Malena, 2009)

The evidence offered by Hickey and Borges-Sugiyama suggests that while voice and participation have long been acknowledged as important elements within development practice, meaningful social accountability cannot rely solely upon participatory mechanisms and must take into account the broader political economy and institutional dynamics at play. Without greater attention to these factors, and without establishing the means to provide adequate and accessible information systems, feedback loops and monitoring and evaluation procedures, there will be limited scope for individuals, house-holds and communities to have their needs and priorities heard and responded to.

Finally, securing transformative social protection is resource- and time-intensive, particularly given the need for careful contextualisation in terms of geography, political systems, decentralisation structures and conflict/post-conflict-related dynamics. Indeed, findings from some of the case studies profiled in this special issue make the point that progress towards this goal is unlikely to be linear given the complexities of the political environments in which programmers are working. Broader structural obstacles also stand in the way of achieving transformative results from these programmes. Economic crises and fiscal deficits set up financial barriers to taking programmes to the scale needed; investment in longer-term processes may be discouraged, including in those required to empower citizens and strengthen capacities of service providers. There is therefore some way to go if social protection programmes are to do more than offer some respite from destitution for the poorest and realise the promise held out by 'transformative' social protection.

Disclosure statement

No potential conflict of interest was reported by the authors.

Notes

1. Nancy Birdsall (when Director of the Centre for Global Development), quoted in Adato and Hoddinott, (2010, p. 4).
2. For a review of the literature on CTPs see Arnold et al. (2011). Among the continuing debates over CTs are those between opponents and advocates of conditionalities and targeting (see articles by Barrientos and Hinojosa-Valencia [2009] and Lomeli [2008] for contrasting views). For other debates over CTPs see the special issue of Global Social Policy on Cash Transfers, August 2009:9 (2).
3. Even where human development conditionalities were included in programme design (as in the Latin American child-centred programmes) the poor quality of the educational and health services on offer limited the positive effects (Morley & Coady, 2003; Sandberg, 2012), while fulfilling the conditionalities imposed additional burdens on the beneficiary mothers (Molyneux, 2006; Bradshaw with Quiros Víquez, 2008; Benderly, 2011).
4. See for example the opening address by the President to the 69th Annual Session of the UN General Assembly http://www.un.org/apps/news/story.asp?NewsID=48729#.VPH092ZcSDo (accessed 28 Feb 2015).
5. Of course all interventions have effects so there is much scope for disagreement, depending on the theory and evidence offered over whether the changes are significant or not.
6. For one of the few studies of CT effects on social mobility see Sandberg (2012).
7. Chile Solidario and its Puentes programme are examples of a multi-pronged approach to tackling extreme poverty, providing a range of services to households from job seeking support to specialised counseling. See Barrientos (2010).
8. The five case studies and other reports of this research project can be found at http://transformingcashtransfers.org/. Maxine Molyneux was the project Research Director, and Nicola Jones and Fiona Samuels led fieldwork teams in Africa and the Middle East.
9. For overviews of the impacts of Social Accountability see Claasen and Alpin-Largies (2010), Goldring, Holla, Koziol, and Srinivasan (2012), and Malena et al. (2004).
10. As Gupta has argued in his analysis of Indian anti-poverty programmes, if these have no links to political processes they can serve to 'shore up the legitimacy of ruling regimes' (Gupta, 2012, p. 278).
11. Corbridge et al. (2005) were among the first to conduct in depth longitudinal research on social audits finding some evidence of greater citizen activism and contestation on the part of programme members.

References

Ackerman, J. M. (2005). Human rights and social accountability. *Social Development Papers no. 86*. Washington, DC: World Bank.

Adato, M., & Hoddinott, J. (2010). Conditional cash transfer programmes: A 'magic bullet'? In M. Adato & J. Hoddinott., Eds., *Conditional cash transfers in Latin America*. Baltimore, MD: Johns Hopkins University Press.

Adato, M., Roopnaraine, T., & Becker, E. (2011). Understanding use of health services in conditional cash transfer programs: Insights From qualitative research in Latin America and Turkey. *Social Science & Medicine, 72*, 1921–1929. doi:10.1016/j.socscimed.2010.09.032

Adato, M. (2000). *The impact of PROGRESA on community social relationships* (Final Report). Washington, DC: Institute of Food Policy Research Institute.

Arnold, C., Conway, T., & Greenslade, M. (2011). Cash transfers: A literature review. *DFID Policy Division Paper*. London: UK Department for International Development. Retrieved from http://r4d.dfid.gov.uk/PDF/Articles/cash-transfers-literature-review.pdf

Baird, S., De Hoop, J., & Özler, B. (2011). Income shocks and adolescent mental health. *World Bank Policy Research Working Paper no. 5644*. Washington, DC: World Bank.

Barrientos, A. (2010). Protecting capability, eradicating extreme poverty: Chile Solidario and the future of social protection. *Journal of Human Development and Capabilities: A Multi-Disciplinary Journal for People-Centred Development, 11*(4), 579–597. doi:10.1080/19452829.2010.520926

Barrientos, A., Gideon, J., & Molyneux, M. (2008). New developments in Latin America's social policy. *Development and Change, 39*(5), 759–774. doi:10.1111/dech.2008.39.issue-5

Barrientos, A., & Hinojosa-Valencia, L. (2009). *A review of social protection in Latin America*. Brighton, UK: Centre for Social Protection.

Benderly, B. L. (2011). *A bargain or a burden? How conditional cash transfer (CCT) program design affects the women who participate in them* (World Bank Results-Based Financing for Health (RBFH) Report). Retrieved February 24, 2014, from http://www.rbfhealth.org/news/item/477/bargainburdencctprogramdesignaffectswomen

Bourdieu, P. (1986). The forms of capital. In J. G. Richarson (Ed.), *Handbook of theory and research for the sociology of education* (pp. 241–258). New York, NY: Greenwood Press.

Bradshaw, S., & Víquez, A. Q. (2008). Women beneficiaries or women bearing the cost? A gendered analysis of the red de protección social in Nicaragua. *Development and Change, 39*(5), 823–844. doi:10.1111/dech.2008.39.issue-5

Cecchini, S., & Madariaga, A. (2011). *Conditional cash transfer programmes: The recent experience in Latin America and the Caribbean*. Chile: Economic Commission for Latin America and the Caribbean.

Claasen, M., & Alpin-Largies, C. (2010). *Social accountability in Africa: Practitioners' experiences and lessons*. Pretoria: IDASA-ANSA Africa.

Corbridge, S., Williams, G., Srivastava, M., & Veron, R. (2005). *Seeing the state: Governance and Governmentality in India*. Cambridge: Cambridge University Press.

Devereux, S., & Sabates-Wheeler, R. (2004). Transformative social protection. *IDS Working Paper 232*. Brighton: Institute of Development Studies.

Engberg-Pedersen, L., & Webster, N. (Eds). (2002). *The name of the poor: Contesting political space for poverty reduction*. London: Zed Books.

Ferguson, J. (2015). *Give a man a fish: Reflections on the new politics of distribution*. Durham, NC: Duke University Press.

Fiszbein, A., Schady, N., Ferreira, F. H. G., Grosch, M., Keleher, N., Olinto, P., & Skoufias, E. (2009). *Conditional cash transfers: Reducing present and future poverty*. Washington, DC: World Bank.

Fox, J. (2015, August). *Social accountability: What does the evidence really say?* (World Development, No. 72). Washington, DC: GPSA.

Fultz, E., & Francis, J. (2013). *Cash transfer programmes, poverty reduction and empowerment of women: A comparative analysis. Experiences from Brazil, Chile, India, Mexico and South Africa*. Geneva: International Labour Office.

Gammage, S. (2011). *Conditional Cash Transfers and Time Poverty: An Example from Guatemala*. Retrieved from http://www.cepal.org/mujer/noticias/noticias/1/43711/GAMMAGE_Conditiona_Cash_Transfers_and_Time-Poverty_03102011.pdf

Goldring, E., Holla, A., Koziol, M., & Srinivasan, S. (2012). *Citizens and service delivery: Assessing the use of social accountability approaches in human development*. Washington, DC: World Bank Publications.

Gonzalez De La Rocha, M. (2006). *Procesos Domésticos y Vulnerabilidad: Perspectivas Antropológicas de los Hogares con Oportunidades*. Mexico City: Publicaciones de la Casa Chata.

Gupta, A. (2012). *Red tape: Bureaucracy, structural violence and poverty in India*. Durham, NC: Duke University Press.

Haushofer, J., & Shapiro, J. (2013). '*Policy brief: Impacts of unconditional cash transfers*' Jamil Abdul Poverty Action Lab (J-PAL). Cambridge: MIT. Retrieved February 23, 2013, from http://web.mit.edu/joha/www/publications/Haushofer_Shapiro_Policy_Brief_UCT_2013.10.22.pdf

Hickey, S., & Mohan, G. (2008). The politics of establishing pro-poor accountability: What can poverty reduction strategies achieve? *Review of International Political Economy, 15*(2), 234–258. doi:10.1080/09692290701869712

Holmes, R., & Jones, N. (2013). *Gender and social protection in the developing world, beyond mothers and safety nets*. London: Zed Books.

Holzmann, R., & Jørgensen, S. (2000). Social risk management: A new conceptual framework for social protection and beyond. *World Bank Social Protection Discussion Papers no. 21314*. Washington, DC: World Bank.

Hossain, N. (2009). Rude accountability in the unreformed state: Informal pressures on frontline bureaucrats in Bangladesh. *IDS Working Paper no. 319*. Brighton: Institute of Development Studies.

Kabeer, N. (1999). Resources, agency, achievements: Reflections on measurement of women's empowerment. *Development and Change, 30*, 435–464.

Koehler, G. (2011). Transformative social protection: Reflections on South Asian policy experiences. *IDS Bulletin, 42*(6), 96–103. doi:10.1111/idsb.2011.42.issue-6

Lomeli, E. V. (2008). Conditional cash transfers as social policy in Latin America: An assessment of their contributions and limitations. *Annual Review of Sociology, 34*, 475–499.

MacAuslan, I., & Riemenschneider, N. (2011). Richer but resented: What do cash transfers do to social relations? *IDS Bulletin, 42*(6), 60–66. doi:10.1111/idsb.2011.42.issue-6

Malena, C. (Ed.). (2009). *From political won't to political will: Building support for participatory governance*. Sterling VA: Kumarian Press.

Malena, C., Forster, R., & Singh, J. (2004). Social accountability: An introduction to the concept and emerging practice. *Social Development Paper 76*. Washington, DC: World Bank.

Mansuri, G., & Rao, V. (2013). *Localizing development: Does participation work?* Washington, DC: World Bank.

McGee, R., & Norton, A. (2000). Participation in poverty reduction strategies *IDS Working Paper 109*. Brighton.

Molyneux, M. (2006). Mothers at the service of the new poverty agenda: PROGRESA/Oportunidades, Mexico's conditional transfer programme. *Journal of Social Policy and Administration*, *40*(2/3), 2006.

Morgan, R., & Yablonski, J. (2011, April 13–15). *Addressing, not just managing vulnerability: Policies and practice for equity and transformation*. Paper presented at the International Conference, 'Social Protection for Social Justice', Sussex.

Morley, S., & Coady, D. (2003). *From social assistance to social development: Targeted educational subsidies in developing countries*. Washington, DC: Centre for Global Development, International Food Policy Research Institute.

Pellissery, S. (2010). Process deficits in the provision of social protection in Rural Maharashtra. In A. Barrientos & D. Hulme (Eds.), *Social protection for the poor and poorest: Concepts, policies and politics university of Manchester chronic poverty research centre*. Basingstoke: Palgrave Macmillan.

Pouw, N., & McGregor, A. (2014). An economics of wellbeing. What would economics look like if it were focused on human wellbeing? *Institute of Development Studies Working Paper no. 436*. Brighton: Institute of Development Studies.

Putnam, R. D. (2000). *Bowling alone: The collapse and revival of American community*. New York, NY: Simon & Schuster Ltd.

Reiners, F., Da Silva, C., & Trevino, E. (2005). Where is the education in the conditional cash transfers in education? *UNESCO Institute for Statistics Working Paper no. 4*. Montreal: UNESCO.

Ringold, D., Holla, A., Koziol, M., & Srinivasan, S. (2012). *Citizens and service delivery: Assessing the use of social accountability approaches in human development*. Washington, DC: IBRD.

Rose-Ackerman, S. (2005). The challenge of poor governance and corruption. *Revista Direitogv Special Issue*, *1*, 207–266.

Sandberg, J. (2012). Conditional cash transfers and social mobility: The role of asymmetric structures and segmentation processes. *Development and Change*, *43*(6), 1337–1359. doi:10.1111/dech.2012.43.issue-6

Sen, A. (1999). *Development as freedom*. Oxford: Oxford University Press.

Shah, A., & Schacter, M. (2004). Combating corruption: Look before you leap. *Finance and Development*, *41*(4), 40–43.

Slater, R., & Farrington, J. (2006). Introduction: Cash transfers: Panacea for poverty reduction or money down the drain? *Development Policy Review*, *25*(5), 499–511.

Slater, R. (2011). Cash transfers, social protection and poverty reduction. *International Journal of Social Welfare*, *20*(3), 250–259. doi:10.1111/j.1468-2397.2011.00801.x

Soares, F. V., Soares, S., Medeiros, M., & Guerreiro Osório, R. (2006). Cash transfer programmes in Brazil: Impacts on inequality and poverty. *International Poverty Centre Working Paper no. 21*. New York, NY: UNDP.

Stewart, F. (2002). Horizontal inequalities: A neglected dimension of development. *Working Paper 81*. Oxford: University of Oxford, Queen Elizabeth House.

United Nations Development Programme. (2013). *The global conversation begins: Emerging views for a new development agenda*. Retrieved from http://www.undp.org/content/undp/en/home/librarypage/mdg/global-conversation-begins.html

White, S., & Ellison, M. (2006). Wellbeing, livelihoods and resources in social practice. *Wellbeing in Developing Countries (WeD) Working Paper no. 23*. Bath: University of Bath and Economic and Social Research Council.

White, S. C., Gaines, S. O., & Jha, S. (2013). Inner wellbeing: Concept and validation of a new approach to subjective perceptions of wellbeing—India. *Social Indicators Research*, *14*(2), 1–14.

World Bank. (2004). *World development report: Making services work for poor people*. Washington, DC: World Bank and University of Oxford.

'Being Able to Breathe Again': The Effects of Cash Transfer Programmes on Psychosocial Wellbeing

FIONA SAMUELS* & MARIA STAVROPOULOU**

*Overseas Development Institute, London, UK, **Independent consultant, London, UK

ABSTRACT *The multidimensional nature of poverty and vulnerability and the role of psychosocial dimensions in achieving wellbeing are increasingly being recognised, yet development programme assessments still tend to focus on material outcomes. We situate this article within a wellbeing framework and after reviewing evidence on the psychosocial effects of cash transfer programmes, we explore findings from a qualitative and participatory study on beneficiary experiences of unconditional cash transfers in the Middle East and Sub-Saharan Africa. Narratives reveal how cash transfers can improve psychosocial wellbeing at individual level and in relation to others suggesting that psychosocial dimensions need to be considered when planning, implementing and evaluating cash transfer programmes.*

1. Introduction

In 1986 the United Nations Declaration on the Right to Development defined development as 'a [...] process, which aims at the constant improvement of the well-being of the entire population and of all individuals' (UN, 1986). However, the prominence given to economic growth as the fundamental requirement for development resulted in it becoming for many not only the key means of raising people's incomes and reducing poverty, but the ultimate aim of international development policy (International Organization for Migration [IOM], 2013; World Bank, 2013). Accordingly, development interventions and their evaluations have largely focused on tackling income poverty and economic vulnerability. More recently, however, the concept of wellbeing has been attracting growing interest. Faced with the limitations of the dominant paradigm and drawing on established trends for a more human-centred approach, researchers, policy-makers and governments have increasingly acknowledged that development and social progress cannot be narrowed down to economic performance and related indicators, but people's experiences and subjective assessments of what matters in their lives also need to be considered (Stiglitz, Sen, & Fitoussi, 2009; UN, 2011, 2013). Thus a wellbeing approach seems to have a promising potential for a more holistic understanding of human progress, despite its conceptual and methodological challenges (IOM, 2013; World Bank, 2013).

This article contributes to these debates by showing that, in addition to improving the economic situation of their beneficiaries, cash transfer programmes can also have often unintended, mostly positive, non-material effects on people's lives and particularly on their psychosocial wellbeing. Drawing on a qualitative and participatory study of beneficiary perceptions and experiences of five unconditional cash transfer programmes in the Middle East and Sub-Saharan Africa, this article presents narratives of how these programmes improved beneficiary sense of wellbeing. The study did not use the concept of wellbeing to frame the research from the outset, nor did it aim to explore psychosocial wellbeing in particular; nevertheless, using a grounded theory approach, findings related

13

to these concepts emerged when analysing cash transfer beneficiary narratives. Additionally, findings also resonated with other literature on wellbeing, including frameworks for analysis and interpretation.

We first situate our findings within current psychosocial wellbeing theory in international development. We then review existing evidence on the impact of cash transfers on individual and community wellbeing. Moving on to our data, after providing an overview of the cash transfer programmes and our methodology, we present the psychosocial dimensions of poverty and vulnerability in each country context. Drawing on the wellbeing approach developed by the Wellbeing in Developing Countries (WeD) research group and the related concept of Inner Wellbeing, we then show how cash transfers, through alleviating some of the multiple dimensions of poverty and vulnerability, can also improve beneficiary sense of wellbeing. The article ends with a brief discussion of the potential benefits of integrating a wellbeing perspective into social assistance programmes.

2. Development and Psychosocial Wellbeing

Although the concept of wellbeing is still relatively new in development policy and practice, it engages with well-established approaches that question the dominance of income and economic growth, define poverty and development in multidimensional terms, emphasise people's strengths and consider the role of the personal and the social (White, 2009a). Notably, amongst others, Sen's (1999) capability approach included the notion of wellbeing assessed in terms of one's capability to achieve valuable 'functionings', both elementary and complex, such as achieving self-respect, participating in community life and 'appearing in public without shame'. Work on participation and agency as well as on gender and empowerment also made influential contributions (White, 2009a).

Despite its promising potential, the concept of wellbeing presents two major challenges (International Organization for Migration, 2013). The first has to do with its definition (Camfield, Streuli, & Woodhead, 2008) as this concept is 'notoriously difficult to define' (White, 2009a). Social scientists have understood it in different ways, often using related but not identical terms such as happiness, subjective wellbeing, quality of life or life-satisfaction. Economists who made the first contributions to the study of wellbeing have focused on happiness and its linkages to income. On the other hand, psychologists explore the 'good life' in terms of people's ability to find pleasure, meet basic psychological needs such as autonomy, competence and relatedness, or achieve 'optimal psychological functioning' (White, Gaines, & Jha, 2012). Given the affinity between such concepts and mental health, some mental health practitioners have narrowed the concept of wellbeing and investigate the linkages between poverty, mental illness and development (Helliwell, Layard, & Sachs, 2013; Lund et al., 2011; Patel & Kleinman, 2003).

The second challenge has to do with measuring and analysing wellbeing (Camfield et al., 2008; International Organization for Migration, 2013). So far a diverse range of methods have been used including brain scans or measuring saliva-cortisol levels,[1] with the most common tools being surveys based on self-report questionnaires and quantitative analytical methods. Moreover, while there are a few exceptions (for example Clark, 2003; Trani, Bakhshi, & Rolland, 2011; White, 2009b; White, Gaines, & Jha, 2014), most of these research tools have been developed in high-income Western countries, and thus the extent to which they are able to capture the experience of people in developing country contexts remains to be seen.

Influenced by the dominance of the economic growth paradigm and the conceptual and methodological challenges of wellbeing, development interventions have explicitly focused on tackling the material dimensions of poverty and vulnerability. Accordingly their evaluations have been preoccupied by measuring changes in beneficiaries' income, nutrition, health or education as they are not only clearly linked to economic growth, but also relatively easier to measure and quantify. Concentrating on these material effects, evaluations of cash transfers have indeed produced robust evidence that these programmes do work in terms of material wellbeing (Devereux et al., 2013; MacAuslan & Riemenschneider, 2011). However, it is increasingly acknowledged that not only do poverty and vulnerability have multiple, including psychosocial, dimensions (Walker et al., 2013), but also that cash transfers can have effects that exceed their original material objectives (Devereux et al., 2013).

Early and ongoing research on the multidimensional nature of poverty and particularly its non-material aspects highlighted the psychosocial dimensions of poverty and vulnerability and their negative impact on people's lives and wellbeing. In several studies, poor people described what it means and feels to be poor and, despite considerable context-related differences, they spoke not only in terms of material deprivation but also of frustration, shame, humiliation, lack of dignity and confidence, and hopelessness: the shame of the father who is unable to feed his family, the rejection of children at school due to their poor clothes, the humiliation of people by rude social assistance staff, the social isolation, distress and low self-esteem due to people's inability to fulfil their social obligations and participate in social events (Narayan, Patel, Schafft, Rademacher, & Koch-Schulte, 2000a; Walker et al., 2013). Respondents also identified what psychosocial well-being means to them: peace of mind and confidence in the future, autonomy, self-respect and dignity, ability to fulfil social expectations and participate in community life (Narayan, Chambers, Shah, & Petesch, 2000b).

Other studies led by mental health professionals and taking a more medicalised approach explored the relationship between poverty and mental health in developing countries without reaching consensus on their causal linkages (Das, Do, Friedman, McKenzie, & Scott, 2007; Lund et al., 2011; Patel & Kleinman, 2003). Combined with the concept of psychosocial wellbeing, the mental health focus also appears in assessments of humanitarian interventions, which aim to address the multiple mental health needs of communities affected by conflict or disaster (Strang & Ager, 2003).

Researchers working in international development, however, have tended towards formulating and employing a broader concept of wellbeing. Amongst others, the ground-breaking work of the Wellbeing in Developing Countries (WeD) research group (See http://www.welldev.org.uk/ for details and studies) and the current related work at the University of Bath (See www.wellbeingpath ways.org; White, 2009b; White et al., 2014) have helped in conceptualising and developing a concrete model to explore and analyse subjective perceptions of wellbeing. It is also useful as a way of framing the findings from our study not least because, like our study, they also focus on people's own experiences and perceptions about their lives, giving them an active voice.[2] Bringing together scholarship in psychological wellbeing and international development and based on field research in developing countries, they put forward an approach grounded on psychological literature, but emphasising the importance of the particular context and the relational aspect of wellbeing (White et al., 2014). Developing the concept of Inner Wellbeing that expresses what people think and feel they can be and do, they stress that 'wellbeing is not the property of an individual, it emerges in relationship', and thus any assessment of wellbeing needs to consider how people interact with each other and their wider environment (White, 2013, p. 4). They also identify seven distinct but closely interrelated domains through which to view wellbeing: economic confidence, agency and participation, social connections, close relationships, physical and mental health, competence and self-worth, and values and meaning (White et al., 2014). As will be seen in the analysis of our findings, while our study did not start with this framing, our instruments covered some of these elements and consequently many of the themes emerging around psychosocial wellbeing can fit into these domains and indeed bring us closer to their concept/approach of Inner Wellbeing.

3. Cash Transfers and Psychosocial Wellbeing: Reviewing the Evidence

Having located our study within this wellbeing framework, we now turn to consider existing evidence of the effects of cash transfers beyond their material benefits. We first explore studies that use a quantitative methodology and tend to adopt a medicalised perspective; we then discuss qualitative studies which are smaller in scale and less systematic, but have included material on broader and relational aspects of wellbeing. Although both types of research highlight the positive effects of cash transfers on psychosocial wellbeing, a few qualitative studies also reveal some potentially negative effects.

3.1. Quantitative and Medicalised Approaches

Although still limited, the evidence base on the non-material effects of cash transfers is growing. Most of the existing and more systematic evidence has been generated through studies using quantitative methodologies and explicitly focusing on mental health issues such as stress, anxiety, and depression, measured mainly by self-reported questionnaires but also saliva cortisol levels.

The majority of these studies assess the impact of conditional cash transfers in Latin American countries. Using experimental or quasi-experimental designs, they measure and find changes on beneficiary child psychosocial and cognitive development, and maternal mental health although they are unable to identify the exact causal pathways. Thus, the Mexican Oportunidades cash transfer was found to modestly reduce child aggressive behaviour (Ozer, Fernald, Manley, & Gertler, 2009), reduce child emotional problems (Fernald, Gertler, & Neufeld, 2009), and lower child cortisol levels indicating reduced exposure to stressors (Fernald & Gunnar, 2009). Cash transfers were also found to have small but positive improvements in maternal depression and stress in Ecuador (Paxson & Schady, 2007) and Nicaragua (Macours, Schady, & Vakis, 2008).

A number of similar studies in Asia and Sub-Saharan Africa have also reported mostly positive changes. In Cambodia, a study using two 12-item screening instruments[3] found that a cash transfer for poor secondary school students had a small positive effect on beneficiary mental health (Filmer & Schady, 2009). In South Africa, another study using a depression index showed that the social pension reduced household stress levels (Case, 2004). In Kenya, a randomised controlled trial of an unconditional cash transfer programme found that the intervention increased happiness and life satisfaction (Haushofer & Shapiro, 2013). Finally, a study in Malawi that mainly used the General Health Questionnaire[4] found that the cash transfer reduced psychological distress among schoolgirls offered the conditional transfer by 17 per cent and by 38 per cent amongst those offered the unconditional cash transfer. The researchers attributed the difference to the 'heavy burden' the regular attendance conditionality imposed on adolescent girls and their mental health (Baird, De Hoop, & Özler, 2011).

3.2. Towards a More Holistic, Relational and Contextual Approach

A small number of studies focusing on the social effects of cash transfer programmes and using qualitative methodologies also provide some insights into their psychosocial wellbeing effects. More in line with our research, such studies take into account contextual factors, but also beneficiary perceptions of wellbeing and the role of relationships with others. Thus, respondents in small-scale assessments of social pensions in India and Nepal reported that despite its small value, the transfer enabled them to cover household and health-related expenditures, depend less on their relatives and even contribute to the family; it, therefore, provided considerable relief from the 'worries of daily existence', increased their dignity and self-confidence and improved their social relationships (HelpAge International, 2009a, p. 7; 2009b). Likewise, the Bangladeshi Old Age Allowance made its beneficiaries and particularly women 'feel happy, peaceful, and tension-free' (Begum & Wesumperuma, 2012, p. 200).

In Malawi, beneficiary children also reported an improved sense of psychosocial wellbeing. While before they had felt 'ashamed of' themselves and 'shy to mix with' peers, the transfer enabled them to buy new clothes and soap and thus to look better. They were 'proudly able to go to school' and were treated better by their peers and teachers. Apart from their increased self-esteem, they also admitted to being more optimistic about the future, having hopes and dreaming of a job (Miller, Tsoka, Reichert, & Hussaini, 2010).

In South Africa, recipients of the child cash transfer acknowledged that the transfer saved them from the shame of begging and enabled them to become self-reliant. As a result, they felt a sense of dignity and pride, control over their lives and reduced stress – 'poverty that I used to think about before is no longer in my mind' (Hochfeld & Plagerson, 2011, p. 15). Finally, female recipients of a Nicaraguan conditional cash transfer said that this regular source of income reduced their stress levels, increased their self-confidence and improved their psychosocial wellbeing (Adato & Roopnaraine, 2010a).

3.3. Some Limitations in Terms of Psychosocial Wellbeing

Cash transfers may also have some adverse effects on psychosocial wellbeing, and it is essentially the qualitative approaches that allow these issues to emerge. Thus, for instance, in the aforementioned study in Nicaragua, despite the reported positive psychosocial effects of the transfer, some mothers also revealed increased stress due to programme conditionalities related to children's health and inadequate knowledge about programme rules (Adato & Roopnaraine, 2010a). This coincides with the similar observation in Malawi (see above) (Baird et al., 2011). More research is needed, however, to explore the potential negative psychosocial effects of conditionalities, research which so far has been absent from debates over whether cash transfer programmes should include conditions or not (Department for International Development [DFID], 2011).

Some studies have found that cash transfers increased household tensions and domestic violence as well as tensions between beneficiaries and non-beneficiaries with negative wellbeing effects (Devereux et al., 2013). Thus in South Africa, female recipients of the child transfer reported being looked down on by non-recipients and facing negative comments such as being lazy or unwilling to work (Hochfeld & Plagerson, 2011). Women receiving cash transfers in Peru and Ecuador also faced stigma and rejection by non-beneficiaries (Molyneux & Thomson, 2011). In Nicaragua, while beneficiaries experienced envy and gossip, non-beneficiary adults reported a loss of self-esteem and their children sadness or annoyance when seeing their beneficiary classmates with new clothes and supplies (Adato and Roopnaraine, 2010b). A similar situation was noted in Peru (Jones, Vargas, & Villar, 2008) with some attributing the tensions and disappointment to lack of clarity in the targeting process (Streuli, 2012). Finally, negative feelings of envy and resentment between beneficiaries and non-beneficiaries also emerged in Malawi and Zimbabwe along with reduced support through traditional networks to beneficiaries (MacAuslan & Riemenschneider, 2011).

These studies have also highlighted another important but often-neglected issue: the interactions between staff and beneficiaries during programme implementation and their impact on beneficiary sense of wellbeing and response to the intervention. Evidence from several countries show that people are not always treated in a respectful and dignified way with negative consequences on their self-esteem and willingness to make full use of the programme. Research carried out on the Peruvian Juntos found that participants complained of being frequently mistreated or even insulted by programme staff with negative impact on their self-esteem (Molyneux & Thomson, 2011; Streuli, 2012). Likewise, in Bolivia and Ecuador female beneficiaries also reported mistreatment by health service providers with negative impact on their confidence (Molyneux & Thomson, 2011).

This section has therefore shown that while there is a small but growing body of literature exploring the psychosocial effects of cash transfers, many of the studies adopt relatively narrow, quantitative and medicalised approaches to wellbeing and use individual diagnostic tools developed in Western clinical settings with no or limited concern over their accuracy in different cultural contexts (Kleinman, 1987). As such, not only do they often miss the relational and contextual dimensions of psychosocial wellbeing, but also the potentially negative impact that cash transfers can have. We now turn to our study findings, which are more in line with the qualitative studies that explore the contextual and relational effects of cash transfers. However, this article explicitly uses a wellbeing framework and gives centre stage to the psychosocial dimension as a critical component to achieving broader wellbeing, rather than as a 'by the way' finding.

4. Towards a Wellbeing Framing for Exploring the Psychosocial Effects of Cash Transfers

4.1. Programme Description and Methodology

Our research explored beneficiary and community perceptions of five unconditional cash transfer programmes: two in the Middle East and three in Sub-Saharan Africa (see Table 1 for programme details). Each country study focused on a specific vulnerable social group: female-headed households in Palestine, young people in Yemen, orphans and vulnerable children in Kenya, older people and people living with a disability in Mozambique, and older people in Uganda. This was partly guided by the particular focus of each programme, but also by the interests of the research team and the intention to fill information/data gaps and provide added value to the study.

The research methodology combined secondary and primary data collection, review and analysis. Secondary data included reviewing existing quantitative data sets and qualitative data gathered through an in-depth literature review of government policy documents and other studies on key vulnerabilities, gender, social protection, and cash transfers, in the research countries and beyond. Primary data collection took place between July and September 2012. In each country two study sites were selected and in each site a set of qualitative and participatory data collection methods were applied. The methodology was developed in a participatory manner with all country teams, and included the following tools: community/institutional mapping (total of 24), focus-group discussions (total of 74), in-depth interviews (total of 140), key informant interviews (total of 147), life histories/case studies (total of 74) and structured observations (total of 38). Programme beneficiaries, other community members and service providers were amongst those interviewed by local teams supported by a member of the international research team. Ethical clearance was obtained in each country and appropriate informed consent was obtained from all study participants (for details see Samuels & Jones, 2013).

Each country study first identified the particular vulnerabilities of its focus group within the specific historical, economic, political and cultural context, and then explored beneficiary perceptions of the effects of cash transfers in their lives. While the research questions did not specifically ask about or measure psychosocial wellbeing, when describing their situation respondents themselves often spoke about it using terminology that best equates with personal and relational wellbeing. The next section first presents the psychosocial vulnerabilities and the ways that people cope across the five countries, and then explores the psychosocial effects of cash transfers on people's lives, drawing on the wellbeing framework outlined above. In order to capture as much as possible from the detailed five country studies,[5] relatively short but highly indicative narratives are drawn on here.

4.2. Psychosocial Vulnerabilities and Coping Strategies

Before presenting the effects of the cash transfers on beneficiary psychosocial wellbeing, it is useful to explore the extent to which poverty and vulnerability is perceived and spoken about beyond its material dimensions, how the psychosocial dimension is critical to people's lives and what strategies they use to cope with these kinds of stresses in each setting.

The context of each country study ranges widely, from the two Middle Eastern countries which experience ongoing conflict and insecurity, to the three Sub-Saharan Africa countries which, despite their diversity, face similar challenges related to HIV and AIDS, climate, geography and remoteness, and either pockets of sporadic conflict or a history of conflict. As such, it might be assumed that the ways and the extent to which people face psychosocial challenges and similarly the ways they are able to cope with them will vary. Nevertheless, while the triggers may be different, interestingly our study found that respondents across all countries had similar ways of talking about them.

Other factors that are also likely to affect the kind of psychosocial stresses people experience, often interacting to produce enhanced effects, include gender, age, health status and disability. Mental health literature contends that girls and women experience higher levels of stress and anxiety than boys and men due to gender discrimination, restricted rights and economic opportunities, lack of support, limited power and higher exposure to violence (Astbury, 2001; Dennerstein, Astbury, & Morse,

Table 1. Programme overview

Country	Kenya	Mozambique	Occupied Palestinian Territories		Uganda	Yemen
			West Bank	Gaza		
Name	Cash Transfer for Orphans and Vulnerable Children (CT-OVC)	Basic Social Subsidy Programme (PSSB)	Palestinian National Cash Transfer Programme (PNCTP)		Senior Citizen Grant (SCG)	Social Welfare Fund (SWF)
Start date	2009	1992	2010	2011	2011	1996
Transfer amount and frequency	KSh 4000 ($48) per household, per two months. Paid every two months	130mzn (approx. $4.5) to 380mzn ($1.8) for each dependant. Increments of 50mzn ($1.8) for each dependant. Monthly	From 750–1800 NIS ($195–468). Quarterly		UGX 24,000 ($8.70) per individual, per month. Paid monthly	Maximum benefit of YER 4000 ($20) for a family of six people. Quarterly
Target group	Extremely poor Households supporting at least one OVC under 18 and not benefiting from a similar scheme	Permanently labour-constrained households: households headed by older people with no/unable to work dependants, households with members with chronic degenerative illnesses, disabled person	Extremely poor households: female-headed households, people with disabilities, people with chronic illnesses, older people		People aged 65 years and above (60 and above in Karamoja) in rural areas	Vulnerable groups: orphans, women with no caretaker, disabled people, older people, female-headed households, families missing household head, families below poverty line
Programme reach	Approx. 145,000 households	261,519 (169,542 female direct beneficiaries and 91,977 male direct beneficiaries), as of 2012	120,000 hhs by end 2013	Approx. 48,000 families	Approx. 60,000 beneficiaries	Approx. 1,500,000 beneficiaries
Payment mechanism	Post office	Cash	Bank accounts	Payment slip, exchanged at bank or Ministry of Social Affairs (MoSA)	MTN Mobile Money account	Post office, bank account or cash from mobile cashiers
Recipient	Household head but households can nominate alternative recipient	Household head but households can nominate alternative recipient	Paid to household representative accepted as a beneficiary		Beneficiary	Official beneficiary

1993). Physical health problems along with isolation and declining support networks experienced by older people (World Health Organization [WHO], 2013) may cause them much greater stress than younger people who are more concerned with finding employment and generating a livelihood. For children, inadequate clothing and lack of peer approval may not only result in feelings of shame and exclusion, but also discourage them from attending school, thus further limiting their future prospects and compromising their wellbeing (Miller et al., 2010; Walker et al., 2013). Finally, high stress levels, stigma and discrimination may heighten the psychosocial difficulties people with HIV face (World Health Organization [WHO], 2010).

Turning to our research findings, and taking into account both context and individual differences, respondents in all countries did not only talk about their lack of income and resources, inadequate food, education and healthcare or poor living conditions, as daily stressors, but they also spoke about feelings of stress, anxiety, helplessness, and low self-esteem that compounded their problems. Respondents attributed these feeling to their poverty and economic insecurity as well as to the particular situation they experienced: the blockade and ongoing violence in Gaza and West Bank; the limited prospects for the future in Yemen; being an orphan or being HIV-positive and often facing associated stigma and discrimination in Kenya; disability, old age and the impact of HIV and AIDS in Mozambique; and old age and erosion of traditional support structures in Uganda.

Thus in Gaza and West Bank men spoke of their frustration and helplessness due to lack of employment and their subsequent inability to fulfil the traditional breadwinner role and related obligations: *'I feel helpless when my wife demands money or food for the family'* (man, Beit Lahia); *'As a father, I would say that the hardest thing is when I see my child sick and I can't help, it breaks my heart'* (man, Jenin). They also spoke about the constant struggle to control their feelings, maintain dignity and avoid losing face in front of their family and friends. Many frequently mentioned feelings of stress and anxiety in relation to the Israeli occupation and ongoing tensions, with several respondents even reporting being traumatised and having mental health problems which increased their social isolation due to the cultural stigma surrounding mental illness.

Women's increased psychosocial vulnerability emerged particularly acutely in Palestine, possibly because of the restrictive gendered norms affecting the behaviour of study respondents. In both Gaza and West Bank, divorced and separated women heading households reported carrying a large psychosocial burden: apart from their economic problems and the stigma of divorce, they are expected to conform to mobility and social restrictions, live under the constant surveillance of their relatives and communities, and prioritise their children's needs without the right to ever enjoy themselves. Such conditions generated feelings of humiliation and distress among these women: *'We are under the eyes of our society. People observe us when we move, they want us to be prisoners at our homes!'* (female household head, Rafah). In Kenya, widows often faced HIV and AIDS-related stigma and even neglect from family members on suspicion that they may have passed the disease to their husbands. Hence, not only did knowing their HIV status cause stress, but the need to support their dependents when they were lacking both strength and assistance added to this stress and anxiety.

In Yemen, young people were frustrated and humiliated by unemployment, poverty and inability to buy good clothes and improve their social status: *'Being poor means desperation, humility and disrespect'* (young man, Taiz); *'I want to have better clothes like other girls. I want to go to the school cafeteria to eat like them [...] I go to get ice cream and eat it in front of my classmates at breakfast time so they believe I have already had my food'* (adolescent girl, Taiz).

In Uganda, older people felt isolated and powerless when experiencing lack of respect and support in their communities: *'Nowadays, as people grow older, they lose respect from others; lose control over resources; and lose support from other family members'* (community worker, Kiboga district). Many elderly were considered an additional burden for their families; some were mistreated and others even abandoned by their children, relatives or neighbours. Such attitudes left them humiliated, frustrated and even wishing to die to reduce the family burden. Finally, in Mozambique, many disabled people spoke of increased stress levels and loss of dignity due to their disability. At the same time, family members who cared for them also reported stress and emotional strain.

In each context people also spoke about the various strategies they use to cope with psychosocial challenges. In terms of negative coping strategies, men in Palestine and Yemen reported resorting to alcohol, drugs and smoking for a short escape from limited prospects and feelings of powerlessness: *'People are getting mad because of the siege and the lack of income; they will either lose their minds or escape by taking hallucinating drugs* [sic]*'* (man, Beit Lahia). Respondents also revealed that stress and anger increased intra-household tensions, and often resulted in domestic violence towards spouses, children or siblings as a way of releasing daily tension. Thus a husband in Gaza admitted that: *'I can't provide them with what they need and I can't go and ask people for help as if I was a beggar. When my wife insists, I beat her.'* An orphaned girl in Yemen also faced domestic tensions and violence: *'I miss the old days of my father and being able to smile at home. This is now a dream because of the daily fight among my siblings over food, clothes and sleeping sheets and mattresses. My dream is to see my brothers respect me, my mother and my sisters, and for them to stop beating us.'*

Given mobility restrictions and high levels of social control, many Palestinian women reported 'practising patience', minimising social relations and isolating themselves in order to avoid 'people talking' about them. Self-imposed isolation was also mentioned by women and men as a mechanism to save their scarce resources or avoid losing face due to their inability to fulfil the expected principles of hospitality and provide a wide range of food and drinks to their guests. Finally, crying emerged as a common way of coping with negative feelings, particularly amongst widowed women in Palestine: *'We cry and keep everything in our heart'* (widow, Jenin).

Apparently more positive coping strategies to deal with psychosocial burdens included turning to other people for support and comfort. In Gaza several men mentioned that they leant on their wives, while many women in West Bank spoke about turning to female family members, relatives or friends for support: *'Those with daughters who keep their secrets and feel with their mothers and use crying as one of the common strategy for coping'* (woman, Hebron). In Yemen, respondents talked about resorting to prayer or getting involved in political activism. In Kenya and Uganda, participation in informal groups provided not only some financial, but also social support.

4.3. Effects of the Cash Transfers on Psychosocial Wellbeing

Drawing on the wellbeing framework and its domains presented earlier, and focusing at both personal and relational levels, we first explore the positive effects of the cash transfers on beneficiary psychosocial wellbeing and then discuss some of their limitations.

4.3.1. Improved financial security reducing stress and anxiety (economic confidence/mental health)..

Although the cash transfer was insufficient to cover all needs (see Table 1), it did help recipients to cope with daily challenges and cover food, medical and education costs, or even pay their debts. Additionally, its regularity and predictability provided a sense of financial security and led to a reported reduction in stress and anxiety. In the West Bank a beneficiary man said: *'After the cash transfer my wife says to me: "Now you can give your brain a break and stop worrying."'* Likewise, in Gaza many remarked that although inadequate to satisfy all their needs, the transfer allowed them to 'breathe again'. In particular, female-headed households, who, according to study respondents, usually face increased vulnerability, often spoke about 'feeling a sense of security', 'improving the morale', and 'decreasing anxiety and worry' as a result of the cash transfer. In Kenya beneficiaries spoke of how the transfer ended previous feelings of hopelessness when they were unable to cover their needs, noting its regularity as its most important feature. In Mozambique the predictability of the transfer allowed people to plan ahead. And in Uganda the transfer stopped beneficiaries being 'afraid of tomorrow', with respondents noting that they were feeling 'happy and satisfied', because the cash provided them with some economic security and opportunities to meet basic needs.

4.3.2. Reduced dependency leading to increased control over lives (economic confidence/agency).

Compared to other forms of assistance, the transfer was considered to be better in terms of reducing people's dependency on others, offering freedom in deciding how to spend it, and enabling beneficiaries to establish some control over their lives. It has, thus, also provided some of them with a sense of empowerment. In Gaza people commented that more than any other form of assistance the cash allowed them to meet their own priorities. In Kenya people recognised that the transfer offered them the ability to make choices contrary to other forms of assistance that made them look like 'dependants'. In Mozambique and in Uganda disabled and older beneficiaries respectively also found that the transfer reduced their dependency on their families and gave them the chance to set their own priorities and spend money according to their own needs.

4.3.3. Improved household relationships (close relationships). Although the cash is given to one individual, it is usually shared with other household members and thus strengthens intra-household relationships. In the West Bank people spoke about the increased collaboration among family members and reduced tension and violence due to lower stress levels. In Yemen a young man bluntly said: *'When coming to the house with money, family members will like you, the wife will be happy and everything is OK. Money is the main source of happiness.'*

A positive impact was reported not only between spouses but also between parents and children as parents were now able to better support their families. In the West Bank a middle-aged father revealed that his ability to fulfil his breadwinner role reduced his stress and negative attitude and improved his relationship with his children: *'I feel closer to my kids when the payment comes. I can meet their needs. Other times when they ask for money I become angry.'* And a female beneficiary added: *'My son is so happy, he comes with me to the bank to help in carrying what I will buy [from the cash] for the house.'* Respondents also noted that spending part of the transfer on children was a priority not only in terms of buying their school supplies but also for giving children some pocket money to buy snacks *'so that their children do not feel excluded compared to their peers'* (female beneficiary, Ramallah). Likewise, in Yemen a father noted that the transfer enabled the purchase of foods, which improved his image in front of the children.

Because the transfer enabled older people in Uganda to contribute to household needs, it also improved their relations with other family members as they were no longer viewed as a burden or 'worthless' but as persons who can contribute and help their family: *'Some children who had abandoned their parents are now coming back because they know that parents are worth something and have something to give them back'* (programme implementer, Nebbi district); *'My elder son, who collects this money on my behalf, has become the most humble because he knows that he will always receive something from me on pay days'* (male beneficiary, Nebbi district). In Mozambique the transfer also enabled disabled recipients to become more independent and less of a burden for their families, thus improving their family relationships: *'Among the positive effects of the programme is that I'm now able to contribute to some basic household expenses'* (female beneficiary, Chokwe).

4.3.4. Decreasing social isolation and increasing integration (social connections/agency and participation). Many respondents also spoke about how the transfer enabled them to break their isolation and feel more integrated in their communities and thus less vulnerable. In Kenya the transfer contributed to the social acceptance of orphans and vulnerable children in the wider community. While in the past orphans were perceived to be a burden to fostering households and were often discriminated, the transfer resulted in their relatives being more willing to become foster parents and share its benefits. Orphans are therefore no longer seen as a burden, but as a valuable addition to a household, and thus enjoy a better status. Children themselves spoke about feeling more accepted even in school and by other children and having more friends than before.

In Uganda beneficiary older people found that their social life improved considerably and they were no longer alone: *'My social relations with my friends have become stronger because once I receive this money, my friends come here and we share good moments together'* (male beneficiary, Nebbi district). Some recipients also used part of the transfer to contribute to religious ceremonies, festivals and community activities, which gave them 'personal fulfilment'. Likewise, respondents in West Bank, Gaza and Yemen noted that they used the money to participate more in community events by buying new clothes for their children, attending weddings or other family and religious celebrations, or inviting relatives and friends.

Payment days also provide opportunities to socialise and feel part of a community. In Palestine many beneficiaries emphasised that during these days and when queuing for the cash transfer, they can meet each other and share their experiences and problems, thus not only increasing their knowledge about assistance channels but also communicating and feeling closer with others who face similar challenges. Similarly, in Uganda payment day *'brings re-union among the elderly – they will meet and talk and socialise. The first payment was like an elders' convention* [. . .] *This meeting means more to them than just money. They also share ways of how to deal and cope with their diseases'* (community officer, Nebbi district).

4.3.5. Restored dignity and self-esteem (competence and self-worth). Respondents often explicitly recognised that the transfer improved their social status, restored their dignity and increased their self-esteem by enabling them to establish some control over their lives, become less dependent on others, avoid getting involved in humiliating activities, improve their relationships and increase their social interactions. In the West Bank women said that the transfer accorded them greater respect and helped them to feel more confident as *'people respect us more for having some money, unlike when we didn't have anything'*. Female household heads particularly stressed the importance of the cash transfer as it *'protects us from begging and burdening our families'* (female beneficiary, Jenin) and offers them some comfort as they *'feel there is someone who cares about us'* (female beneficiary, Ramallah). In Kenya beneficiary children going to school (instead of being chased away) and being better clothed and fed, reported increased self-confidence, self-worth and aspirations about the future. Being able to eat, wear decent clothes, go to school and have friends made them feel stronger and able to hope and plan for the future in terms of leading a better life. Their caregivers also admitted that they did not feel inferior anymore but were treated equally during village meetings and participated in mutual assistance groups where members contribute money and support. Many of these groups also in fact offer psychosocial support to HIV-positive widows and counselling to grandmothers on how to manage orphans.

In Mozambique the transfer also improved the social position of its older recipients: *'Before I received the help [transfer] my life was not going well* [. . .] *With the help, many things have improved. My relationship with other people has improved. Before, nobody wanted to have anything to do with me. Now, nobody looks down on me'* (male beneficiary, Chokwe). Similarly, its disabled beneficiaries reported more self-confidence: *'It means I can cook for myself for the first time in a long time. Before, I hardly ate anything – just when it was given to me'* (male beneficiary, Chokwe).

Finally, in Uganda many recipients also reported increased self-esteem and social status as they were no longer viewed as a burden, but as an active member of their household and community: *'Before, we were treated as if we were dead* [. . .] *Now, people respect me'* (male beneficiary, Nebbi district). Change also occurred as beneficiaries reported becoming more 'presentable' by buying soap, new clothes and shoes and thus more confident to interact with other community members without feeling shame: *'Soap that used not to be available, you can now buy it and your body smell becomes better'* (female beneficiary, Angal Lower parish). Even beneficiary body stature depicts this positive change: *'Before, they were crooked and bent under the burden of their problems; now that the problems have been reduced, the physical change is striking'* (community officer, Kiboga district).

The importance of the transfer in transforming beneficiary lives found an extreme expression in the words of an old man in West Bank: *'If the programme stops, I have no reason to live anymore and I keep a bottle of poison on the top of my closet and I think of drinking it if things get worse'* (80-year-old beneficiary, Jenin).

4.4. Limitations of Cash Transfers on Psychosocial Wellbeing

Although the majority spoke about positive experiences, some respondents revealed that the transfer triggered or exacerbated pre-existing intra-household and community tensions, potentially increasing their distress. They also commented on programme delivery and how their interactions with staff members had a negative impact on their dignity and self-respect. These findings, therefore, provide useful insights on how cash transfer programmes can compromise beneficiary psychosocial wellbeing

4.4.1. Effects on close relationships. Intra-household tensions surfaced in a minority of households around the use of the new income source: in the West Bank violent husbands or sons demanded female recipients to hand over the cash to buy alcohol or drugs; in Yemen not only did some men use it to purchase drugs, but tensions also arose between recipients and their husbands or parents who typically control household cash; in Kenya and Uganda some spouses fought over how the money was used with accounts of men spending it on alcohol; and in Kenya tensions arose between orphans and vulnerable children (the programme target group) and the biological children of caregivers, but also between orphans and caregivers who accused beneficiary orphans of becoming 'arrogant' and 'disrespectful'.

4.4.2. Effects on social connections. Some tensions were also reported with extended family members and at community level: in Uganda where the general feeling was that the transfer strengthened relationships, there were a few cases where children stopped supporting their parents who received the transfer; in the West Bank envious in-laws sabotaged the possibility of certain family members participating in the programme and in other cases relatives stopped supporting beneficiaries; in Gaza some respondents also spoke of 'envy' on behalf of both their relatives and communities; and in Kenya some tensions arose between beneficiaries and non-beneficiaries.

4.4.3. Effects on competence and self-worth. In Palestine some respondents felt that the transfer increased dependency and social stigma. Acceptance of the transfer was viewed as a humiliating act, equating beneficiaries with beggars. Some children felt stigmatised that their mothers received the transfer: *'My oldest son shouted at me and tried to prevent me from becoming a beneficiary of the cash transfer because, he said, "my peers said your mother is a beggar and also servant and cleaner of houses" so he tried to stop me and also to stop me working'* (female beneficiary, Jenin). Partly due to limited programme information and transparency, widows, already a vulnerable group, became targets of community envy and resentment and felt that their dignity suffered a further blow: *'They name us beggars. We wish to give up this stigma but we don't have any other choice'* (female beneficiary, Hebron); *'The cash transfer has impacted on our dignity'* (female beneficiary, Jenin). People also commented on their increased dependency on assistance with negative impact on their psychosocial wellbeing: *'We are losing our dignity. I wish all support ends and we have jobs instead'* (female beneficiary, Beit Lahia).

4.4.4. Effects on competence and self-worth arising from interactions with implementers. Several beneficiaries noted the insensitive behaviour of programme implementers and its negative effects. In the West Bank respondents complained that social workers coming once a year to assess their economic situation did not have time to talk with beneficiaries about their problems, let alone provide any support. Some respondents also complained of being treated in a disrespectful way by bank employees who *'are mean and sometimes they call us beggars'* or *'they call this* [payment] *day "the beggars' day" and so ordinary people typically don't go to the bank on the same day'* (male beneficiary, Hebron). A few beneficiaries acknowledged their sensitivity to other people's comments and reactions, as they *'are vulnerable and there for assistance, any word could hurt us'* (female beneficiary, Jenin). In Gaza lack of information created a considerable amount of stress and frustration among applicants, recipients and social workers. Although most recipients spoke positively about social workers, some also described them as disrespectful. Likewise, there were a few complaints about the degrading treatment they faced at the bank, generating high levels of stress and feelings of humiliation as *'We wait long and we feel some sort of discrimination as we stand in a special queue known to be for beneficiaries of MoSA* [the Ministry implementing the programme]*'* (male beneficiary,

Beit Lahia). A few respondents in Mozambique and Yemen also complained of being treated by programme staff members with inadequate sensitivity to their particular vulnerabilities and 'with no respect'.

5. Conclusion

There is growing recognition of the need to take a more holistic perspective to human progress, one in which both material and non-material dimensions attract equal attention. This is mirrored by increasing acceptance that poverty and vulnerability have multiple, including psychosocial dimensions, and consequently can only be addressed through a multidimensional approach such as the one developed around the concept of wellbeing. While this concept presents several conceptual and methodological challenges, its framing by the WeD programme and current work at the University of Bath has pushed the debate forward, by highlighting the contextual and relational dimensions of wellbeing and the importance of a mixed methods approach where people's own voices and perceptions are also critical.

Cash transfer programming provides a good example of a development intervention where the above debates can be explored. Thus while the majority of such programmes and their evaluations have focused on the material benefits of the transfer, cash transfers also have a range of, often unintended, and largely positive non-material, including psychosocial, impacts. Similarly, when people are asked their perceptions and experiences of poverty and the effects of the cash transfers on this, non-material, including psychosocial, dimensions emerge alongside discussions on the material aspects. Despite the increasing number of studies exploring the psychosocial effects of cash transfers, as this paper has shown, many tend to take a quantitative and narrow approach, focusing mostly on the personal rather than on the relational, let alone the contextual.

This paper argues that taking a more holistic approach, drawing on a wellbeing framework, looking at wellbeing from a personal and relational perspective, and listening to how people speak about their experiences can help us understand the wider effects of cash transfer programmes in each context. In line with existing literature, our study confirms the psychosocial effects of poverty and finds, amongst other things, that failure to maintain control over lives and fulfil gender and social expectations, generates feelings of distress, shame, humiliation and low self-esteem. Not only did this lead to social isolation, but also to people engaging in negative coping strategies that often exacerbated existing problems. However, as our study shows the injection of cash into vulnerable households and communities has largely positive psychosocial effects through the close interaction of the material with the non-material. Hence respondents spoke about how the transfer offered them some financial security, reduced dependency on others, restored dignity and self-esteem, and enabled them to make choices and establish control over their lives. Our study also confirmed the important role of social relationships for wellbeing. Much of people's sense of wellbeing originates in their ability to relate satisfactorily with others, break out of isolation and engage with their community members on an equal basis. Similarly, the cash transfer enabled many beneficiaries to improve their family and community interactions. All these changes have arguably translated into an improved sense of wellbeing.

However, cash transfers are limited in what they can achieve and may not be the most appropriate intervention in certain contexts, particularly for dealing with heightened psychosocial stresses. In such cases, it is important to link to complementary interventions, such as specific psychosocial support services. To some extent this is already happening in Palestine with some cash transfer beneficiaries being referred to such services; additionally in Mozambique, plans are underway to improve the relevant skills of the social workers involved in the programme to also deal with specific psychosocial issues.

Although the study did not set out to explore wellbeing per se through using a wellbeing framework, retrospectively such an approach and framing has provided valuable insights for conceptualising and contextualising the non-material effects of cash transfer programmes as they emerged in beneficiary narratives. Aspects of this approach can also, arguably, potentially improve programme outcomes and effectiveness. Thus, as explored above, relational dimensions are key aspects of psychosocial wellbeing, including interactions between programme beneficiaries and implementers. The sometimes disrespectful attitudes of implementers towards beneficiaries, not only reinforced beneficiaries' feelings of shame, humiliation and low self-esteem, but even threatened their participation in the programme (see also Walker et al., 2013; World Bank, 2013). Thus both understanding and improving interactions between beneficiaries and service providers through, for instance, creating spaces for dialogue and exchange, training implementers in recognising and easing psychosocial stresses, and/or through regular monitoring and supervision of implementers could increase programme uptake as well as have a positive effect on psychosocial wellbeing of beneficiaries.

A wellbeing perspective has also allowed for the non-material effects, including the psychosocial effects, of development interventions, in this case cash transfers, to take centre stage. In future studies, it would be interesting to start with this framing when designing the study and to explore in further depth, for instance, how wellbeing may be variously defined both within and across different contexts and according to different groups of people. From a programme perspective, it would be useful to incorporate wellbeing, and more specifically psychosocial wellbeing, dimensions into programme design, implementation and monitoring. Thus not only should vulnerability assessments that are critical in the programme design phase include an exploration and analysis of psychosocial wellbeing, but indicators to track this, need to be developed and monitored during the lifetime of the programme. Similarly, appropriate methods for collecting this kind of information within the particular social and cultural context need to be identified – such methods would largely include qualitative and participatory approaches which are more adapted to uncovering these often hidden and sensitive non-material and psychosocial dimensions of wellbeing. Last, but not least, in order to ensure that implementers are aware of the multidimensional nature of poverty, and similarly both the material and non-material effects of development programmes, in this case cash transfers, appropriate capacity building and awareness raising amongst implementers at different levels would also be important to support and increase programme uptake and success.

Disclosure statement

No potential conflict of interest was reported by the authors.

Notes

1. Magnetic resonance imaging (MRI) is a brain scan technology mapping the flow of blood to parts of the brain in relation to feelings of happiness. On the other hand, elevated cortisol levels are linked to stress and anxiety.
2. They also advocate for a mixed methods approach that recognises the importance of qualitative research to capture subjective experiences and complements it with objective/quantitative measures.
3. They used an adaptation of the General Health Questionnaire 12 along with another 12-item scale developed for Hurricane Katrina survivors in the United States.
4. The GHQ 12 is a 12 item instrument widely used to assess general mental health.
5. Further details can be found in the country reports: Abu Hamad And Pavanello (2012), Bagash, Pereznieto, and Dubai (2012), Bukuluki and Watson (2012), Jones and Shaheen (2012), Onyango-Ouma and Samuels (2012), Selvester, Fidalgo, and Taimo (2012).

References

Abu Hamad, B., & Pavanello, S. (2012). *Transforming cash transfers: Beneficiary and community perspectives on the Palestinian national cash transfer programme. Part 1: The case of the Gaza strip*. London: ODI.

Adato, M., & Roopnaraine, T. (2010a). Women's status, gender relations, and conditional cash transfers. In M. Adato & J. Hoddinott (Eds.), *Conditional cash transfers in Latin America* (pp. 284–314). Washington, DC: IFPRI.

Adato, M., & Roopnaraine, T. (2010b). Conditional cash transfer programs, participation and power. In M. Adato & J. Hoddinott (Eds.), *Conditional cash transfers in Latin America* (pp. 315–347). Washington, DC: IFPRI.

Astbury, J. (2001). *Gender disparities in mental health* (Ministerial Round Tables 2001, 54th World Health Assembly). Geneva: WHO.

Bagash, T., Pereznieto, P., & Dubai, K. (2012). *Transforming cash transfers: Beneficiary and community perspectives of the social welfare fund in Yemen*. London: ODI.

Baird, S., De Hoop, J., & Özler, B. (2011). *Income shocks and adolescent mental health* (Policy Research Working Paper 5644). Washington, DC: World Bank.

Begum, S., & Wesumperuma, D. (2012). Overview of the old age allowance programme in Bangladesh. In S. W. Handayani & B. Babajanian (Eds.), *Social protection for older persons: Social pensions in Asia* (pp. 187–213). Mandaluyong City: ADB.

Bukuluki, P., & Watson, C. (2012). *Transforming cash transfers: Beneficiary and community perspectives on the senior citizen grant (SCG) in Uganda*. London: ODI.

Camfield, L., Streuli, N., & Woodhead, M. (2008). *Children's wellbeing in contexts of poverty: Approaches to research, monitoring and participation* (Young Lives Technical Note No. 12). Oxford: Oxford Department of International Development.

Case, A. (2004). Does money protect health status? Evidence from South African pensions. In D. A. Wise (Ed.), *Perspectives on the economics of aging* (pp. 287–305). Chicago, IL: University of Chicago Press.

Clark, D. A. (2003). Concepts and perceptions of human well-being: Some evidence from South Africa. *Oxford Development Studies, 31*, 173–196. doi:10.1080/13600810307428

Das, D., Do, Q.-T., Friedman, J., McKenzie, D., & Scott, K. (2007). Mental health and poverty in developing countries: Revisiting the relationship. *Social Science and Medicine, 65*, 467–480. doi:10.1016/j.socscimed.2007.02.037

Dennerstein, L., Astbury, J., & Morse, C. (1993). *Psychosocial and mental health aspects of women's health*. Geneva: WHO.

Department for International Development. (2011). *Cash transfers evidence paper*. London: Author.

Devereux, S., Roelen, K., Béné, C., Chopra, D., Leavy, J., & McGregor, J. A. (2013). *Evaluating outside the box: An alternative framework for analysing social protection programmes* (Working Paper 431). Brighton: IDS.

Fernald, L. C. H., Gertler, P., & Neufeld, L. M. (2009). 10-year effect of oportunidades, Mexico's conditional cash transfer programme, on child growth, cognition, language, and behaviour: A longitudinal follow-up study. *The Lancet, 374*, 1997–2005. doi:10.1016/S0140-6736(09)61676-7

Fernald, L. C. H., & Gunnar, M. R. (2009). Poverty-alleviation program participation and salivary cortisol in very low-income children. *Social Science and Medicine, 68*, 2180–2189. doi:10.1016/j.socscimed.2009.03.032

Filmer, D., & Schady, N. (2009). *School enrollment, selection and test scores* (Policy Research Working Paper 4998). Washington, DC: World Bank.

Haushofer, J., & Shapiro, J. (2013). *Impacts of unconditional cash transfers* (Policy Brief). Retrieved from http://www.princeton.edu/~joha/publications/Haushofer_Shapiro_Policy_Brief_2013.pdf

Helliwell, J. F., Layard, R., & Sachs, J. (Eds.). (2013). *World happiness report 2013*. New York, NY: UN Sustainable Development Solutions Network.

HelpAge International. (2009a). *The social pension in India: A participatory study on the poverty reduction impact and role of monitoring groups*. London: Author.

HelpAge International. (2009b). *The universal social pension in Nepal: An assessment of its impact on older people in Tahanun district*. London: Author.

Hochfeld, T., & Plagerson, S. (2011, April). *The social construction of the cash transfer mother in Soweto, South Africa: The emergence of social stigma?* Paper presented at the International Conference 'Social Protection for Social Justice', Institute of Development Studies, Brighton.

International Organization for Migration. (2013). *World migration report 2013: Migrant well-being and development*. Geneva: Author.

Jones, N., & Shaheen, M. (2012). *Transforming cash transfers: Beneficiary and community perspectives on the Palestinian national cash transfer programme. Part 2: The case of the West Bank*. London: ODI.

Jones, N., Vargas, R., & Villar, E. (2008). Cash transfers to tackle childhood poverty and vulnerability: An analysis of Peru's Juntos programme. *Environment and Urbanization, 20*, 255–273. doi:10.1177/0956247808089162

Kleinman, A. (1987). Anthropology and psychiatry. The role of culture in cross-cultural research on illness. *The British Journal of Psychiatry, 151*, 447–454. doi:10.1192/bjp.151.4.447

Lund, C., De Silva, M., Plagerson, S., Cooper, S., Chisholm, D., Das, J., & Patel, V. (2011). Poverty and mental disorders: Breaking the cycle in low-income and middle-income countries. *The Lancet, 378*, 1502–1514. doi:10.1016/S0140-6736(11)60754-X

MacAuslan, I., & Riemenschneider, N. (2011, April). *Richer but resented: What do cash transfers do to social relations and does it matter?* Paper presented at the International Conference 'Social Protection for Social Justice', Institute of Development Studies, Brighton.

Macours, K., Schady, N., & Vakis, R. (2008). *Cash transfers, behavioral changes, and cognitive development in early childhood: Evidence from a randomized experiment* (Policy Research Working Paper 4759). Washington, DC: World Bank.

Miller, C. M., Tsoka, M., Reichert, K., & Hussaini, A. (2010). Interrupting the intergenerational cycle of poverty with the Malawi social cash transfer. *Vulnerable Children and Youth Studies, 5*, 108–121. doi:10.1080/17450120903499452

Molyneux, M., & Thomson, M. (2011). *CCT programmes and women's empowerment in Peru, Bolivia, and Ecuador* (Policy Paper). London: CARE.

Narayan, D., Chambers, R., Shah, M. K., & Petesch, P. (2000b). *Voices of the poor: Crying out for change*. New York, NY: Oxford University Press for the World Bank.

Narayan, D., Patel, R., Schafft, K., Rademacher, A., & Koch-Schulte, S. (2000a). *Voices of the poor: Can anyone hear us?* New York, NY: Oxford University Press for the World Bank.

Onyango-Ouma, W., & Samuels, F. (2012). *Transforming cash transfers: Beneficiary and community perspectives on the cash transfer for orphans and vulnerable children programme in Kenya*. London: ODI.

Ozer, E. J., Fernald, L. C. H., Manley, J. G., & Gertler, P. J. (2009). Effects of a conditional cash transfer program on children's behavior problems. *Pediatrics*, *123*, e630–e637. doi:10.1542/peds.2008-2882

Patel, V., & Kleinman, A. (2003). Poverty and common mental disorders in developing countries. *Bulletin of the World Health Organization*, *81*, 609–615.

Paxson, C., & Schady, N. (2007). *Does money matter? The effects of cash transfers on child health and development in rural Ecuador* (Policy Research Working Paper 4226). Washington, DC: World Bank.

Samuels, F., & Jones, N. (2013). *Holding cash transfers to account: Beneficiary and community perspectives*. (Briefing). London: ODI.

Selvester, K., Fidalgo, L., & Taimo, N. (2012). *Transforming cash transfers: Beneficiary and community perspectives on the basic social subsidy programme in Mozambique*. London: ODI.

Sen, A. (1999). *Development as freedom*. Oxford: Oxford University Press.

Stiglitz, J. E., Sen, A., & Fitoussi, J.-P. (2009). *Report by the Commission on the Measurement of Economic Performance and Social Progress*. Retrieved from http://www.stiglitz-sen-fitoussi.fr/documents/rapport_anglais.pdf

Strang, A. B., & Ager, A. (2003). Psychosocial interventions: Some key issues facing practitioners. *Intervention*, *1*(3), 2–12.

Streuli, N. (2012). *Children's experiences of Juntos, a conditional cash transfer scheme in Peru* (Young Lives Working Paper 78). Oxford: Oxford Department of International Development.

Trani, J.-F., Bakhshi, P., & Rolland, C. (2011). Capabilities, perception of well-being and development effort: Some evidence from Afghanistan. *Oxford Development Studies*, *39*, 403–426. doi:10.1080/13600818.2011.620089

UN. (1986). *United Nations General Assembly Declaration on the Right to Development*. A/RES/41/128.

UN. (2011). *United Nations General Assembly 65/309 Resolution, Happiness: Towards a holistic approach to development*. A/RES/65/309.

UN. (2013). *United Nations General Assembly, Happiness: Towards a holistic approach to development* (Note by the Secretary General). A/67/697.

Walker, R., Bantebya Kyomuhendo, G., Chase, E., Choudhry, S., Gubrium, E. K., Yongmie Nicola, J., & Ming, Y. (2013). Poverty in global perspective: Is shame a common denominator? *Journal of Social Policy*, *42*, 215–233. doi:10.1017/S0047279412000979

White, S. C. (2009a). *Analyzing wellbeing: A framework for development practice* (WeD Working Paper 09/44). Bath: University of Bath.

White, S. C. (2009b). *Bringing wellbeing into development practice* (WeD Working Paper 09/50). Bath: University of Bath.

White, S. C. (2013). *An integrated approach to assessing wellbeing* (Wellbeing and Poverty Pathways Briefing 1). Bath: University of Bath.

White, S. C., Gaines, S. O., & Jha, S. (2012). Beyond subjective well-being: A critical review of the Stiglitz report approach to subjective perspectives on quality of life. *Journal of International Development*, *24*, 763–776. doi:10.1002/jid.v24.6

White, S. C., Gaines, S. O., & Jha, S. (2014). Inner wellbeing: Concept and validation of a new approach to subjective perceptions of wellbeing—India. *Social Indicators Research*, *119*, 723–746. doi:10.1007/s11205-013-0504-7

World Bank. (2013). *Inclusion matters: The foundation for shared prosperity*. Washington, DC: Author.

World Health Organization. (2010). *Mental health and development: Targeting people with mental health conditions as a vulnerable group*. Geneva: Author.

World Health Organization. (2013). *Mental health and older adults* (Fact sheet No 381). Retrieved from http://www.who.int/mediacentre/factsheets/fs381/en/

Can Social Protection Affect Psychosocial Wellbeing and Why Does This Matter? Lessons from Cash Transfers in Sub-Saharan Africa

RAMLATU ATTAH, VALENTINA BARCA, ANDREW KARDAN, IAN MACAUSLAN, FRED MERTTENS & LUCA PELLERANO

Oxford Policy Management Ltd., Oxford, UK

ABSTRACT *Social protection interventions have been demonstrated to improve traditional measures of poverty by protecting people from risk. Less research has been conducted on their impacts on psychosocial dimensions of wellbeing – self-acceptance, autonomy and purpose in life among others –, that are both intrinsically and instrumentally important. This paper provides evidence from a mixed method evaluation of a cash transfer in Kenya, and from systematic cross-country qualitative research from Ghana, Zimbabwe and Lesotho. It shows that cash transfers can have positive impacts on psychosocial wellbeing leading to further positive impacts on educational performance, participation in social life and empowerment for decision-making.*

Introduction: Why Psychosocial Wellbeing Matters

There is reasonable consensus that development ultimately aims to improve people's wellbeing (Alkire, 2007; Chambers, 1997; Stiglitz, Sen, Fitoussi, & Sarkozy Commisison, 2009). Wellbeing is a final goal in a way that other traditional developmental outcomes – say, income, expenditure, educational qualifications, or health – are not. All of these may contribute to wellbeing and can be considered intrinsically good, but the notion of wellbeing rests on more fundamental and often subjective (yet strongly relational) dimensions: evaluation of one's life and satisfaction with it, positive feelings and emotional states in relation to experiences (for example feeling happy, not feeling stressed or shamed, and so on.) and 'having a sense of meaning and purpose in life' (for example linked to self-worth, agency and empowerment, having fulfilling relationships, and so on.) (OECD, 2013). It is also widely accepted and proven that poverty restricts the 'ability of people to achieve the things expected of them and which they expect of themselves', leading to feelings of shame and ultimately withdrawal, depression and 'reductions in personal efficacy' (Walker et al., 2013, p. 222).

A growing body of literature is starting to show how different dimensions of subjective wellbeing (for example lack of stress and shame, believing one's actions can affect one's life, and so on) can also have an instrumental value: for example improving decision-making and enhancing productivity (see for example Mani, Mullainathan, Shafir, & Zhao, 2013; Shah, Mullainathan, & Shafir, 2012), or improving educational (see for example Goodman & Gregg, 2010; Gutman & Vorhaus, 2012; Outes, Sanchez, & Molina, 2010) and health outcomes (for example Marmot, 2005; Wilkinson & Marmot, 2003). In this sense, subjective wellbeing, or lack of it along any of its various dimensions, could potentially affect pathways of change of traditional development policies either positively or negatively.

Yet, despite the centrality of these 'non-material' dimensions of wellbeing being largely acknowledged, there is not always agreement on how exactly the concept can be fully operationalised, captured and used in research and policy development (Alkire, 2007; McGregor, 2007; Taylor, 2011; White, 2009). Recent efforts have been made to overcome this limitation, the most notable of which is the 2013 OECD 'Guidelines on Measuring Subjective Wellbeing' (OECD, 2013). However these guidelines are primarily directed at statistical agencies within OECD member countries who wish to standardise their approach to measuring subjective wellbeing and (as a consequence) they mainly focus on the collection of comparable quantitative data across countries. They also do not acknowledge the importance of mixed methods and qualitative research methods in assessing subjective wellbeing.

Because of all these complexities, impact evaluations of development interventions generally fail to disentangle the pathways through which subjective wellbeing is affected by, and can affect, the outcomes of a given programme. This is evident if one looks at the one particular type of development intervention that has received possibly the most extensive research attention in the social protection field over the past two decades: cash transfers.[1]

Social protection interventions have been demonstrated to improve 'material' wellbeing by protecting people from risk through, for example, regular transfers or insurance. Theory tells us that social protection interventions that reduce exposure to risk should improve psychosocial wellbeing as well. However, less research has been conducted on impacts on psychosocial dimensions of wellbeing, and on the implications of these impacts. A great number of impact evaluations of cash transfer programmes have been conducted across all continents, yet most of these studies assess impact on simpler, more tangible and usually quantitative metrics, such as poverty (in developing countries often proxied by expenditure), food consumption, or health and education outcomes. Indeed, very often the objectives of cash transfers are expressed in purely these terms, and theories of change don't include an explicit reference to subjective wellbeing.[2]

This approach to programme design and evaluation is partial at best and can be misleading: progress against 'standard' objectives and measurements used within cash transfer impact evaluations does not always mean improved wellbeing. In some cases, people receiving a cash transfer can spend more money, but this could result in weakened social networks due to resentment by non-recipients. A combination of these two changes could lead to an overall reduction in their wellbeing (Adato, 2000; MacAuslan & Riemenschneider, 2011). Other evidence shows that cash transfers can have a positive effect on participation in social organisations and the creation of social capital (Attanasio, Pellerano, & Reyes, 2009), a potential contribution to wellbeing which is often disregarded in the analysis of cash transfers' effectiveness.

This paper aims to address some of these shortcomings by developing a conceptual framework and providing evidence of the **effects of cash transfer interventions on 'psychosocial' aspects of wellbeing**: those aspects that are intrinsically subjective yet mediated by a social context. We present material from a large mixed method evaluation of a cash transfer programme conducted in Kenya, and from systematic cross-country qualitative research in Ghana, Zimbabwe and Lesotho. While these studies were not explicitly designed to focus on psychosocial wellbeing, they elicit, first, important evidence on how cash transfer programmes can have significant and positive psychosocial impacts on those they support, and second, how such improvements in psychosocial wellbeing have an instrumental bearing on economic decision-making, schooling, and participation in social networks.

The evidence presented in this paper adds to a small but growing sub-field of literature on this topic. In Kenya, for example, the impact evaluation of the cash transfer programme for orphans and vulnerable children (CT-OVC) included measures of risk preferences, expectations of the future, and perceptions on quality of life. It found 'strong and positive effects of the cash transfer on current subjective well-being and perceptions about future well-being' (Handa, Martorano, Halpern, Pettifor, & Thirumurthy, 2014a, p. 18, 2014b). In the past, similar results had been reported in Nicaragua (Macours, Schady, & Vakis, 2012), Zambia (Handa, Seidenfeld, & Tembo, 2013) and Kenya (Haushofer & Shapiro, 2013)[3] Together with this relatively new body of literature, we argue that psychosocial aspects of wellbeing should be more regularly and systematically examined as part of the assessments of development interventions such as cash transfers, as they are both intrinsically and instrumentally important.

The next section outlines a conceptual framework for the analysis of the impact of cash transfers on psychosocial wellbeing. We then briefly give an overview of the four programmes analysed in this paper and the methodology adopted for the studies. Key findings are presented in two sections, first focusing on education and then analysing psychosocial impacts of cash transfers in other realms. A discussion section presents the implications of these findings, before a summary conclusion.

A Conceptual Framework for the Analysis of Psychosocial Wellbeing

Recent conceptualisations – most notably those by the ESRC Research Group at the University of Bath and by the Institute of Development Studies (IDS) – define wellbeing as a multidimensional concept (McGregor, 2007; White, 2009). For example, McGregor's definition focuses on the interplay between three dimensions (3D) of wellbeing: material, subjective and relational wellbeing (McGregor, 2007; IDS, 2009). 'Psychosocial wellbeing', as we define it, lies at the cross-section between these two latter aspects, relating to subjective perspectives in a context of human relationships. While this does not mean that material aspects (such as having enough money or housing) should be neglected, this approach helps to draw more attention to other less-studied dimensions of wellbeing.

In practice, 'psychosocial' wellbeing mixes the concept of psychological and subjective wellbeing and an attempt to draw more attention to social influences on wellbeing. 'Psychosocial' therefore refers to the dynamic relationship between internal psychological processes and external social processes.[4] This interaction generates a state of psychosocial wellbeing when it leads to self-esteem, self-respect, and self-reliance (psychological processes), the mental health to function to a person's fullest capacity and cope with normal stress (a psychological state) and the ability to engage in meaningful and effective relationships with others – including public institutions (a social process).[5]

To develop a framework to analyse psychosocial wellbeing, we borrow from the classic formulation of psychological wellbeing, born in the field of psychotherapy. Specifically, this framework includes six dimensions (Ryff & Singer, 1996)[6]:

- Self-acceptance, including positive attitudes towards oneself (this also implies self-respect, self-esteem and self-reliance, as well as lack of shame[7])
- Positive relations with others (warm, trusting and reciprocal interpersonal relations)
- Autonomy (including self-determination and independence)
- Environmental mastery
- Purpose in life (related to hopefulness – and having goals, intentions and a sense of direction)
- Personal growth

This framework allows the identification of psychosocial wellbeing as both effect (it is good to have increasing values on any of those six dimensions) and cause of further positive effects (increasing values on those six dimensions is likely to lead to improvements in other areas of wellbeing). This is useful for our purposes because we seek precisely to draw attention to those components of wellbeing that are both intrinsically and instrumentally important, that is, which simultaneously represent both cause and effect. For instance, greater purpose in life is likely to lead to greater investment in the future, which in children may mean trying to perform better in school, and in adults could lead to a greater willingness to save, or maintain health. Having more positive relations with others is likely to improve people's ability to give and obtain help in times of need.

We also use this framework to illustrate the social or 'relational' dimension of wellbeing, high-lighting the *inter-subjective* (Giddens, 1976; Habermas (1981/1987)) nature of some key elements of our conceptions and construction of wellbeing. The Psychosocial Assessment of Development and Humanitarian Interventions (PADHI), identifies three levels of wellbeing: personal, communal and institutional. PADHI conceives wellbeing as something that must be actively achieved, and that it is understood differently in different social and cultural contexts (White, 2009). Indeed all the six dimensions included in the framework can affect and be affected by an individual's social, cultural and political environment. This is easily seen for positive relations with others, but it is also clear that self-acceptance, autonomy, environmental mastery, purpose and personal growth are all firmly embedded in a social, cultural and political construct. In the context of cash transfer programmes, the design and implementation of the programme itself can also affect these dimensions, either positively or negatively.

Figure 1 illustrates this framework graphically. Its principal purpose is to emphasise the psychological and social channels through which wellbeing is mediated, and the importance, therefore, of locating our analysis of cause and effect of social protection interventions – specifically cash transfers – at this level.

The framework in Figure 1 is mostly 'eudaimonic' in nature – focused on the 'functioning and realisation of a person's potential' and 'concerned with capabilities as much as with final outcomes' – according to the definition provided by the OECD guidelines on measuring subjective wellbeing (OECD, 2013). Nevertheless, it is based on the additional acknowledgment of how affective states – experienced feelings at a particular time – ultimately influence all of the relevant dimensions.

Overview of Case Study Programmes and Methodology

The evidence presented in this paper draws from case studies of four distinct unconditional cash transfer programmes operating in sub-Saharan Africa. All programmes provide regular cash grants to poor households, though with some variations in objectives, targeting, amounts and institutional arrangements that are summarised in Table 1.

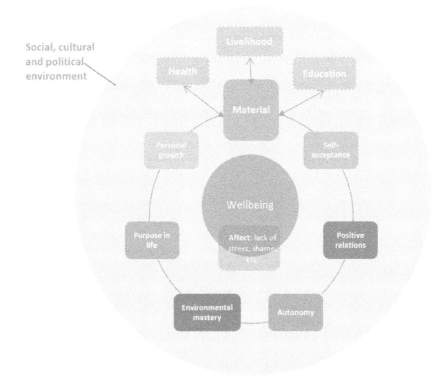

Figure 1. Overall conceptual framework, psychosocial wellbeing.

For the Kenya Case Study, the information provided is based on an independent impact evaluation of the Hunger Safety Net Programme (HSNP) conducted by Oxford Policy Management (OPM) in partnership with IDS. The evaluation utilised a mixed methods approach, underpinned by a quantitative Randomised Controlled Trial (RCT) design and extensive qualitative research conducted over the three-year duration of the pilot. For the quantitative survey, a sample of just over 5000 beneficiary and non-beneficiary households was randomly selected at baseline (prior to the programme roll-out) for interview on an annual basis in 48 evaluation sub-locations (of which 24 had been randomly assigned to the treatment and 24 to serve as a control group). The baseline data collection was completed in November 2010, and the evaluation was designed to assess impact at two distinct points: after one year of programme operations and after two years.[8] For the qualitative component, focus groups and key informant interviews (KIIs) were undertaken in a selection of sub-locations from each of the four counties, with respondents including beneficiary and non-beneficiary households, school children, educational professionals and other community leaders such as local government and health workers. For more details on the methodology, see OPM & IDS (2011a).

For the Case Studies in Ghana,[9] Zimbabwe[10] and Lesotho,[11] we draw on findings from a six country systematic qualitative study performed by OPM which forms part of the 'From Protection to Production' (PtoP) project, a collaboration between DFID, UNICEF and FAO. The PtoP seeks to provide the evidence base on the social and economic impacts of social cash transfers by promoting a mixed methods approach to research on these two areas. Specifically, the study focused on household and local economy impacts, analysing how these were mediated by social networks. Sampling for the study followed a three-stage protocol and led to the selection of four communities in two distinct regions/districts of each country. Five days were spent in each community, during which focus groups and KIIs were conducted adopting a range of participatory tools including social mapping and community wellbeing analysis, household income and expenditure analysis, institutional mapping (Venn diagramming), and livelihood matrices. For more details of the study methodology, see OPM (2013a).

Psychosocial Impacts in the Realms of Education

To analyse the complex pathways through which cash transfers can affect psychosocial wellbeing and psychosocial wellbeing can affect educational outcomes we focus on Kenya's HSNP.

HSNP: No Impact on Education Enrolment, Attendance or Expenditure, but Impact on Performance

While the quantitative impact evaluation found a statistically significant impact of the HSNP pilot on consumption expenditure for beneficiary households, and on poverty and depth and severity of poverty,[12] no impact was observed on education enrolment, attendance or expenditure.[13] These findings, taken in context, were unsurprising, given that the survey also revealed that barriers to schooling in the HSNP counties were largely driven not by cost and access, but rather by livelihoods and cultural attitudes toward education. For example, the study showed that, amongst children aged 6–17 who had never attended school, only 6 per cent claimed not to have done so due to cost; 2 per cent due to lack of school; and just 1 per cent because the school was considered too far. In fact, the most common reasons given for having never attended school were domestic duties (49%), working for household's own production (13%), and parental attitudes (15%). These findings were corroborated by various testimonies produced by the qualitative research, which highlighted expectations that children participate in livestock rearing (the dominant livelihood strategy of people living in the arid and semi-arid lands (ASAL) of northern Kenya) and household chores, ambivalent attitudes of many households towards the value of education, views on girls and marriage,[14] as well as negative perceptions of education quality.[15]

A significant positive impact of the HSNP that was observed, however, was on the performance of children that were in school. This positive impact was manifest in a greater mean highest grade

Table 1. Overview of the four cash transfer programmes: Kenya, Ghana, Zimbabwe, and Lesotho

Programme	Description and objectives	Institutional arrangements	Targeting and number of beneficiaries	Amount provided
Hunger Safety Net Programme (HSNP), Kenya	Unconditional cash transfer programme rolled out in northern Kenya. The overall goal of the HSNP is to reduce poverty, food insecurity and malnutrition, and promote asset retention and accumulation for beneficiary households.[a] It operates in four counties in the arid and semi-arid lands (ASALs) of the country.[b]	Under its pilot phase (2009–2012), the programme operated under the Ministry of State for the Development of Northern Kenya and Other Arid Lands and was delivered by several contracted service providers, with financial support from DFID.	During the pilot phase approximately 300,000 beneficiaries (69,000 households, many of which are pastoral and nomadic) were targeted under three different targeting mechanisms, Community-based (CBT), Dependency ratio (DR), and Social pension (SP).[c]	The HSNP originally provided a flat rate of KES 2150 (around US$27 at time of first transfer) to each beneficiary household every two months. Now (in phase 2) the transfer stands at KES 4900.
The Ghana Livelihood Empowerment Against Poverty programme (LEAP), Ghana	Unconditional cash transfer that started in 2008 and aims to reduce poverty by increasing consumption and promoting access to services and opportunities among the extreme poor and vulnerable.[d]	The programme – which is considered the flagship programme under Ghana's National Social Protection Strategy – is being implemented by the Department of Social Welfare (DSW) under the Ministry of Gender and Social Protection (MGSP)	LEAP covers some 70,191 beneficiary households across 100 districts in Ghana using a range of targeting methods including geographical, community based, categorical and proxy means testing.[e]	The bi-monthly transfer value ranges from a minimum of 24 Ghana Cedis (US$12.5) per household per month to a maximum of 45 Ghana Cedis (US$24.6) The payment level represents at least 37% of food consumption for eligible households. Severe delays in payment are present.
The Harmonised Social Cash Transfer (HSCT), Zimbabwe	Unconditional cash transfer, started in 2011 with the objective of enabling labour-constrained households to increase consumption to above the food poverty line, reducing the number of ultra-poor households.	Developed by the Ministry of Labour and Social Services (MoLSS) in support of the Government's National Action Plan for Orphans and Vulnerable Children, together with the Child Protection Fund (CPF) – a multi-donor funding mechanism.	During Phase 1 of the programme (from 2011 to 2012) 10 districts were targeted for HSCT coverage. In total 236,458 households were surveyed and 18,637 households were identified as labour-constrained and food poor.	The value of the bi-monthly cash transfer varies depending on the size of the household, ranging from US$10 for a one-person household to US$25 for households with four or more members.[f]

(continued)

Table 1. (*Continued*)

Programme	Description and objectives	Institutional arrangements	Targeting and number of beneficiaries	Amount provided
The Child Grants Programme (CGP), Lesotho	Unconditional cash transfer targeted at poor and vulnerable households in Lesotho. The primary objective of the CGP 'is to improve the living standards of Orphans and Vulnerable Children (OVC) so as to reduce malnutrition, improve health status, and increase school enrolment among OVCs'.	The programme is managed by the Ministry of Social Development with financial support from the European Commission and technical support from UNICEF.	The households are selected through a combination of PMT and community validation.[g] The pilot programme was designed and implemented in three rounds. By the end of 2012, the pilot programme covered about 10,000 households in 21 Community Councils.	Provides a regular transfer of Maloti 360 (US$36) every quarter to poor households with children.

Notes: [a] In addition, it was anticipated that the programme would also have positive impacts on a wider range of indicators of wellbeing and wealth, such as resilience to shocks, health and education uptake, and access to financial services. [b] It should be noted these are among the poorest areas of the country, with some 85 per cent of the population falling below the national poverty line at the time of the 2005/6 Kenya Integrated Household Budget Survey (KIHBS) and some 54 per cent falling into the bottom national decile. [c] In CBT the community collectively selects households they consider most in need of cash transfers, up to a quota of 50 per cent of all households. In DR households are selected if the proportion of members under 18 or over 55 years old, disabled or chronically ill exceeds a specified number. In SP any individual aged 55 or over is eligible for cash transfers (so one household could receive multiple transfers). [d] More specifically, it aims to improve basic household consumption and nutrition, increase access to health care services among beneficiary households, and increase basic school enrolment, attendance and retention of beneficiary children between 5 and 15 years of age. Access to a broader range of complementary services such as the National Health Insurance Scheme (NHIS), free school uniforms, microcredit and agriculture inputs is also envisaged for beneficiary households. [e] Districts and communities are selected using poverty maps and locally defined poverty criteria that prioritise 'deprived' districts and communities. Beneficiaries are selected firstly through a Community Based Targeting process to identify extremely poor households. A Proxy Means Test (PMT) is then administered, after which categorical filters are applied, prioritising households with members that are elderly (over 65 years old), disabled or caring for Orphans and Vulnerable Children (OVC). [f] The value of the transfer was aligned with the prevailing 'food basket' offered by the World Food Programme (WFP) to vulnerable households and the payment offered by the Public Works scheme run by the Zimbabwe Government. [g] The PMT was applied to a census carried out in the targeted communities to categorise households into five distinct groups: ultra-poor (NISSA 1), very poor (NISSA 2), poor (NISSA 3), less poor (NISSA 4) and better off (NISSA 5). Following the NISSA categorisation, a community validation process was carried out by a community structure known as the Village Assistance Committee (VAC), established by the programme. The VACs were given the household list collected through the census (without the PMT ranking) and asked to verify those who were the poorest in their community based on a set of criteria provided by the programme implementers.

achieved for children aged 6–17, and, after controlling for community, household and individual factors, and in an increased proportion of children aged 10–17 that passed grade Standard IV. As with most of the other programme impacts the evaluation analysed, these results were again driven by poorer households and households for whom the cumulative per capita value of transfers received was larger.[16]

Thus, as these impacts do not appear to be driven by increased educational expenditure or attendance, the question is: what is driving them? A qualitative study was designed to enquire into the possible reasons for this potentially counter-intuitive finding and to better understand the causal pathways for the observed impact. The findings from this research are presented below.

HSNP: How Psychosocial Wellbeing Affected School Performance

How does this impact pathway work? Improved performance is driven by reduced stigma and increased self-acceptance. On one hand, children who pay their fees and come properly equipped to class elicit more favourable treatment by teachers and other classmates, which can contribute to improved education outcomes. On the other, the self-acceptance and self-esteem that derive from owning proper education materials and being well presented in school can also boost children's confidence and reduce their sense of shame, helping to explain their improved performance. Numerous testimonies from the research bore witness to this psychosocial dimension of impact:

> *These children who are coming from homes where they are getting this money, there is a difference. They look smart, they are smiling, because they can automatically tell the teacher they got the money and I have bought this and this. In fact, they enjoy it very much. (KII with teacher, Mandera)*

> *They have improved in performance because they are fully equipped with learning materials and they are doing more assessment exams. They also feel confident because they have uniforms. (KII with teacher, Turkana)*

> *Before children were chased from school when their shirts were dirty. Since the shirt is not dirty as there is soap for washing uniforms, children are taken to school. (Focus Group Discussion (FGD) with children, Mandera)*

> *Where parents are able to buy their children school materials, their performance increases. A child who has an essential textbook required by the school will improve his or her performance. (KII with teacher, Marsabit)*

National school feeding programmes, coupled with HSNP impact on increased food intake and dietary diversity, also help children to concentrate better in schools:

> *When [a child] has those basic needs, and, for example, he has eaten lunch, he is not hungry and is then motivated to learn and therefore there is improvement in terms of mean scores in exams. (KII with teacher, Marsabit)*

It should be noted that, although these statements seem to imply increased expenditure on education, the aggregate results from the quantitative study reveal no such effect. In fact, as the quotes above indicate, it was increased household expenditure elsewhere, such as on food and basic consumer items like soap, which had the most significant bearing on children's sense of wellbeing (being clean and smart and 'presentable').[17]

By way of conclusion, a community leader in Wajir usefully summarises the trajectory that leads from increased satisfaction and decreased stress to improved cognitive outcomes:

Parents are never stressed about meeting the fees and can even go to the head teacher and pledge to pay at a given time when they get the money. Thus, performance now depends on the hard work and discipline of the child. And when they are satisfied at home and have eaten enough food, they are able to perform well. Children also concentrate better on their studies, unlike before this programme when children were also involved in looking for food. (KII with community leader, Township, Wajir)

Findings in Zimbabwe and Lesotho Confirm the Impact Pathway

In Zimbabwe, parents reported that their increased credit worthiness enabled them to negotiate payment plans with schools. This had an effect not only on their children's enrolment, but also on their sense of self-worth from being able to provide for their basic needs. Similarly, increased household expenditure on soap and uniforms was perceived as enabling children to go to school without the fear of being teased or stigmatised.

They can afford to buy uniforms, soap. These children are now bathing. There is a notable change in attendance and their appearance. (KII with Child Protection Committee member, Chivi district)

Similarly, in Lesotho, several comments during FGD discussions were focused around the fact that 'children are now clean and have clothes and manage to eat three meals a day',[18] affecting their attitude towards school and their self-esteem ('Before, children were not able to go to school because they didn't have proper clothes or uniforms'[19]). Preliminary results confirm that the CGP contributed to a highly significant 25.5 percentage point increase of the proportion of pupils who had both uniform and shoes to go to school with (OPM, 2014b). The effect of a change of this significance on children's sense of self is substantial, as one 13-year-old in Leribe district candidly explained:

Before, some children at school would talk about me, saying bad things about my torn uniform. But now I feel better and never sleep in class, and have improved to being in the second position in my class from previously being only tenth. I am also going to be able to attend the school field trip to South Africa this year. (KII with beneficiary child, Leribe district)

The comment of a non-beneficiary is also telling, showing how physical appearance affects others' perceptions and behaviour, and highlighting the way subjective wellbeing is socially constructed (that is 'inter-subjective'):

We see a lot of changes in their [beneficiaries'] children because their children are now better dressed and have school uniforms and they look a lot brighter [more lively]. (Female non-beneficiaries FGD, Leribe district)

The interplay between sense of self-worth and social relations is further highlighted by the comment of the a child who noted that, since the receipt of the CGP, friends started to come home with him after school, also because they can get something to eat at his house, while before his mother 'would sometimes have to ask neighbours to borrow maize meal' (KII with beneficiary child, Leribe district).

The Intrinsic and Instrumental Values of Psychosocial Wellbeing for Educational Outcomes

Overall, in line with the conceptual framework for this study, school children benefitting from the cash transfer programmes appear to have improved psychosocial wellbeing in as far as they have better self-acceptance (they are at ease and more confident), more positive relations with their teachers and class mates (they are no longer 'chased away' from school), more autonomy and mastery over their environment (their performance now depends only on their hard work and discipline rather than being constrained by lack of food and school materials), and more purpose in life (in as far as parents are increasingly more willing to send children to school as a means of trying to secure for them greater life opportunities). These improvements in psychosocial wellbeing, in turn, had the instrumental value of improving children's performance in school and their standing within the community (with possible effects on their economic outlook).

Wider Impacts on Psychosocial Wellbeing

Evidence from systematic qualitative fieldwork in Ghana, Zimbabwe and Lesotho highlighted further impacts on psychosocial wellbeing (as described in the conceptual framework) that are worth exploring.

Hopefulness and 'Purpose in Life'

In Ghana, across all study communities, and in the context of severe delays in cash payments, the anticipation and expression of certainty that support would arrive created a strong sense of hopefulness among Livelihood Empowerment Against Poverty (LEAP) beneficiary households. Despite the delays in delivery, respondents remained adamant that the cash would eventually come to enable them to meet their basic needs, offset debts, or possibly even invest. This sense of hopefulness gave these elderly beneficiaries a longer-term perspective on life, where before they were perceived to be simply 'waiting for death'.[20] Overall, beneficiaries were reported to be 'looking happier and hopeful'[21] in contrast with non-beneficiaries who described life as 'tipping down'.[22]

'Self-Acceptance' and Reduced Shame Leading to 'Positive Relations'

In all locations across the study countries beneficiaries – and not only their children – were able to be better clothed, clean, and appear 'presentable' in public. This increased their sense of worth and consequently their sociability and interaction with other community members. As one key informant in Dompoase, Ghana, put it concisely: 'LEAP has allowed beneficiaries to mingle'. A female beneficiary in Goromonzi district (Zimbabwe) explained that going to the nearby market in Surrey in proper clothes gave her dignity and more confidence. More generally, the cash transfer had given her a sense of relief: 'Now I sleep better' she concluded.

Increased 'Autonomy' Also Leading to 'Positive Relations', and in Turn to Self-Respect

Newly found self-esteem and self-acceptance, together with the availability of financial resources on a predictable basis, also enabled beneficiaries to assert individual agency and autonomy by reducing reliance on their families. Rather than being a burden and a drain on already scarce resources, programme beneficiaries across the study locations were now seen to be financially independent individuals with a capacity to contribute to household or family income. As a male beneficiary in Tali, Ghana, noted: 'Before I used to rely on other people, now I give to others.' Harmonised Social Cash Transfer (HSCT) beneficiaries also reported a higher sense of self-esteem and autonomy emanating from their ability to better meet their own needs and 'stand on their two feet'.[23] As one group of non-beneficiaries explained:

> Now they [beneficiaries] are also in a position to share since they have begun receiving cash transfers. (Non-beneficiary FGD, Chivi district)

In Lesotho, CGP beneficiaries similarly stressed the importance of being increasingly self-reliant and able to return things they had borrowed (rather than just receive with no reciprocation):

Before the transfer the beneficiaries used to rely on others for things, but now they are less reliant. And also when they borrow things now they are expected to return them, whereas before there were no expectations for them to return the things that they had borrowed. (Male beneficiaries FGD, Mafeteng District)

In some instances, these changes also helped beneficiaries to strengthen or re-build links with risk sharing networks in their community. For example, many respondents spoke of more active participation in savings groups,[24] religious activities (paying church tithes, attending prayer meetings), naming ceremonies, weddings and so on. Importantly, this is because participation in these is not merely about attendance, but also about ability to contribute financially. Not being able to make these contributions is perceived as 'shameful'. As one beneficiary in Ghana explained:

In fact, it's rather embarrassing [. . .] if something [birth, wedding or death] happens you cannot even show your face – what would you take there? (Female Beneficiary FGD, Tolon Kumbungu District)

This enhanced ability to meet social obligations in turn affected beneficiaries' sense of worth and self-respect, thus constituting a positive cycle. For example, in the Fante society of Ghana's Central Region, LEAP enabled beneficiaries to contribute to the family levy system (*'abusua tow'*), which helps extended family members to defray costs associated with life cycle events such as funerals. Those who do not contribute regularly 'are buried without a coffin',[25] constituting a shameful circumstance in a context where 'people pay more respect to your coffin than when you are alive',[26] and where the importance of a decent burial cannot be overstated. During the discussions, a few elderly beneficiary women boasted of the funerals that would be given to them because of their regular contributions. One elderly beneficiary spoke rather proudly about saving towards a shroud for her burial, and about how much respect this would bring to her and her household.

Similarly, in Zimbabwe, many felt greater self-worth due to increased respect and deference shown to them by the wider community – 'they now see us as real people with worth'[27] – and better respected by business people – 'We are now their kings'.[28]

Discussion and Policy Implications

Several important observations can be made on the basis of these findings. From a conceptual point of view, the case studies clearly show that psychosocial wellbeing is a useful concept in the context of evaluating the impact of social interventions, and cash transfers specifically. In practice, it is difficult to distinguish subjective/psychological wellbeing from social wellbeing, as the two dimensions are intertwined and mutually reinforcing ('co-constructing', according to Chase & Walker, 2012). In fact, improvements in psychological wellbeing are most often manifest in the form of social interactions. In the words of respondents, inner feelings of increased self-esteem and purpose in life are strongly linked, as both cause and effect, to respect and social status, independence or acceptance by others in the family and community, and engagement with peers and institutions (schools, churches, community groups). In this sense, it is acknowledged that psychosocial problems cannot simply be 'fixed' through clinical treatment as they are rooted in stigmatisation, lost hope, chronic poverty, inability to meet basic needs (and the related stress that leads to), and inability to fulfil expected social roles. As the case studies show, these are all dimensions of people's existence that cash transfers and other social protection interventions can help to address.

Similarly, the intrinsic and instrumental value of psychosocial wellbeing was clearly demonstrated by all case studies. The evidence suggests that there's a self-reinforcing cycle that leads from increased material wellbeing towards increased self-esteem (for example, ability to be clean and wear good clothes, ability to pay into risk-sharing arrangements, and so on), which then has effects on social integration and interactions (for example, diminished stigma from teachers, increased respect gained from other community members, and so on), which in turn can positively affect other relevant development outcomes (for example, improved performance in school, increased support from the community at a time of need, and so on). This 'virtuous circle' (as opposed to the more frequently evoked 'vicious circle') is implicit in Townsend's definition of poverty as the inability to 'play the roles, participate in the relationships and follow the customary behaviour which is expected of them by virtue of their membership of society' (Townsend, 1973, p. 36), and is referenced in recent cross-country research on the ties between shame and poverty (Walker et al., 2013).

From a policy and practical perspective, these considerations have important consequences. Firstly, policy interventions – particularly but not exclusively in the area of social protection – could benefit from building considerations of psychosocial wellbeing more explicitly into their theory of change. This is not only because development interventions should aim at improving all dimensions of wellbeing in a holistic way, but also because psychosocial wellbeing is potentially a powerful driver for the achievement of material gains, and thus for achieving larger and more sustainable impacts on 'traditional' outcomes by virtue of the positive circular process described above.

It is also important to acknowledge that beneficiaries' experience of social protection pro-grammes can further enhance or undermine the positive effects discussed within this paper.[29] This holds true for programme design and implementation alike. When considering design aspects, it would be important to disentangle the differential impact on dignity and psychosocial wellbeing of poverty versus categorical targeting (for example, means tested vs. child grants, grants for elderly or pregnant mothers, and so on; see for example Van Oorschot, 2002), of conditional versus unconditional cash transfers (Chase & Walker, 2012) or different payment modalities (for example, in public at pay points or through mobile phone payments/banks; see Barca, Hurrell, MacAuslan, Visram, & Willis, 2013).

When considering implementation, the quality of beneficiaries' interaction with programme officers at crucial times of a cash transfer operation (targeting, enrolment, payment, graduation, and so on) can strongly affect their psychosocial wellbeing. The ways in which beneficiaries are informed about the programmes objectives and rules, about their duties and rights, and provided opportunities to express their complaints, all represent opportunities of social interaction through which a programme can build or deplete beneficiaries' dignity, self-respect and autonomy. In this sense, the development of case management or 'grievance' systems (aimed at collecting and responding to complaints and questions by community members), and 'integrated communication strategies' (aimed at socialising information on the programme, including programme rights and responsibilities), is essential, but not always an element of the design of cash transfer programmes that seems to receive adequate attention.

A finding from the case study in Lesotho[30] brings an additional element to this discussion: in the communities visited the grant had created tensions between beneficiaries and non-beneficiaries due to people's limited knowledge of the selection criteria, their own sense of entitlement and the perceived exclusion of many deserving households. Social tensions of this sort can be damaging to psychosocial wellbeing of individuals as well as to communities *en mass*. The analysis of psychosocial pathways of change should therefore not necessarily be restricted to beneficiaries, but should look at the social dynamics produced by the programme in the community as a whole.

Finally, it should be noted that this under-researched strand of impacts are particularly relevant for children, who are far more likely to suffer from the consequences of early deprivations (Barrientos & Dejong, 2006). The psychosocial wellbeing of children, insofar as it attains to their social and emotional development, should be valued as importantly as their cognitive development, particularly in the early years of life, as both are crucial determinants of wellbeing as an adult. The findings considered here are largely consistent with literature on this topic, which stresses that 'what concerns children [... is the] exclusion from activities that other children appear to take for granted, and embarrassment and shame at not being able to participate on equal terms with other children' (Redmond, 2008, p. i). Children in several studies conducted in the UK,

United States and Australia report being bullied, teased and excluded in other ways because they do not have the 'right' clothes, for example, and it has been shown that policies aimed at reducing intangible barriers to schooling linked to social exclusion and stigma can have significant effects (Redmond, 2008; Ridge, 2002).[31]

Conclusions

Findings from the four case studies presented in this paper have highlighted the multiple pathways through which a cash transfer intervention can affect beneficiaries' psychosocial wellbeing. We focused our attention mainly on the realm of education, where we found that children's improved cleanliness, clothing and ability to pay for fees and other school materials affected their overall self-acceptance (they were at ease and more confident), improved relations with their teachers and class mates (as they are no longer 'chased away' from school and stigmatised), increased their sense of autonomy and mastery over their environment (their performance now depended only on their hard work and discipline rather than being constrained by lack of food and school materials), and gave them more purpose in life. In turn, this improved education performance, as was clearly visible in the Kenya HSNP quantitative impact evaluation and described by respondents in Lesotho.

In Ghana, Zimbabwe and Lesotho, albeit to different extents, we also found compelling evidence that the cash transfer had helped to re-inject hope ('purpose in life') and affect the overall level of autonomy of many beneficiary households, who were now increasingly self-reliant. It is interesting to read this result in the context of recent studies in social psychology, showing that mental distress associated with poverty and resource-scarcity can also be instrumental to hinder cognitive outcomes and decision-making. In other words, 'poverty-related concerns consume mental resources, leaving less for other tasks'[32] (Mani et al., 2013, p. 976; Shah et al., 2012).

Similarly, evidence from Ghana, Zimbabwe and Lesotho shows that the transfers helped beneficiaries to become active and contributing participants in social life in their respective communities ('positive relations' and increased 'autonomy'), rather than being 'ashamed' of their inability to meet social obligations and feeling like a burden to their family members. This had the intrinsic consequence of increasing self-respect and self-esteem, but also the instrumental value of allowing households to enter risk-sharing arrangements that improved their capacity to cope in cases of shock.

Based on this evidence, and on a growing body of research on the impacts of cash transfers on subjective wellbeing (Handa et al., 2014a), this paper calls for more systematic study and attention to be placed on this newly acknowledged topic. Subjective wellbeing is an intrinsic but essential measure of programme success. When analysed within the social, cultural and political environment that builds or depletes it, it is revealed to be even more important, potentially leading to wider 'instrumental' gains (or losses) that multiply programme impact along traditionally conceived lines, sometimes even provoking new impacts in areas that might not have been anticipated by policy-makers. Importantly, programme design and implementation choices can further enhance or undermine the effects of development interventions on psychosocial wellbeing.

The pathways through which social protection can contribute to increasing psychosocial wellbeing need to be more comprehensively analysed and understood. Ignoring such dimensions can leave significant gaps in the understanding of interventions' impact. What this means in practice is the need for standard impact evaluations of policy interventions to incorporate questions on subjective and relational wellbeing, building on the methodological guidelines developed by the OECD (2013). Yet quantitative assessments of such a complex phenomenon would not be sufficient. As trialled within the HSNP evaluation, a triangulated mix-method approach is the most suitable approach for tracing how and why impact pathways develop (Garbarino & Holland, 2009). Within qualitative evaluation research itself, moreover, there is a need to build on the inter-disciplinary tools and methods adopted by academics (for example, sociologists, psychologists, and so on) whose focus has been on appreciating the role of shame, dignity and other dimensions of psychosocial wellbeing in poverty alleviation.

Notes

1. Welfare programmes that provide predictable amounts of cash transferred to poor households on a regular basis.
2. As the Sarkozy Commission observes, the conceptual models and measures that address the material dimensions of wellbeing are the best developed and are well tailored to the structures of policy deliberation and implementation (Stiglitz et al., 2009).
3. Based on the evaluation of the Give Directly programme (see https://www.givedirectly.org/). A special mention should also be made of the ground-breaking evidence provided by the Young Lives international study on childhood poverty – ongoing for 15 years – which focuses on psychosocial wellbeing as one strand of children's experiences of poverty, including measures such as 'agency and self-efficacy, self-esteem, aspirations and respect' (see for example Dercon & Krishnan, 2009).
4. http://psychosocial.actalliance.org/default.aspx?di=66177, accessed December 2013.
5. Note that this reflects the approach of several organisations that focus on psychological wellbeing in practice, including often those working with children in difficult situations (see UNICEF's work on psychosocial support), or emergencies (Williamson & Robinson, 2006).
6. These dimensions differ from conceptions of psychological wellbeing as reflecting happiness, on the basis that measuring happiness alone could just reflect satisfaction or intoxication, and that a more useful measure should include some normative statement about a 'good' life.
7. See for example (Walker et al., 2013).
8. See Attah, Farhat, and Kardan (2013), Merttens et al. (2013), Merttens and Morris (2013), OPM (2012), OPM & IDS (2011a, 2011b, 2011c, 2012a, 2012b, 2012c).
9. See OPM (2013b) for the full Ghana case study report.
10. See OPM (2013c) for the full Zimbabwe case study report.
11. See OPM (2014b) for the full Lesotho case study report.
12. Significant positive impacts were also found on food security and health expenditure, as well as asset retention. All these results were driven by smaller and poorer households, and by households who had received a greater cumulative per capita value of transfer (given that implementation of the transfer wasn't always even).
13. This last finding was consistent after one year and two years of programme operations.
14. Marriage strongly affects girls' access to education because it has a significant economic value and can be viewed as an economic transaction between the bridal family and the groom's household. The transaction is a negotiated bridal price (dowry) given to the family of the daughter based on certain social, economic and cultural expectations (such as standing in community, household wealth, and chastity). Once the transaction has taken place, the future benefits of the marriage accrue to the husband's household. In this context girls' education is seen as a threat to the value of the bride due to the girl's exposure to other males and the consequent risk of dishonouring the family.
15. The number and quality of teachers, the condition and size of facilities, the availability of appropriate sanitation and drinking water, even the lack of provision of school boarding, all influence parent's and carers' propensity to send their children to school.
16. This conclusion is further supported by the analysis of a panel of children aged 6–17 who were attending school at baseline. While the sample size shrinks for this panelled cohort, so that change is not able to be detected with statistical significance, the trends are again in the same direction, with beneficiary children aged 6–17 at baseline some 3.5 per cent more likely to have passed Standard IV at follow-up. In addition, amongst this panel cohort, children from poorer and smaller households also achieve a higher grade on average – a statistically significant result – and this result persists with statistical significance after controlling for other factors.
17. A further aspect to be considered is that beneficiaries were able to use the HSNP transfer as a guarantee of payment – demonstrating their increased credit-worthiness – allowing school authorities to accept fees due on credit, whereas previously households had to resort to sale of assets such as livestock to pay for children's education (this was again evidenced by the quantitative study which found a positive impact of the programme on asset retention). 'If I did not have the payment then I would have been forced to sell my small stock to buy my children uniform, books and pens. But due to the programme I am able to send both my boys and girls to school' (Beneficiary, Marsabit); 'Since HSNP started I can talk to the teacher and tell him that I'll pay the fees when I get paid so he doesn't send the children home' (Beneficiary, Wajir).
18. Female beneficiaries FGD, Leribe District.
19. Male beneficiaries FGD, Mafeteng District.
20. KII Komenda district – 'before LEAP, life was simply about survival and many beneficiaries were waiting for their death'.
21. KII, Komenda District.
22. Non beneficiaries FGD, Komenda District.
23. Beneficiary, Goromonzi.

24. Interestingly, this was not the case for women's savings groups (Fushai) in Zimbabwe, as the capital required to enter was still perceived as excessive for beneficiary households.
25. Female Beneficiary FGD, Komenda District.
26. Female Beneficiary FGD, Komenda District.
27. Beneficiaries, Chivi.
28. Beneficiaries, Chivi.
29. As Paragraph 3 of the ILO's Recommendation 202 on setting up Social Protection Floors clearly states, governments should have 'respect for the rights and dignity of people covered by the social security guarantees' (ILO, 2012; Walker, Chase, & Lødemel, 2012).
30. Also in Zimbabwe the programme had created some tension and jealousy amongst community members in targeted districts, but this had not resulted in visible changes in the relationship between beneficiary and non-beneficiaries in areas visited by the research team.
31. Ridge also notes that policies relating to clothing to be worn at school (whether uniforms or ordinary) are particularly important for children and adolescents, as these have strong significance at that age (2002).
32. According to this line of thought, 'the poor must manage sporadic income, juggle expenses, and make difficult trade-offs. Even when not actually making a financial decision, these preoccupations can be present and distracting. The human cognitive system has limited capacity. Preoccupations with pressing budgetary concerns leave fewer cognitive resources available to guide choice and action' (Mani et al., 2013, p. 976).

Disclosure statement

No potential conflict of interest was reported by the authors.

Funding

This research was supported by funding from FAO. We would like to acknowledge the financial and intellectual support provided by several members from the 'from Protection to Production' (PtoP) team, primarily Pamela Pozarny and Ben Davis.

References

Adato, M. (2000). *The impact of PROGRESA on community social relationships*. Washington, DC: International Food Policy Research Institute.

Alkire, S. (2007). *The Missing Dimensions: An Introduction*. (OPHI Working Paper 00). Oxford: University of Oxford.

Attah, R., Farhat, M., & Kardan, A. (2013). *Kenya hunger safety net programme monitoring and evaluation component: Qualitative impact evaluation report: 2011–2012*. Oxford: Oxford Policy Management.

Attanasio, O., Pellerano, L., & Reyes, S. (2009). Building trust? Conditional cash transfer programmes and social capital. *Fiscal Studies*, 30(2), 139–177. doi:10.1111/fisc.2009.30.issue-2

Barca, V., Hurrell, A., MacAuslan, I., Visram, A., & Willis, J. (2013). Paying attention to detail: How to transfer cash in cash transfers. *Enterprise Development and Microfinance*, 24(1), 10–27. doi:10.3362/1755-1986.2013.003

Barrientos, A., & Dejong, J. (2006). Reducing child poverty with cash transfers: A sure thing? *Development Policy Review*, 24(5), 537–552. doi:10.1111/dpr.2006.24.issue-5

Chambers, R. (1997). *Whose reality counts? Putting the first last*. London: Intermediate Technology Publications.

Chase, E., & Walker, R. (2012). The co-construction of shame in the context of poverty: Beyond a threat to the social bond. *Sociology*, 47(4), 739–754. doi:10.1177/0038038512453796

Dercon, S., & Krishnan, P. (2009). Poverty and the psychosocial competencies of children: Evidence from the young lives sample in four developing countries. *Children, Youth and Environments*, 19(2), 138–163.

Garbarino, S., & Holland, J. (2009). *Quantitative and qualitative methods in impact evaluation and measuring results*. Birmingham: University of Birmingham.

Giddens, A. (1976). *New rules of sociological method*. London: Hutchinson.

Goodman, A., & Gregg, P. (2010). *Poorer children's educational attainment: How important are attitudes and behaviour?* York, UK: Joseph Rowntree Foundation.

Gutman, L., & Vorhaus, J. (2012). *The impact of pupil behaviour and wellbeing on educational outcomes*. London: Department of Education.

Habermas, J. (1981/1987). *Theory of communicative action. Volume Two: Liveworld and system: A critique of functionalist reason*. Translated by Thomas A. McCarthy. Boston, MA: Beacon Press.

Handa, S., Martorano, B., Halpern, C., Pettifor, A., & Thirumurthy, H. (2014a). *Subjective wellbeing, risk perceptions and time discounting: Evidence from a large-scale cash transfer programme* (Innocenti Working Paper No. 2014-02). Florence: UNICEF Office of Research.

Handa, A., Martorano, B., Halpern, C., Pettifor, A., & Thirumurthy, H. (2014b). *The impact of the Kenya CT–OVC on parents' wellbeing and their children.* Florence: UNICEF Office of Research.

Handa, S., Seidenfeld, D., & Tembo, G. (2013). *The impact of a large scale poverty targeted cash transfer program on intertemporal choice.* Chapel Hill: Carolina Population Center, University of North Carolina.

Haushofer, J., & Shapiro, J. (2013). *Household response to income changes: Evidence from an unconditional cash transfer program in Kenya* (Working Paper). Princeton, NJ: Princeton University.

IDS. (2009). *After 2015, '3D Human Wellbeing', Issue 9, IDS in focus policy briefing, June 2009.* Brighton: Insititute of Development Studies.

ILO. (2012). *Text of the recommendation concerning national floors of social protection.* Geneva: International Labour Organisation.

MacAuslan, I., & Riemenschneider, N. (2011). Richer but resented: What do cash transfers do to social relations? *IDS Bulletin, 42*(6), 60–66. doi:10.1111/idsb.2011.42.issue-6

Macours, K., Schady, N., & Vakis, R. (2012). Cash transfers, behavioral changes, and cognitive development in early childhood: Evidence from a randomized experiment. *American Economic Journal: Applied Economics, 4*(2), 247–7.

Mani, A., Mullainathan, S., Shafir, E., & Zhao, J. (2013). Poverty impedes cognitive function. *Science, 341*(6149), 976–980. doi:10.1126/science.1238041

Marmot, M. (2005). Social determinants of health inequalities. *The Lancet, 365*, 1099–1104. doi:10.1016/S0140-6736(05)74234-3

McGregor, J. A. (2007). researching wellbeing: From concepts to methodology. In I. Gough & I. A. McGregor (Eds.), *Wellbeing in developing countries.* Cambridge: Cambridge University Press.

Merttens, F., HUrrell, A., Marzi, M., Attah, R., Farhat, M., Kardan, A., & MacAuslan, I. (2013). *Kenya hunger safety net programme monitoring and evaluation component: Impact evaluation final report: 2009 to 2012.* Oxford: Oxford Policy Management.

Merttens, F., & Morris, R. (2013). *Kenya hunger safety net programme monitoring and evaluation component: Operational monitoring final report: 2009–2012.* Oxford: Oxford Policy Management.

OECD. (2013). *OECD guidelines on measuring subjective well-being.* Paris: OECD publishing.

OPM. (2012). *Kenya hunger safety net programme monitoring and evaluation component: Qualitative impact evaluation report: 2011 to 2012.* Oxford: Oxford Policy Management.

OPM. (2013a). *Qualitative research and analysis of the economic impact of cash transfer programmes in sub Saharan Africa: A research guide for the from protection to production (PtoP) project, FAO.* Oxford: Oxford Policy Management.

OPM. (2013b). *Qualitative research and analysis of the economic impact of cash transfer programmes in sub Saharan Africa: Ghana country case study report, FAO.* Oxford: Oxford Policy Management.

OPM. (2013c). *Qualitative research and analysis of the economic impact of cash transfer programmes in sub Saharan Africa: Zimbabwe country case study report, FAO.* Oxford: Oxford Policy Management.

OPM. (2014a). *Qualitative research and analysis of the economic impact of cash transfer programmes in sub Saharan Africa: Lesotho country case study report, FAO.* Oxford: Oxford Policy Management.

OPM. (2014b). *Child grants programme impact evaluation - Follow-up impact report.* Oxford: Oxford Policy Management.

OPM & IDS. (2011a). *Kenya hunger safety net programme monitoring and evaluation component: Baseline report.* Oxford: Oxford Policy Management.

OPM & IDS. (2011b). *Kenya hunger safety net programme monitoring and evaluation component: Targeting effectiveness evaluation report.* Oxford: Oxford Policy Management.

OPM & IDS. (2011c). *Kenya hunger safety net programme monitoring and evaluation component: Payments monitoring report.* Oxford: Oxford Policy Management.

OPM & IDS. (2012a). *Kenya hunger safety net programme monitoring and evaluation component: Impact analysis synthesis report.* Oxford: Oxford Policy Management.

OPM & IDS. (2012b). *Kenya hunger safety net programme monitoring and evaluation component: Quantitative impact evaluation report: 2009/10 to 2010/11.* Oxford: Oxford Policy Management.

OPM & IDS. (2012c). *Kenya hunger safety net programme monitoring and evaluation component: Consolidated operational monitoring report.* Oxford: Oxford Policy Management.

Outes, I., Sanchez, A., & Molina, O. (2010). *Psychosocial status and cognitive achievement in Peru* (Working Paper n. 65). Oxford: Young Lives, Department of International Development, University of Oxford.

Redmond, G. (2008). *Children's perspectives on economic adversity: A review of the literature* (Discussion Paper 2008–01). Florence: UNICEF Innocenti Research Centre

Ridge, T. (2002). *Childhood poverty and social exclusion: From a child's perspective.* Bristol: Policy Press.

Ryff, C., & Singer, B. (1996). Psychological weil-being: Meaning, measurement, and implications for psychotherapy research. *Psychotherapy and Psychosomatics, 65*(1), 14–23. doi:10.1159/000289026

Shah, A. K., Mullainathan, S., & Shafir, E. (2012). Some consequences of having too little. *Science, 338*(6107), 682–685. doi:10.1126/science.1222426

Stiglitz, J., Sen, A., Fitoussi, J., & Sarkozy Commisison. (2009). *Report of the commission on the measurement of economic performance and social progress.* Paris

Taylor, D. (2011). Wellbeing and welfare: A psychosocial analysis of being well and doing well enough. *Journal of Social Policy, 40*(4), 777–794. doi:10.1017/S0047279411000249

Townsend, P. (1973). *The International Analyis of Poverty*. Hemel Hempstead: Harvester Wheatsheaf.

Van Oorschot, W. (2002). Targeting welfare: On the functions and dysfunctions of means testing in social policy. In P. Townsend and D. Gordon (Eds.), *World poverty: New policies to defeat an old enemy*. Bristol: Policy Press.

Walker, R., Chase, E., & Lødemel, I. (2012). The indignity of the Welfare Reform Act. *Poverty, 143*, 9–12.

Walker, R., Kyomuhendo, G., Chase, E., Choudhry, S., Gubrium, E. K., Nicola, J., ... Ming, Y. (2013). Poverty in global perspective: Is shame a common denominator? *Journal of Social Policy, 42*, 215–233. doi:10.1017/S0047279412000979

White, S. (2009). *Bringing wellbeing into development practice* (WeD Working Paper 09/50). Bath: Wellbeing in Developing Countries Research Group, University of Bath.

Wilkinson, R., & Marmot, M. (2003). *The solid facts: Social determinants of health*. Copenhagen: World Health Organization.

Williamson, J., & Robinson, M. (2006). Psychosocial interventions, or integrated programming for well-being? *Intervention, 4*(1), 4–25.

Accessing the 'Right' Kinds of Material and Symbolic Capital: the Role of Cash Transfers in Reducing Adolescent School Absence and Risky Behaviour in South Africa

MICHELLE ADATO*, STEPHEN DEVEREUX** & RACHEL SABATES-WHEELER**

*Poverty, Health and Nutrition Division, International Food Policy Research Institute, Washington, DC, USA[1], **Centre for Social Protection, Institute for Development Studies, Brighton, UK

ABSTRACT *This article investigates how well South Africa's Child Support Grant (CSG) responds to the material and psychosocial needs of adolescents, and the resultant effects on schooling and risky behaviour. One driver of schooling decisions is shame related to poverty and the 'social cost' of school, where a premium must often be paid for fashionable clothes or accessories. The other driver relates to symbolic and consumptive capital gained through engaging in sexual exchange relationships. The anticipated impacts from the CSG are partial because of these non-material drivers of adolescent choices. Non-material transmission mechanisms must be better understood and addressed.*

1. Introduction

Cash transfer programmes, both unconditional and conditional, have been designed to address the basic consumption and human capital needs of poor people. There is growing interest, however, in how cash transfers could help to address the psycho-social needs of poor children, integrated with other child protection and social services, though more has been written on their potential than on actual examples to date (see Barrientos, Byrne, Villa, & Peña, 2013; Richter, 2012). More generally, Sabates-Wheeler and Roelen (2011) consider whether cash transfer programmes are child-sensitive, emphasising the need to look at practical as well as strategic needs of different population groups – needs that relate to, and derive from, social status, position within society or in relation to other groups (for instance, women in relation to men). Addressing the psychosocial conditions and needs of children through a cash transfer programme requires first an understanding of what these are, then a programme design that responds to them. But cash transfer programme designs, particularly conditional transfers, are predominantly based on economic assumptions about the role of cash in enabling and incentivising behaviour change (Behrman & Skoufias, 2010). While much of the evidence suggests that cash incentives often do play this role successfully (Adato & Hoddinott, 2010; Fiszbein et al., 2009), there are also many psycho-social, sociocultural and structural influences on people's practices and decisions, which cash transfer programmes are generally not designed to address (Adato, Roopnaraine, & Becker, 2011).

This article looks at how well South Africa's Child Support Grant responds to the material and psychosocial needs of adolescents, and the effects on their participation in school and risky behaviour.

Our empirical analysis draws on qualitative research conducted as part of a mixed-method evaluation of the Child Support Grant (CSG) commissioned by the South African government's Department of Social Development (DSD), the South African Social Security Agency (SASSA), and UNICEF.[2] The CSG is the largest cash transfer programme in Africa, reaching nearly 11 million poor children in 2013 (South African Social Security Agency [SASSA], 2013). It is a means-tested unconditional grant. Although it was designed primarily to ensure a basic level of subsistence within South Africa's rights-based social policy, there has been a long-standing interest among its government architects and champions, researchers and programme evaluators, regarding its potential to increase school attendance and reduce dropouts.

The evaluation sought to test this theory of change: that cash transfers allow recipients to improve their wellbeing on several dimensions, including education and risky behaviours such as transactional sex or substance abuse (DSD, SASSA, & UNICEF, 2011). This would occur directly through material support, and indirectly through early childhood human capital investment when the grant was received early in life. The direct transmission mechanisms are not self-evident. The implied theory of change is that education constraints are mainly cash-related, that risky behaviours are functions of both income poverty and social marginalisation, and that cash transfers simultaneously alleviate poverty and reduce economic and social dependence on risky behaviours.[3]

Our research findings suggest that these effects are partial, because of the powerful non-material drivers of education and behavioural choices, which the CSG can help to address, but only up to a point. One of these drivers is shame related to poverty: for poor children, the food they bring (or don't bring) to school, the quality of their clothing and shoes, and their hairstyles can be significant sources of embarrassment, even keeping them away from school. Shame, peer pressure, the need for social status, and the articulation of material and non-material needs and desires, also drive 'risky behaviour' – non-professional sexual exchange relationships, where girls and young women engage in sexual relationships in exchange for financial support, gifts and status.[4] Our findings contain strong echoes of Bourdieu's (1986) seminal work on the 'forms of capital' and the (conditional) convertibility of symbolic and social capital into economic capital, discussed below, but with caveats. We conclude that future social transfer initiatives to transform beneficiary wellbeing must be intentionally designed to identify synergies between these different capitals.

This article first proposes a theoretical framework for understanding the significance of psycho-social drivers of adolescent behaviour, and their relationship to material drivers, drawing primarily on Bourdieu's concept of symbolic capital. It further draws on social capital theory to explain constraints on the conversion of social capital to economic capital. We distinguish three levels of 'needs' to explain why the CSG is or is not effective at breaking the constraints on the convertibility of symbolic capital to economic opportunity. After reviewing relevant literature on the constraints on school attendance, the relationship between shame and poverty, and the drivers of risky sexual practices, we provide a brief overview of the CSG, and the research design for the evaluation on which this article is based. Next, we present our findings, focusing first on the role of stigma and peer pressure on schooling decisions, then on the hierarchy of risky sexual exchange relationships and the complex interplay of material and non-material needs. We conclude with a call for a more nuanced understanding of the non-material causal pathways of behaviour, and how programmes might respond.

2. Material and Non-Material Assets: the Importance of Symbolic and Social Capital

One way to frame the choices of adolescents from very poor homes and communities around schooling and risky behaviours is through the work of Bourdieu and other sociologists who seek to explain how different forms of capital and resources produce and reproduce inequality and opportunity through affecting psycho-social drivers of these choices. Wearing socially acceptable clothes, for instance, costs more than wearing ordinary or old clothes. This can be modelled as investing in symbolic capital. A narrow analysis would criticise the purchase of 'status' goods, such as a particular brand of shirt or shoes by or for schoolchildren from poor families as 'extravagant' and 'wasteful'. But an understanding of the non-economic values attached to these goods recognises that children may skip school or drop out unless they are socially accepted by their peers, that social acceptance is critical in determining access to opportunities, and that this requires spending extra on such 'status' goods.

Bourdieu, in his classic work *The Forms of Capital* (1986), expands the concept of capital to include assets formed by access to culturally valuable symbols, ways of life and social networks. Money carries powerful symbolic properties that confer meaning, dignity and relevance to people's lives (see Carruthers & Espeland, 1998). By thinking of worth only as economic value we overlook (1) other important measures of wealth and (2) other economically important types of exchange. In relation to the first point, as we will show below, adolescents in South Africa indicate that they obtain self-worth and dignity through a range of 'status' goods, such as clean clothes, accepted hairstyles, the 'right' shoes. The cost of obtaining these 'status' goods often exceeds what a poor family's budget can afford. Without such goods children feel less inclined to show up at school, fearing embarrassment and marginalisation. Bourdieu makes a further point: that all capitals (social, assets, cultural [symbolic]) are, under certain conditions, convertible to economic capital or monetary value. Evidence from Ethiopia and the UK shows that material resources can acquire symbolic and emotional power; for instance, when children ascribe importance to items of clothing, such as branded trainers in the UK (Ridge, 2002) or hair decorations in Ethiopia that signify the festival Meskel (Camfield & Tafere, 2009). In relation to our CSG case, many assets to which adolescents ascribe important value, such as hairstyles, uniforms and clothing brands, can be converted into 'status capital', which facilitates inclusion into social networks and ultimately opportunities that convert to economic capital. That is, these status goods potentially increase the likelihood that children will show up and stay in school, allowing them access to the economic opportunities that education provides.

In terms of Bourdieu's point about other economically important types of exchange, we can draw on social capital theory to understand why many adolescents from very poor homes engage in 'risky behaviours' and unproductive peer groups: simply because they are a more profitable type of exchange than anything else on offer. These behaviours offer them an immediate way to relieve a material or financial constraint, but also a form of exchange that allows them to access wealth and worth.

Social capital is the capital gained from personal connections, such as membership in groups, including families, clubs, and solidarity groups. These connections can lead to jobs, loans, valuable connections, and investment opportunities. In other words they can alleviate material constraints in an indirect way. They are sustained through exchange of material goods (such as gifts) and symbolic goods (such as mutual recognition). In fact, 'the profits which accrue from membership in a group [network] are the basis of the solidarity which makes them possible' (Bourdieu, 1986, p. 286). There is however a downside to social capital, not addressed by Bourdieu but usefully discussed by Portes and Landolt (1996). They argue that social capital can have downward levelling pressures, that is, pressure to conform within a social network can mean that individuals may be kept back from reaching their aspirations, or even successfully converting their social means of exchange into economically beneficial worth. Durlauf (1999) usefully defines social capital as 'the influence which the characteristics and behaviours of one's reference groups has on one's assessment of alternative courses of behaviour' (p. 2). This indicates that any presumption concerning the virtues of social capital is questionable.

In the case of the social networks and peer groups related to sexual exchange relationships (for example, 'sugar daddies'), adolescents are unable to convert these 'negative' social networks into positive, socially desirable outcomes. They derive some short-run gains related to material benefits and belonging, but the effects are perverse. The question we ask is whether the CSG has the potential to break these constraints to capital convertibility and also to reduce the likelihood that adolescents will engage in social mechanisms that enforce undesirable types of community behaviour. Potentially, even the small CSG payment can make inroads on two fronts: (1) it can alleviate constraints to access to symbolic capital and (2) it can break the lock-in into negative social capital.

Both of these outcomes could allow conversion to access to opportunities, economic capital and socially desirable behaviours.

We find that the CSG can make these inroads, but only partially. This is because first, the grant is either too small to provide access to the necessary cultural/symbolic capital, or it is not used to that end because of the spending choices of caregivers. Second, in some circumstances, it does not respond sufficiently to the drivers of negative social capital. In both cases, the CSG's convertibility, from economic to symbolic capital and back again, is limited. The distinctions can be understood through a categorisation of three levels of 'needs' revealed in our research, which map onto Bourdieu's conceptualisation of capitals. The first level, which we call 'basic subsistence', is basic material needs, such as food, transportation, and school expenses – needs that the CSG is directly designed to address. The second level, which we refer to as 'basic symbolic', is material social needs, which confer a sufficient degree of dignity that enables children to go to school without humiliation – symbolic capital in the form of a morning bath, a new uniform, warm clothes, a respectable lunch or hairstyle. The CSG can help to meet these needs, though our data suggests that in practice it does so only marginally. The third level of need, which we refer to as 'consumptive symbolic', is for higher levels of consumption – expensive clothes, jewellery, cell-phones, specialty foods, rides in luxury cars. All three levels drive sexual exchange relationships, reflecting Hunter's (2002) distinction between 'sex linked to subsistence' and 'sex linked to consumption' (p. 101). It is in addressing this last level that the CSG is most limited. This is because, first, the payment is far too small, and second, the drivers of these consumptive needs are too deeply rooted in historical, sociocultural, and psychosocial processes. A different kind of intervention is required, one that directly addresses non-material drivers in a way that the CSG does not.

3. Material and Non-Material Drivers of Schooling and Sexual Exchange Relationships in South Africa

In South Africa, the primary reason for not completing high school is unaffordability. For 7–15 year-olds, the main reason is insufficient money to pay fees, followed by being too young to attend, and then illness. For 16–18 year-olds, the main reason is also lack of money, followed by the belief that education was useless or uninteresting, then pregnancy (South African Department of Education, 2006).

A literature review (Hunt, 2008) on dropping out of school concluded that few studies on this subject are available, particularly from the point of view of children and the processes that lead to drop-out or absenteeism.[5] We were unable to find literature on the impact of peer pressure and social status on school attendance and retention in South Africa, but this issue emerged very strongly in our qualitative data, as will be seen below.

There is theoretical and empirical work that links shame to poverty (though not to education outcomes). As we are interested in the way that poverty can affect education choices by adolescents, and given that adolescents in our qualitative research on the CSG indicated that shame, embarrassment and self-worth were important factors influencing the desire to attend school, this literature is instructive. The presence or absence of dignity is part of a multi-dimensional well-being and poverty framework, and the 'ability to go without shame' is a basic capability pointed out by Sen (1983; see also Reyles, 2007). Other research identifies shame, guilt and humiliation as missing dimensions of poverty (Narayan, Chambers, Shah, & Petesch, 2000; Reyles, 2007). Walker et al. (2013) explore the contention that shame is a universal attribute of poverty that is common to people experiencing poverty in all societies The research investigated Sen's contention that the experience of shame lies at the 'irreducible absolutist core in the idea of poverty' (p. 4), is always present, and arises from the inability fully to participate in society. Based on fieldwork in seven countries, Walker et al. found that adults and children in all study settings often felt ashamed because of their poverty. Respondents frequently reported that poverty caused them social and psychological pain, which in turn led them to engage in pretence, withdrawal, self-loathing and scapegoating.

In addition to analysing the role that shame and dignity play in driving the material and symbolic needs of South African adolescents, this article focuses on one of the most salient responses to those needs – that of risky sexual practices in the form of sexual exchange relationships. A literature review by Eaton, Flisher, and Aarø (2003) found that psychosocial factors explaining these practices include beliefs around HIV and AIDS, self-esteem, and the psychosocial dimensions of unequal gender and power relations. Research in South Africa finds that low self-esteem is associated with earlier onset of sexual activity and having more sexual partners (Goliath, 1995, as cited in Eaton et al., 2003; Perkel, Strebel, & Joubert, 1991).

Psychosocial factors interact closely with structural factors, foremost of which is pervasive poverty. Lack of material necessities and status-conferring symbolic capital can itself create or reinforce low self-esteem, leading to risky behaviour. Kelly and Parker (2000, as cited in Eaton et al., 2003) suggest that socio-economic background is the most significant vector for predicting adoption of risk prevention measures. Poverty is a strong driver of commodified sex, whereby poor women engage in sexual relationships in exchange for financial support, as well as less overt exchange relationships, where older boyfriends with money offer status, gifts and financial benefits that parents are too poor to afford. The prevalence of sexual exchange relationships and their role in the social and economic fabric of the lives of men and women is seen in the large literature on non-professional sexual exchange that emerged in the 1990s (Leclerc-Madlala, 2003), including much research in South Africa. This practice is very distinct from that of prostitution, and involves the giving of gifts in everyday relationships between 'boyfriends' and 'girlfriends' that involve sex. Much of this literature is focused on relationships between younger women or girls and older men, the so-called 'sugar daddies', though these exchanges are also common among school-aged youth (Kaufman & Stavrou, 2004) as well as women of varying ages. One study of women seeking antenatal care in Soweto health clinics found that 21 per cent reported having had sex with a non-primary male partner in exchange for material goods or money (Dunkle et al., 2004).

Research by Hunter (2002) in KwaZulu-Natal, South Africa, illustrates how 'sugar daddy' relationships derive from the historically rooted economically privileged positions of men, and socioculturally-rooted expectations that men will have multiple partners, as well as extreme poverty and its gendered dimensions. Importantly, however, the relationships of power are not one-sided: young women, particularly in urban areas where they have a greater element of choice, do not perceive themselves as victims but rather as choosing and using these relationships to access power and resources. An important distinction made by Hunter (2002) is between 'sex linked to subsistence' and 'sex linked to consumption' (p. 101). In the former, sex is traded to meet basic subsistence needs. In the latter sex is linked to consumption, where subsistence needs are taken care of by parents or guardians, leaving fashion and cell-phones with high sexual-exchange value. In these circumstances young women exercise more agency, using men to fulfil their consumptive needs, sometimes pursuing multiple partners and deriding men who cannot afford them (Hunter, 2002). Sex linked to consumption is also the focus of research by Leclerc-Madlala (2003), who attributes it in part to a globalising, modernising world where young women pursue ideals fuelled by the media.

The literature on risky sexual exchange relationships makes clear that the three levels of need we described in the previous section – basic material, basic symbolic, and consumptive symbolic – all drive these relationships, with 'sex linked to subsistence' responding to the first level, and 'sex linked to consumption' (Hunter, 2002, p. 101) responding to the third. This literature says little about the second level, straddling the first and third in that it can be seen as a need for 'basic symbolic capital', which came out strongly in our qualitative research as a factor influencing school attendance decisions, and in making the experience of school either humiliating or affirming.

4. The Child Support Grant

The Child Support Grant (CSG) is the single largest social grant programme in sub-Saharan Africa, reaching close to 11 million beneficiaries by late 2013. It was introduced in 1998, soon after South

Africa's transition to democracy in 1994. In the 2013 financial year, a flat rate of R290 (US$26) was paid each month to every child under 18 living in households that satisfy the means test: monthly income less than R2,900 (US$260) for a single parent or caregiver, or less than R5,800 (US$527) for a married couple. Eligibility was initially restricted to children under seven years old, but the age threshold has been steadily lifted until it reached 18 years in 2012, meaning that households with adolescents also receive the CSG (Proudlock, 2011). The designated recipient of the CSG is the child's primary caregiver, usually the mother but often – due especially to South Africa's high HIV and AIDS prevalence – other relatives or even non-related carers. This has implications for how – by whom, on whom and on what – the grant money is spent, as discussed below.

With respect to impacts on schooling, earlier studies found that access to the CSG resulted in higher school enrolment and attendance rates (Budlender & Woolard, 2006; Case, Hosegood, & Lund, 2005; Samson et al., 2004). The 2011 quantitative evaluation of the CSG (DSD, SASSA, & UNICEF, 2012) linked to our study found that current adolescent recipients are absent for fewer days than those who do not receive the grant. This impact was particularly strong for males. It also found positive impacts on grade attainment, and mathematics and reading scores for children enrolled at a young age. The quantitative evaluation also found that CSG receipt does significantly reduce sexual activity and number of partners among adolescents. This effect was strongest when the grant had been received since early childhood.

5. Methodology and the Qualitative CSG Evaluation

The qualitative fieldwork was undertaken in 2010 in 12 urban, peri-urban and rural localities in four provinces of South Africa: Eastern Cape, Gauteng, KwaZulu-Natal and Limpopo. In each locality, seven focus group discussions (FGDs) were conducted with primary caregivers (mostly women) and their male partners, with separate groups for women and men, and CSG recipient and non-recipient households, and with adolescent girls and boys. All focus group participants gave their informed consent, and the research was reviewed by an institutional review board. Four key informant interviews (KIIs) were also conducted in each locality with SASSA staff,[6] education workers, health workers and community leaders.

Semi-structured interview guides were designed, pre-tested and revised for the FGDs and KIIs, covering the following topic areas: grant access, pay-point, use of grant, education, health, child labour, risky behaviours, social welfare, and early childhood development. Discussions and interviews lasted 60–90 minutes on average, and were recorded subject to respondents giving their informed consent. After the fieldwork was completed the data were transcribed and translated, then coded and analysed using NVivo, a qualitative data analysis software.

This study formed part of a mixed-method evaluation that also included a representative household survey in five provinces, and the qualitative sample was a sub-sample of communities and households, purposively drawn from the quantitative sample. Eighty-four focus groups were conducted averaging about eight people each, thus including roughly 670 participants, and additional key informants. Despite these substantial numbers, focus groups do not produce statistically representative data; rather, they provided a rich, textured dataset for social analysis. Thus, for instance, this qualitative data is not intended to claim with statistical confidence that the CSG does or does not reduce risky behaviour. Instead, we are able to analyse the complex, multi-layered social phenomena that explain why the CSG may or may not reduce this behaviour, and under what circumstances.

6. Research Findings on the Psychosocial Dimensions of Schooling and Risky Behaviour Decisions: The Interplay of Material and Non-Material Influences on South African Adolescents

Understanding the impact of the CSG on schooling requires understanding the motivations behind the decisions of caregivers and children with respect to children's education. While the evaluation survey looked at the quantitative impacts of the CSG on school attendance and retention, the qualitative research examined the reasons why children do and don't go to school. Material factors – the financial costs associated with schooling – were the most widely cited obstacles in the qualitative research with respect to why children dropped out of school. This is consistent with analysis of national household survey data, where lack of money for fees is by far the main reason preventing attendance or continued education for children 7–18 years of age (South African Department of Education, 2006). 'Fees' is not broken down in these surveys, and is intended to encompass the various financial expenses associated with school attendance. In our research the breakdown of these expenses is indicated by what people said they spent the CSG on, with 'education' mentioned even more frequently than food, and education expenses said to encompass school fees (mainly for crèche and pre-school), stationery, transport, food, and clothing.[7] Following financial constraints, other salient factors affecting adolescents' schooling decisions identified in the qualitative research included pregnancy, substance abuse, peer pressure and influence, and the desire to earn money through work explaining drop-outs, and substance abuse, laziness, and illness explaining absences. This is somewhat consistent with national survey data citing pregnancy, the view that 'education is useless/uninteresting' for older children, and illness for younger children (South African Department of Education, 2006).

6.1. The Humiliation of Poverty and 'What Others Think': The Role of Stigma and Peer Pressure in Children's Experience of School

In terms of social and symbolic capital, we were particularly interested in the strength of the findings related to peer pressure, and the way that different types of material constraints affected children's psychosocial well-being, as well as their influence on children's school attendance. Clothing, hairstyle, food types, and other symbols of relative wealth and poverty affect children's image of self in relation to others, and generate respect or derision from peers and even authority figures. 'Peer pressure' was cited in nine out of our 12 qualitative study communities as a reason for missing school, and in all 12 as a reason for dropping out. Peer pressure takes many forms, but one source revolves around having the 'right' clothes and food – direct material constraints which have non-material consequences. In seven of the 12 communities, caregivers and adolescents described children – both girls and boys – as being embarrassed by old or unfashionable clothing and old uniforms, causing them to miss school. Not feeling 'the same as others' was mentioned in several communities as a reason that teenagers drop out, as they seek to fit in. One teenager described her experience of being laughed at for not having a birth certificate or other identification, and the shame she felt. The need to be fashionable is not just an urban experience: a teenager in a rural community discussed how children may drop out of school if others have nice clothes and they do not, or if they do not have the money to get their hair done like other girls. For children of all ages, an old uniform or cheap brand of shoes is a signifier of poverty and lower status. Lack of money for better clothing can create psychosocial access barriers to education. Caregivers in two urban communities explained their children's experiences:

> They need uniforms like any other pupils at school. If she does not have warm clothes, socks to wear and is always laughed at by other pupils she feels isolated and then decides not to go to school. Children want to go to school fully prepared with all the necessary requirements.

Boys are also affected by this peer pressure and shame:

> I need more than the CSG because my child has no jersey to go to school, he is also not allowed to wear 'takkies', he must wear school shoes [...] the principal embarrasses them in front of others and hence they drop out of school. For example when my child was in Standard 9 he was embarrassed by the principal and he dropped.

Uniforms at least provide some levelling effect – there is less opportunity for social differentiation through clothing, apart from uniform quality. A man in Sheshego suggested that schools should eliminate 'casual Fridays', where children wear their own clothes, because some children cannot afford nice clothes, causing envy, embarrassment or competition among them.

Lack of cleanliness is another source of stigma. 'Dirty clothes' was mentioned as a source of embarrassment, as was personal hygiene. One woman explained that when it is cold and there is no electricity or money for paraffin, her daughter cannot bathe and therefore does not go to school. Food is another source of embarrassment, since the food that children bring, or their participation in school lunches, reveals their poverty.

> My child told me that this little boy is in the same school as him but has been missing a lot of school days for the past few weeks. One day I called this boy and asked why he doesn't go to school and he sadly told me that he doesn't go because he no more likes to eat the food that is cooked at school, because other children tease him about it.

Often the boundary between a material constraint (poverty) and a psychosocial constraint (peer pressure) is difficult to disentangle, as in this case of a child who believes his lunch-box is inferior to his classmates': 'The child gets discouraged at school due to that other children come with healthy lunch-boxes. The child complains about having to eat bread and peanut butter every day [...] and so the child decides that he is not going to school at all.' Is this child's decision due to hunger or embarrassment? In other cases the constraint is purely psychosocial (peer pressure): 'Sometimes when you buy them Toughees shoes they will say: "I am no longer going to school because my friends wear Grasshopper shoes."'

At first glance an old uniform or a low-status brand of shoes appears to be a material constraint that the CSG has the potential to alleviate (though one quote above suggests that it is often not sufficient). However, where household income is insufficient, or if a caregiver does not recognise the importance of affirmation by the child's peers at school, the caregiver might insist that the old uniform is still wearable, or the cheapest brand of shoes is sufficient, and allocate the CSG money to other pressing needs instead. This could cause the child to suffer ridicule, dislike school, and skip school or drop out altogether. The reason is that not having a *uniform* is a material barrier to education (the child might not be allowed to attend school), but not having a *new* uniform is a psychosocial barrier (the child can attend school but risks being ridiculed and ostracised by her classmates or teacher).

These material and non-material barriers have different 'costs'. The social cost can be quantified as the margin or premium between basic clothes and higher status labels. In Figure 1 below, the cost of buying social acceptance – and thereby alleviating non-material constraints to education – is R100.

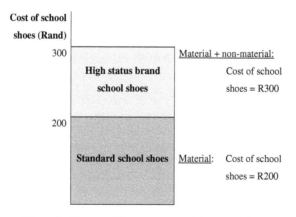

Figure 1. The material and non-material costs of shoes.
Source: Authors.

Whether the CSG is sufficient to cover the social cost of schooling is questionable. Many respondents thought that the CSG helps with keeping children in school through its contributions to school expenses, though some did not see it as enough to cover these. Teenagers in particular did not see the grant as enough, possibly because they are more cognisant of the social cost. Nevertheless, given that education expenses are among the largest grant expenditures, it clearly helps with at least the direct economic costs.

6.2. Material and Symbolic 'Necessities': A Hierarchy of Risky Sexual Exchange Relationships

Among the risky behaviours of adolescents studied in the qualitative evaluation, this article focuses on sexual exchange relationships, for several reasons. First and foremost, the issues related to social status and peer pressure, and the articulation of material and non-material needs and desires that drive education decisions, are closely related to those that drive risky sexual practices. Secondly, these sexual exchange relationships were among the most pervasive risks raised in the qualitative research, with particularly dire consequences for adolescent education and health outcomes. These sexual exchange relationships mostly involve young women, though we found some accounts of young men involved in such relationships with older women.

As discussed above in our conceptual framework, South African adolescents have three levels of 'needs', with material and psychosocial dimensions: 'basic subsistence', 'basic symbolic', and 'consumptive symbolic.' This section examines how all three levels of need have a direct impact on risky sexual behaviour among South African adolescents, but they function in different ways, and for different people across socioeconomic, age, and geographic divides. Furthermore, these sexual exchange relationships are contextualised by needs for status as part of 'negative social capital', networks that adolescent girls are engaged in, providing short-term economic gain but ultimately downward-levelling, often resulting in school drop-out, pregnancy, and/or HIV.

Several of the most widely discussed risks for adolescents in the research relate to sexual relationships, including pregnancy, HIV/AIDS and STIs, dating older men (and to a lesser extent women) for money, and dating teachers. Sexual exchange relationships were described in every study community, frequently and at length. Among the 200 exchanges in the focus groups about the role of income poverty in risky behaviour, the vast majority related to girls' transactional sexual relationships with older men. Some of the literature reviewed earlier explains the normalcy of these relationships and their functionality, in the eyes of the adolescents involved. However, the views of caregivers in the qualitative research, and many of the adolescents themselves, convey powerfully that these are pervasive and indeed pose risks to the health and well-being of adolescents.

Girls' relationships with older partners present a triple risk: first, older men are more likely to be HIV-positive than younger boys (the prospect of dating older men with money makes dating boys less desirable in comparison); second, there is a direct relationship between partner age difference and school drop-out rates among girls aged 15–19 years in South Africa; third, dropping out of school places girls at a higher risk of HIV.

Teenagers who date older men who can provide them with both basic necessities and desired goods such as brand label clothing, are meeting both material needs (financial capital) and non-material needs ('symbolic' capital). These relationships represent strategic choices, whether they are in pursuit of survival or status. Most of our findings were about sexual exchange for material 'basic subsistence' needs – largely food for the girls and their households, as well as 'basic symbolic', clothing and transportation, but more rarely in the 'consumptive symbolic' category. This concentration of examples at the two lower levels of exchange may be because our research was with the very poor – CSG recipients or others who did not receive the grant but were eligible. In Hunter's (2002) example, 'sex for consumption' took place in a lesser context of deprivation where girls had their subsistence needs met by their caregivers. In our research, in a peri-urban community in Gauteng Province, all three types of relationships were mentioned. Men, women and teenagers talked extensively about girls dating older men for money, as a means to obtain both basic necessities – food, school uniforms, household goods and transportation to school, with small amounts of cash gifts described. In other cases higher-end items were described that make teen-agers popular or impressive to their peers, such as brand name clothing, beauty supplies, airtime for cell-phones, or being driven in fancy cars.

> Because of peer pressure, they look at the girl next door and find that she wears expensive clothes, and she ends up falling in love with taxi drivers so that he can buy her clothes. When they date taxi drivers they give them R5 or maybe R20 to buy things. And they date sugar daddies who give them R200 to buy clothes. So they can look as good as their friends, but kids end up being pregnant and HIV-positive.

There is also an age dimension: where very young children were involved the relationships were usually described as being for basic material needs:

> It has become difficult for these kids to report if they are being abused, due to that the perpetrator offers the child money. For example, you find that there is a man who always abuses a 10-year-old child and gives her money to buy [lunch] at school. It's not easy for the child to tell you as a parent because she knows that you will fight with that guy and she will starve because she gets money from him, because she knows that there is no food in the household.

Sometimes the money goes not just to the girl but also to her household, for example, 'buying groceries for her granny', making it less likely that caregivers will object.

On the consumptive end of the continuum, several communities mentioned that girls received as much as R1,000 as gifts from these men. Teenage girls in Limpopo were aware of the HIV risk but engage in the relationship anyway:

> You risk your life because you don't know his status, what you are after is money. That is the main reason because that [money] fools girls immediately – when a man says 'Here is R1,000, let's have sex', you won't say no.

We did not find girls talking about these relationships expressed as an exercise of power or agency, as some of the literature reviewed earlier suggests. Rather, most respondents described the consequences of AIDS and pregnancy, and the risks they have to take to get the things they need.

In addition to the obvious health risks, the negative impact of these relationships on education comes when girls drop out of school, either because they are preoccupied with the material lifestyle on offer, or because of a belief by girls that education is not necessary if a sugar daddy or boyfriend is looking after them. 'This other friend of mine dropped out and when I asked why she is dropping out when she is about to finish, she told me that her boyfriend said that she should because he said he will support her.'

Both the quantitative and qualitative evaluation studies aimed to gain insight on the question of whether the CSG could have an impact on these risky practices. The survey found that receipt of the CSG in the household at the time of adolescence was associated with statistically significant reduc-tions in adolescent engagement in sexual activity and number of sexual partners (DSD, SASSA, & UNICEF, 2012). In the qualitative research, most caregivers, adolescents, and key informants said that they thought the CSG could help, though nearly all responses referred to conditions where the exchange was for basic material necessities like food:

> if there is no income at home […] what will they provide the learners with? […] the CSG can really help a great deal to reduce the sum of risky behaviour because, if the child receives food at home, the child receives basic needs at home, the child receives a uniform, the child receives money to come to school, probably it is definitely going to help a great deal.

Important to note here is that despite the CSG being 'for the child', it is received by the primary caregiver rather than the child her/himself, so the behavioural choices of adolescent CSG beneficiaries cannot be analysed as if they have full decision-making power over 'their' grant money. Our research found, however, that many caregivers do give small amounts of the CSG to adolescent children to spend. When asked whether access to some money could help to reduce teen pregnancy, a non-beneficiary responded that:

> Yes it does because sometimes you will find that your daughter will ask you for money and you'll find that you do not have that kind of money; she gets disappointed and at times doesn't want her friends to laugh, then she meets a guy she knows and she maybe asks for R5 then he gives her R20 and so on then he later realises that he can get sex in exchange for money.

Some adolescent respondents referred to basic symbolic needs that the CSG can help to access. Teenage girls from Gauteng who do not receive the CSG referred to the pressure upon teenagers in their community to have certain kinds of clothes and beauty products, and their perceptions that girls who get the CSG are better able than they are to afford these amenities: CSG girls 'get what they want'. In practice we did not see much evidence of these uses of the grant, with 'beauty' referred to only a handful of times in our data, and mainly for caregivers. While clothing was mentioned frequently, this often referred to school uniforms and clothing for school.

With respect to consumptive symbolic needs, our research found no evidence to suggest that the CSG could undermine sexual exchange relationships where girls get large sums of money, designer clothes, cell-phones, specialty foods, and rides in expensive cars. Furthermore, although the primary motive is economic, the literature on these relationships makes it clear that the social dimensions of these relationships are multiple and complex, and take place among the middle-class as well as the poor, and university students as well as drop-outs. The respondents in our research alluded to this in statements like 'even the ones from wealthy families they do behave wildly' and 'even those who receive CSG money they still have sex for fun', but otherwise did not have much to say on the CSG's potential impact on these higher-end exchange relationships. Their answers to the question focused on subsistence exchange – which itself suggests its limits at the higher end.

7. Conclusions

The Child Support Grant does alleviate some of the material constraints that present barriers to education, a finding shared both by quantitative impact studies of the CSG and by our qualitative research. With respect to psychosocial barriers to education at a level of 'basic symbolic' needs – a new uniform instead of an old one, a bath before school, a respectable meal or hairstyle – the effects are potentially high but partial in practice. Beyond the basic costs of education, food for school and hygiene, a 'premium' must often be paid for 'symbolic capital', by buying the 'right' shoes or clothes or accessories or hairstyles. The CSG money can support these purchases, but is too little to pay for the expensive brands that are required for social acceptance at school, and the caregiver might be unwilling to spend scarce CSG income on 'unnecessarily' expensive items. Yet this may indeed be part of the social costs of education – to enable a child's experience of school to be tolerable, given the social-psychological peer pressures that all children experience, regardless of their socioeconomic background. An increase in the grant may go further toward meeting some of these social costs. However, given competing uses of the grant across household expenditures, and the budgetary and political limits of how high it can go, it is likely to remain a partial solution.

It follows that the CSG is limited in providing enough income directly to adolescent beneficiaries to compete with the income they can earn by engaging in sexual exchange relationships, especially where these relationships provide expensive gifts. If the CSG does not sufficiently substitute for these material benefits, beneficiaries are unlikely to change their preferences for such relationships. Our findings build on a distinction found in previous research between 'sex for subsistence' and 'sex for consumption', but disaggregates the latter category into 'basic symbolic' and 'consumptive symbolic', the latter being characterised by a higher level of material benefits that a social grant cannot begin to compete with. Moreover, although these relationships are primarily driven by material needs and desires, these material drivers are articulated with a powerful set of non-material drivers: historical, sociocultural and social-psychological processes involving the exercise of power by men and women, status, belonging, 'fun', and global culture. These are not easily substituted by a material solution alone. Given that the CSG is targeted at survival, it does have some potential to undermine survival sex, a possibility supported by the responses of our research participants. This may help to explain some of the important survey findings on the CSG's impact on risky behaviour. Given the complexity of these sexual relationships, however, more research is needed to explain the pathways through which that impact occurs.

This article focused on one particularly salient risky behaviour pattern with adverse consequences for children's education and health – sexual exchange relationships – where the material driver is paramount. Children also face many other risks, particularly pregnancy, drug and alcohol abuse, crime, and peer pressure to join gangs, all of which have strong non-material dimensions that cannot be tackled through a cash transfer alone, even if they are deeply rooted in poverty. There are additional factors that affect school attendance, such as illness and caring for younger children or sick relatives, which cash transfers can significantly contribute towards but cannot solve.

The key lesson here is that a simple 'theory of change' approach that fails to account for the complexity of the lives of poor people will limit the ability of social policy to achieve its broader objectives. To better target desired outcomes, a more nuanced theory of change might be needed to better understand the multiple constraints that poor people face. As argued by Camfield, Streuli, and Woodhead (2008) 'when research makes children, their relationships, settings, activities, and material and cultural resources the focus of enquiry; it has demonstrable value in informing evidence based policies to improve the lives of children in resource-poor contexts' (pp. 2–3). Our research findings support this, indicating that policies and programme design must be informed by sociological enquiry. Our research on the CSG reveals that the simple theory of change whereby a cash transfer permits school access or reduction in risky behaviour is too simplistic. Two factors confound the translation of incremental income into these outcomes. The first is the disassociation between CSG beneficiaries and CSG recipients, whereby the cash transferred in the name of the child is inevitably diluted among several spending priorities and often among other household members. The second factor is that people are motivated by social and psychosocial incentives and constraints as well as by material incentives and constraints. Social transfer programmes alleviate material constraints directly but impact only indirectly, if at all, on social and psychosocial constraints.

These non-material causal pathways or transmission mechanisms need to be better understood so that social transfers can be complemented by appropriate interventions. Some approaches are being tested in a few countries, such as cash transfer programmes where all or some of the grant is given directly to the adolescent (in South Africa and Malawi), child saving accounts that accompany cash grants with mechanisms for investment in higher education and other opportunities for the future (in Mexico, Uganda and the United States), and programmes that combine cash transfers with social services for children and their caregivers (in Chile, Malawi and Mozambique). Interventions that are designed to keep girls in school could also have a significant protective effect. Another approach is to design sensitisation and behaviour change components about gender awareness and risky behaviours in conjunction with cash transfer programmes, so as to shift norms along with budget constraints. These approaches increase the chances for social protection systems to meet immediate objectives as well as to have a more transformative impact on individuals and their communities.

Acknowledgements

The authors gratefully acknowledge the following institutions and individuals for their support: Department of Social Development (DSD), the South African Social Security Agency (SASSA) and the United Nations Children's Fund (UNICEF) South Africa for research funding; Fiona Baloyi, Jerry Baloyi, Basithile Dlamini, Wendy Mabasa, Clifford Mabhena, Naledi Mazibuko,Wandile Nyandeni,

Sydney Radebe, and Phumlani Zulu for fieldwork; Jesse McConnell, Michael Samson and Ingrid van Niekerk for study management support; Ashling McCarthy, Amy Hixon and Soomaya Khan for fieldwork support; Elisabeth Becker for assistance with data analysis; Eric Musekene, Rudzani Takalani and Alice Odhiambo from SASSA, Thilde Stevens, Thabani Buthelezi, Maureen Motepe, Tsholofelo Adelekan and Dibolelo Ababio from Department of Social Development; Lucia Knight and Linda Richter from HSRC; George Laryea-Adjei and Nkechi Obisie-Nmehielle from UNICEF; and Patrick Chiroro from Impact Research International. Gratitude is also expressed to the adult and child respondents for their time and contributions.

Disclosure statement

No potential conflict of interest was reported by the authors.

Notes

1. Michelle Adato is currently writing in her personal capacity. At the time the research for this article was conducted, she was with the International Food Policy Research Institute.
2. The authors of this article were the principal authors of the qualitative component of the evaluation. For the qualitative evaluation report, see DSD, SASSA, and UNICEF (2011).
3. A related theory of change is that staying in school itself will lower likelihood of engaging in risky sexual practices (for which there is substantial evidence of association; see Hargreaves et al., 2008; Pettifor et al., 2005), leading to a hypothesis that using cash transfers to keep girls in school will reduce risk. In Malawi, conditional and unconditional cash transfers to girls were associated with lower self-reported sexual activity and younger partners (Baird, Garfein, McIntosh, & Özler, 2012).
4. For this reason, the article focuses on sexual exchange relationships, although there are many forms of risky behaviour. It was not possible in this article to analyse the full range of risky behaviours that we studied in the evaluation, especially those for adolescent boys, such as drug and alcohol abuse, gangs and criminal activity.
5. One such study is Adato et al. (2007), which includes ethnographic accounts of psychosocial and sociocultural factors that cause girls to leave school in south-eastern Turkey, despite the existence of a CCT that incentivises their enrolment. Here shame is experienced by children and their families in relation to their communities where girls are perceived to be interacting with boys or men in or on the way to school.
6. The South African Social Security Agency (SASSA) is mandated by the Department of Social Development to deliver South Africa's social grants.
7. The 2011 quantitative evaluation did not ask about what the CSG was spent on, because the fungibility of cash makes it difficult to assign expenditures to different streams of income. Nevertheless, qualitatively it is helpful to understand what additional spending beneficiaries perceive to be enabled by CSG cash.

References

Adato, M., & Hoddinott, J. (2010). Conditional cash transfers in Latin America: A "magic bullet"? In M. Adato & J. Hoddinott (Eds.), *Conditional cash transfers in Latin America* (pp. 3–26). Baltimore: Johns Hopkins University Press.
Adato, M., Roopnaraine, T., & Becker, E. (2011). Understanding use of health services in conditional cash transfer programs: Insights from qualitative research in Latin America and Turkey. *Social Science & Medicine, 72*, 1921–1929. doi:10.1016/j.socscimed.2010.09.032
Adato, M., Roopnaraine, T., Smith, N., Altinok, E., Çelebioğlu, N., & Cemal, S. (2007). *An evaluation of the conditional cash transfer program in Turkey: Second qualitative and anthropological study* (Final report submitted to the General Directorate of Social Assistance and Solidarity, Prime Ministry, Republic of Turkey). Washington, DC: International Food Policy Research Institute.
Baird, S. J., Garfein, R. S., McIntosh, C. T., & Özler, B. (2012). Effect of a cash transfer programme for schooling on prevalence of HIV and herpes simplex type 2 in Malawi: A cluster randomised trial. *The Lancet, 379*, 1320–1329. doi:10.1016/S0140-6736(11)61709-1
Barrientos, A., Byrne, J., Villa, J. M., & Peña, P. (2013). *Social transfers and child protection* (Working Paper No. 2013-05). Florence: UNICEF Office of Research.
Behrman, J., & Skoufias, E. (2010). The economics of conditional cash transfers. In M. Adato & J. Hoddinott (Eds.), *Conditional cash transfers in Latin America* (pp. 127–158). Baltimore: Johns Hopkins University Press.
Bourdieu, P. (1986). The forms of capital. In J. Richardson (Ed.), *Handbook of theory and research for the sociology of education* (pp. 241–258). New York, NY: Greenwood.

Budlender, D., & Woolard, I. (2006). *The impact of the South African child support and old age grants on children's schooling and work* (Programme Towards the Elimination of the Worst Forms of Child Labour Paper no. 43). Geneva: International Labour Office.

Camfield, L., Streuli, N., & Woodhead, M. (2008). Children's well-being in contexts of poverty: Approaches to research, monitoring and participation. Young Lives Technical Note No. 12. Retrieved from http://economics.ouls.ox.ac.uk/13180/1/TN12-ChildWellBeing.pdf

Camfield, L., & Tafere, Y. (2009). *'Children with a good life have to have school bags': Diverse understandings of well-being among older children in three Ethiopian Communities* (Young Lives Working Paper No. 37). Oxford: Young Lives, University of Oxford.

Carruthers, B. G., & Espeland, W. N. (1998). Money, meaning, and morality. *American Behavioral Scientist, 41*, 1384–1408. doi:10.1177/0002764298041010003

Case, A., Hosegood, V., & Lund, F. (2005). The reach and impact of child support grants: Evidence from KwaZulu-Natal. *Development Southern Africa, 22*, 467–482. doi:10.1080/03768350500322925

Department of Social Development, South African Social Security Agency, & UNICEF. (2011). *Child support grant evaluation 2010: Qualitative research report.* Pretoria: UNICEF South Africa.

Department of Social Development, South African Social Security Agency, & UNICEF. (2012). *The South African child support grant impact assessment: Evidence from a survey of children, adolescents and their households.* Pretoria: UNICEF South Africa.

Dunkle, K. L., Jewkes, R. K., Brown, H. C., Gray, G. E., McIntryre, J. A., & Harlow, S. D. (2004). Transactional sex among women in Soweto, South Africa: Prevalence, risk factors and association with HIV infection. *Social Science & Medicine, 59*, 1581–1592. doi:10.1016/j.socscimed.2004.02.003

Durlauf, S. N. (1999). The case 'against' social capital. *Focus, 20*(3), 1–5. Wisconsin: University of Wisconsin-Madison, Institute for Research on Poverty.

Eaton, L., Flisher, A. J., & Aarø, L. E. (2003). Unsafe sexual behaviour in South African youth. *Social Science & Medicine, 56*, 149–165. doi:10.1016/S0277-9536(02)00017-5

Fiszbein, A., Schady, N., with Ferreira, F. H. G., Grosh, M., Kelleher, N., Olinto, P., & Skoufias, E. (2009). *Conditional cash transfers: Reducing present and future poverty* (World Bank Policy Research Report). Washington, DC: World Bank.

Hargreaves, J. R., Bonell, C. P., Boler, T., Boccia, D., Birdthistle, I., Fletcher, A., … Glynn, J. R. (2008). Systematic review exploring time trends in the association between educational attainment and risk of HIV infection in sub-Saharan Africa. *AIDS, 22*, 403–414. doi:10.1097/QAD.0b013e3282f2aac3

Hunter, F. (2008). *Dropping out from school: A cross country review of the literature* (CREATE Pathways to Access). Research Monograph 16. Brighton: CREATE.

Hunter, M. (2002). The materiality of everyday sex: Thinking beyond 'prostitution'. *African Studies, 61*, 99–120. doi:10.1080/00020180220140091

Kaufman, C. E., & Stavrou, S. E. (2004). 'Bus fare please': The economics of sex and gifts among young people in urban South Africa. *Culture, Health & Sexuality, 6*, 377–391. doi:10.1080/13691050410001680492

Kelly, K., & Parker, P. (2000). *Communities of practice: Contextual mediators of youth response to HIV/AIDS* (Beyond Awareness Campaign Report). Pretoria: South Africa Department of Health.

Leclerc-Madlala, S. (2003). Transactional sex and the pursuit of modernity social dynamics. *Social Dynamics: A Journal of African Studies, 29*(2), 213–233. doi:10.1080/02533950308628681

Narayan, D., Chambers, R., Shah, M. K., & Petesch, P. (2000). *Voices of the poor: Crying out for change.* New York, NY: Oxford University Press.

Perkel, A. K., Strebel, A., & Joubert, G. (1991). The psychology of AIDS transmission — Issues for intervention. *South African Journal of Psychology, 21*, 148–152. doi:10.1177/008124639102100303

Pettifor, A. E., Rees, H. V., Kleinschmidt, I., Steffenson, A. E., MacPhail, C., Hlongwa-Madikizela, L., … Padian, N. S. (2005). Young people's sexual health in South Africa: HIV prevalence and sexual behaviors from a nationally representative household survey. *AIDS, 19*, 1525–1534. doi:10.1097/01.aids.0000183129.16830.06

Portes, A., & Landolt, P. (1996). The downside of social capital. *The American Prospect, 26*, 18–21.

Proudlock, P. (2011). Lessons learned from the campaigns to expand the Child Support Grant in South Africa. In S. Handa, S. Devereux, & D. Webb (Eds.), *Social protection for Africa's children* (pp. 149–175). London: Routledge.

Reyles, D. Z. (2007). The ability to go without shame: A proposal for internationally comparable indicators of shame and humiliation. *Oxford Development Studies, 35*, 405–430. doi:Doi:10.1080/13600810701701905

Richter, L. (2012). The central role of families in the lives of children affected by AIDS. In J. Heymann, L. Sherr, & R. Kidman (Eds.), *Protecting childhood in the AIDS pandemic: Finding solutions that work* (pp. 21–49). Oxford: Oxford University Press.

Ridge, T. (2002). *Childhood poverty and social exclusion. From a child's perspective.* Bristol: Policy Press.

Sabates-Wheeler, R., & Roelen, K. (2011). Transformative social protection programming for children and their carers: A gender perspective. *Gender & Development, 19*, 179–194. doi:10.1080/13552074.2011.592629

Samson, M., Lee, U., Ndlebe, A., MacQuene, K., van Niekerk, I., Gandhi, V., … Abrahams, C. (2004). *The social and economic impact of South Africa's social security system* (Final Report). Cape Town: Economic Policy Research Institute (EPRI).

Sen, A. (1983). Poor, relatively speaking. *Oxford Economic Papers* (New Series), *35*(2), 153–169.

South African Department of Education. (2006). *Monitoring and evaluation report on the impact and outcomes of the education system on South Africa's population: Evidence from household surveys.* Pretoria: Department of Education.

South African Social Security Agency (SASSA). (2013). A statistical summary of social grants in South Africa. Fact sheet: Issue no 12 of 2013. Pretoria: SASSA. Retrieved from http://www.sassa.gov.za/index.php/statistical-reports

Walker, R., Kyomuhendo, G. B., Golooba-Mutebi, F., Lødemel, I., Pellissery, S., & Ming, Y. (2013). *Shame, social exclusion and the effectiveness of anti-poverty programmes: A study in seven countries* (ESRC Impact Report, RES-167-25-0557). Swindon: ESRC.

Effects of Cash Transfers on Community Interactions: Emerging Evidence

SARA PAVANELLO*, CAROL WATSON**, W. ONYANGO-OUMA[†]
& PAUL BUKULUKI[‡]

*Independent Researcher, Malaga, Spain, **Independent Researcher, Nice, France, [†]Institute of Anthropology, Gender and African Studies, University of Nairobi, Nairobi, Kenya, [‡]Department of Social Work and Social Administration, Makerere University, Kampala, Uganda

ABSTRACT *This article examines evidence of the effects of national cash transfer programmes on community interactions and discusses the transformative potential of such programmes. The findings indicate positive effects of social transfers on strengthening 'bonding' social capital and on breaking patterns of exclusion, but also point to negative effects, particularly in fuelling intra-community tensions and generating feelings of unfairness resulting – for the most part – from targeting-related issues. Evidence remains limited on the formation of 'bridging' and 'linking' social capital and on the development of mobilisation processes to drive broader processes of social transformation and changes in the status quo.*

Introduction

Since the late 1990s, social protection has gained increasing attention by governments, donors and civil society partners as a critical policy response to rising levels of poverty and vulnerability in developing countries. More recently, in the context of the ongoing global financial crisis and in light of discussions around international development goals post-2015, social protection is also increasingly viewed as essential to policy responses seeking to promote social justice, of which social inclusion and cohesion are integral parts (Devereux, McGregor, & Sabates-Wheeler, 2011). It is in this context that the social dimensions and effects of social protection policies and of cash transfer programmes in particular as one of the most widely favoured social protection mechanisms, are receiving heightened research and policy attention.

This article seeks to explore the effects of national cash transfer programmes on social cohesion through a focus on social inclusion, social capital and community-level empowerment. It teases out ways in which the transformative potential of social protection programmes is experienced on the ground, particularly among socially excluded groups participating as programme beneficiaries. It draws on theoretical literature on social cohesion and transformative social protection as well as existing evidence of the effects of cash transfers on community dynamics and relations. This serves as background to the presentation and discussion of relevant findings from a qualitative multi-country research project, Transforming Cash Transfers (TCT), which explored micro-level impacts of uncon-ditional cash transfers in Yemen, West Bank and Gaza in the Middle East region and in Kenya, Uganda and Mozambique in sub-Saharan Africa.[1]

In each of these five countries the research sought to elicit beneficiaries' and non-beneficiaries' perceptions of national cash transfer programmes, as well as the views of programme implementers and other national and local stakeholders, to shed light on the economic, psychosocial and political economy dimensions of programme experiences. The manner in which individual, household and community dynamics interacted with structural factors influencing vulnerabilities and capabilities was central to the theory of change guiding the research. While social cohesion per se was not fully developed at the outset of the study, social capital, social inclusion and participation were integral parts of the conceptual framework developed for the research. The framework focused on the multidimensional nature of risk and vulnerability, the importance of structural and political economy parameters at the national level, the drivers of programme impacts at the local level and social justice outcomes.

National cash transfer programmes in the five countries under analysis targeted different population groups exposed to different types of exclusion and vulnerabilities and varied in both design and implementation processes. As such they offered a good mix of context-specific variables and design features to inform analysis of community-level impacts of transfers. Because of resource and time constraints, each case study focused on one specific vulnerable group. Studies in Gaza and West Bank focused on female-headed beneficiaries of the Palestinian National Cash Transfer Programme (PNCTP); in Yemen on young people beneficiaries of the Social Welfare Fund (SWF); in Kenya on Orphans and Vulnerable Children (OVC) under 18 years beneficiaries of the Cash Transfer for OVC (CT-OVC); in Uganda on older people aged 65+ beneficiaries of the Senior Citizens Grant (SCG); and in Mozambique on people living with a disability beneficiaries of the Basic Social Subsidy Programme (PSSB).

The TCT project adopted a qualitative research methodology that combined both secondary and primary data collection, review and analysis. Secondary data included reviews of available quantitative data sets, governmental policy documents and other studies (published and unpublished) on key vulnerabilities, gender, social protection and cash transfers in research countries and beyond. Primary data were collected through in-country fieldwork between July and September 2012 using qualitative and participatory methods and specifically: 124[2] in-depth interviews, 147 key informant interviews, 66 focus group discussions, 25 case studies, 38 structured observations, 49 life histories, 12 institutional mappings and historical timelines, and 12 vulnerability and coping strategies mappings. In each country, fieldwork was conducted in two programme sites, on either two rural, two urban or two peri-urban sites depending on the country context. The number and range of respondents together with the diversity of participatory research techniques enabled the research to acquire in-depth and triangulated information on beneficiary and community perceptions of national cash transfer programmes. Wherever secondary data were available (including quantitative data sets and other monitoring and evaluation data), these were used alongside primary data to provide a more comprehensive picture on which to base policy and programme decision-making (Samuels, Jones, & Malachowska, 2013).

This article (one of a series of articles focusing on different thematic issues arising from the findings of the TCT project) begins by setting out the conceptual framework for analysis, which draws on different bodies of literature and disciplinary perspectives to aid the understanding of the multi-layered concept of social cohesion and its constitutive elements of social capital and social inclusion. It then explores the transformative agenda of social protection, encompassing poverty reduction goals as well as promotion of more cohesive societies, and briefly reviews evidence on the effects of social transfer programmes on social capital, social inclusion and empowerment. Such evidence is still scattered and suggestive, rather than conclusive: the overview provided in this article aims to illuminate some of the emerging findings, rather than provide a systematic review. The core of the article presents the qualitative research findings from the five country case studies that were the focus of the TCT project. The final section concludes and identifies a number of research and policy implications that could contribute to strengthening the design and implementation of cash transfer programmes and increasing their transformative potential.

Conceptual Framings

In recent years, social cohesion, a long-standing core theme in sociological discourse,[3] has been revived in social theory (Chan, To, & Chan, 2006; Easterly, Ritzen, & Woolcock, 2006; Gough & Olofsson, 1999; Green, Janmaat, & Han, 2009; Jenson, 2010) and has been increasingly invoked in international policy dialogues and agendas. At the same time, there is growing interest in social protection policy circles with better understanding the effects of social transfer participation not only on raising living standards but also on tackling socio-political vulnerabilities and improving social relations. Theoretical linkages are also increasingly being drawn between social protection and social cohesion specifically (Babajanian, 2012).

To situate our analysis within these debates, we take social cohesion as the framing concept for our discussion on community interactions and dynamics. We give special emphasis to social capital, seen here as the relational dimension of social cohesion and to social inclusion, seen as the distributional dimension (see also Babajanian, 2012).

Social Cohesion

Social cohesion matters to national public policies. It enables citizens to enjoy a sense of stability, belonging and trust and offers opportunities for upward social mobility. Conversely, the absence of or low social cohesion can trigger or reinforce social instability, civil conflict and crime (DFID, 2005; OECD, 2012). Public programmes such as cash transfers can influence social cohesion. Designed and implemented appropriately, with clear and fair eligibility criteria and with principles of participation and transparency in mind, they can potentially bolster and maintain social cohesion while contributing to strengthening relations of trust, reciprocity and respect among different social groups as well as between citizens and state authorities.[4]

In the literature, social cohesion is widely conceptualised as a composite and multi-dimensional notion, and as a quality or characteristic of societal organisation at the macro level (Babajanian, 2012; Chan et al., 2006; Easterly et al., 2006; Green et al., 2009; Narayan, 1999). According to the Organisation for Economic Co-operation and Development (OECD) a cohesive society 'works towards the wellbeing of all its members, fights exclusion and marginalisation, creates a sense of belonging, promotes trust, and offers its members the opportunity of upward mobility' (OECD, 2012, p. 17).

Defining a complex concept such as social cohesion and operationalising it for research and eventually programmatic purposes is challenging. Several studies have often side-stepped this hurdle by using social cohesion as the framing concept and focusing the discussion on its socially desirable attributes or constitutive elements which include trust, tolerance, reciprocity and shared values, a sense of belonging and participation, inclusion and equality (Babajanian, 2012; Green et al., 2009; Jenson, 2010; OECD, 2012).

Depending on the societal context under scrutiny and the purpose and scope of the analysis, different scholars have given emphasis to different constitutive elements and used different analytical frameworks to study social cohesion. Berger-Schmitt (2002) for instance explores social cohesion by looking at social exclusion and social capital. The 2012 OECD Perspectives on Global Development report examines social cohesion through the lens of social inclusion, social capital and social mobility (OECD, 2012). Babajanian (2012) makes a distinction between the distributional and relational dimensions of social cohesion. The former refers to 'the patterns and extent of distribution of resources and opportunities in a society, and the [latter] concerns the nature and quality of interpersonal and social relations' (Babajanian, 2012, p. 13). The distributional aspect of social cohesion is therefore seen as inherently linked to structural drivers and processes of social inclusion and equality, while the relational aspect to horizontal social relations, interactions and ties which, as discussed below, are the defining elements of social capital.

Given the focus of our analysis on the effects of cash transfers on community interactions and dynamics, this article adopts social cohesion as the umbrella concept to guide the discussion and gives special emphasis to its relational and distributional aspects by focusing on social capital and social inclusion, two overlapping and yet different concepts (see Daly & Silver, 2008).

Social Capital and Social Inclusion

Drawing on earlier research (Banfield, 1958; Bourdieu, 1986; Coleman, 1988), Robert Putnam's (1993) seminal work on community and civic participation brought social capital to the fore of research and policy debates. Social capital refers to 'the glue that holds groups and societies together – bonds of shared values, norms and institutions' (Narayan, 1999, p. 1). A distinction is often made between 'bonding' and 'bridging' social capital, where the former refers to ties and norms of solidarity and trust among members of the same social group (defined by class, caste, religion, ethnicity and so forth) whereas the latter to cross-cutting ties among different social groups (Gittell & Vidal, 1998; Narayan, 1999; Putnam, 2000). 'Linking' social capital is a related concept where the focus is on ties between citizens and representatives of formal institutions with major bearing on citizens' welfare, such as law enforcement officers, social workers and health care providers (Szreter & Woolcock, 2004; World Bank, 2000). Cohesive societies often display a healthy balance of these three forms of social capital and citizens usually enjoy a relatively wide variety of associations with people and groups beyond their immediate social circle and status.

'Bridging' and 'inking' social capital and related ties that cut across status, identity and power differentials can be a powerful force for social transformation. Mansuri and Rao (2013) refer to social movements that arise endogenously within a country's pathway to change as 'organic participation'.[5] Such movements, which include civic associations, community organisations and women's groups, have historically offered routes through which poor and marginalised citizens have come together to pursue a common political agenda of change, pressure power-holders and table their grievances against inequality, oppression and unmet social, political, economic or cultural demands (Batliwala, 2012; Kabeer, 2010; Mansuri & Rao, 2013). Experiences in diverse developing countries across Latin America, South Asia and sub-Saharan Africa indicate how institutions, social structures and political economy dynamics have often been called into question through such routes, in some cases succeeding in engendering social changes (Kabeer, 2010; Leach & Scoones, 2007; Mansuri & Rao, 2013; Szreter & Woolcock, 2004).

The World Bank defines social inclusion as 'the removal of institutional barriers and the enhancement of incentives to increase the access of diverse individuals and groups to development opportunities' (World Bank, 2013, p. 256). The analysis of poverty through a social inclusion (or exclusion) lens draws attention not only to the nature and extent of poverty (outcomes), but also to the deep-rooted structures and processes that produce and reproduce poverty and inequality (drivers)[6] (Babajanian & Hagen-Zanker, 2012). Such processes often relate to formal and informal institutional arrangements which typically reflect the interests of the more powerful and limit access by disadvantaged citizens to productive assets and basic services, while diminishing voice, presence and political representation. The analytical power of social inclusion also serves to bring to the fore the multi-dimensional nature and effects of poverty. Exclusion from sources of income can have significant repercussions on other forms of exclusion including inadequate access to basic services, political rights, voice and representation and the ability to uphold social networks such as participation in familial, social and cultural events (Kabeer, 2010; Levitas et al., 2007; World Bank, 2013).

Social Transfers, Social Cohesion and Transformative Social Protection

The conceptual underpinnings of social cohesion and its two distributional and relational aspects of social capital and social inclusion are important for policies and programmes that not only seek to reduce household economic deprivation and human capital deficits, but to also promote more inclusive and cohesive societies.[7] In this section we discuss specific design aspects and implementation experiences of social transfers and how they affect social cohesion and the two related features under analysis.

To date, the evidence base on how, to what extent and under which conditions social transfers can offer positive potential for strengthening social capital, combating exclusion and solidifying the state-citizen contract is still thin. In part, this has to do with the limited attention in the analysis, design, implementation and evaluation of programmes to social dimensions and to the effects that programmes can have on such dimensions.

According to recent reviews of the literature (Babajanian, 2012; Babajanian & Hagen-Zanker, 2012; Devereux et al., 2013; Dissanayake, Stephenson, & Greenslade, 2012), most evidence on the impacts of social protection programmes, and in particular of cash transfers, highlights immediate effects on poverty reduction (enhanced income for poor households) or human capital development (health, nutrition, education), with less consistent attention to effects on broader social dynamics or transformational social relations. A Deutsche Gesellschaft für Internationale Zusammenarbeit (GIZ) review for example notes that there is little empirical evidence to make inferences about the strengths and limitations of social protection in tackling social exclusion. The same review identifies the dearth of empirical evidence on the impact of social protection policies and instruments on social cohesion and state-building (Babajanian, 2012; See also Dissanayake et al., 2012 and; Devereux et al., 2013).

Nevertheless, a growing body of empirical information is beginning to provide insights on how social transfers are affecting community dynamics in different contexts. Much of this can be analysed through examining the effects on social capital and social inclusion.

Emerging Evidence on the Effects of Social Transfers on Social Capital and Social Inclusion

While a full, systematic review remains to be conducted[8] and is beyond the scope of this article, emerging evidence from a variety of studies in different contexts shed light on some of the ways cash transfers can increase the ability of individual and household beneficiaries to participate in cultural, social and familial activities ('bonding' social capital) (Babajanian & Hagen-Zanker, 2012; Hypher, 2011). In Kenya, a mapping of the social impact of cash transfers found that cash payments strengthened the social networks of participating households in part by enabling recipients to participate in community events, share food and borrow when in need thanks to their enhanced capacity to repay (Ressler, 2008). Other evidence from Latin America documents positive effects on social capital of a conditional cash transfer programme in Colombia (Attanasio et al., 2010). A series of impact evaluations of national cash transfer programmes in selected sub-Saharan African countries conducted by the Food and Agriculture Organization (FAO) found that in Kenya, Ghana, Lesotho, Zimbabwe, Ethiopia and Malawi these programmes 'increased social capital and allowed beneficiaries to "re-enter" existing social networks and/or to strengthen informal social protection systems' (FAO, 2013, p. 3).

That said, cash transfers can also generate feelings of resentment and jealousy towards recipients and trigger or further exacerbate intra-community tensions (Babajanian, 2012; MacAuslan & Riemenschneider, 2011; Roelen, Edstrom, Sabates-Wheeler, & Davies, 2011). An evaluation of the Mchinji Social Cash Transfer Pilot project in Malawi noted problems of jealousy arising between beneficiary and non-beneficiary households (Miller, Tsoka, & Reichert, 2011).

Existing evidence also indicates both positive and negative effects of social transfers on social inclusion. Recipients of the Kalomo social cash transfer in Zambia found that community members were more willing to lend them money, suggesting a revaluation of recipients' social position within the community (Wietler, 2007). Evidence from Malawi, Zimbabwe and Kenya also suggests that where cash transfers lack transparency in targeting criteria or are means-tested, they can lead to problems of stigma, reinforcing the social exclusion of recipients (MacAuslan & Riemenschneider, 2011).

Transformative Social Protection

The potential of social protection to go beyond addressing economic insecurity to foster longer-lasting structural change has been at the core of a shift in the social policy discourse over the past decade. The influential work of Devereux and Sabates-Wheeler (2004) drew on earlier critical studies to highlight the need for social protection policies and programmes to include 'transformative' measures that aim to address equity, empowerment and social justice goals in addition to material needs.

Kabeer's (2010) conceptualisation of empowerment, defined as the ability of individuals to make strategic life choices in the following three interrelated dimensions, further emphasises the relational aspects of well-being and empowerment that are particularly useful for this discussion:

- Resources: including economic, human and social (such as relationships) to enhance the ability to exercise choice;
- Agency: the ability to define one's goals and act on them, thus emphasising the value of individual and collective decision-making;
- Achievements: framed within the context of relational well-being (the extent to which people engage with others to achieve their goals) and subjective well-being (the meanings people give to the goals they achieve) (Jones & Shahrokh, 2013).

While evidence is accumulating on the effects of cash transfers on social capital and social inclusion, there is limited evidence in the literature of positive transformation in social relations resulting from cash transfer participation. What evidence there is seems to point to the importance of specific design features in fostering empowerment. The role that the political and social context, including political systems, social structures and level of elites' control plays in driving different social protection outcomes and a greater appreciation of the conditions under which changes (positive or negative) are observed remain largely unexplored areas.

It is to this growing body of evidence on the different effects of social transfers on community interactions and dynamics that this article seeks to contribute.

Evidence from the 'Transforming Cash Transfers' Project

We now turn to discuss selected findings from the TCT research project on beneficiaries' and non-beneficiaries' perceptions of national cash transfer programmes in West Bank and Gaza, Yemen, Kenya, Mozambique and Uganda. Drawing on the conceptual framework outlined above, we structure the discussion around social capital and social inclusion and we identify evidence of both positive and negative effects of the cash transfer programmes. We conclude this section by discussing the potential of programmes to drive processes of social transformation.

Effects on Social Capital

Strengthening 'bonding' social capital. Echoing the findings of the literature summarised above, the body of evidence drawn from the TCT project points to both positive and negative effects of cash transfers on social capital.

The findings of the research in West Bank and Gaza, Uganda and Kenya brought to the fore positive experiences of beneficiaries' increased social participation as a result of the opportunities that cash transfers provided to meet and interact. These interactions were reported as fostering social connectedness and ties, thus contributing to social capital, while also generating feelings of mutual support and solidarity and alleviating sentiments of shame and increased dignity, with important repercussions on the psychological well-being of beneficiaries.

In West Bank and Gaza, female heads of household beneficiaries of the PNCTP reported that they interacted with other female beneficiaries – mostly when travelling to collect the transfer or at cash disbursement points – using these occasions to discuss personal problems and life experiences, or exchange information on the transfer and other available assistance. Such connections and conversations were perceived as a source of support and comfort, contributing to providing a sense of solidarity and inclusiveness.

Similarly, in Uganda, cash transfers provided an opportunity for elderly beneficiaries to meet and interact with friends, especially during payment days. Beneficiaries valued these opportunities as they reduced feelings of social isolation and enhanced communication on a variety of topics of importance to them. As a community development officer put it: '[The cash transfer] brings re-union among the elderly – they will meet and talk and socialise. The first payment was like an elders' convention[…]. They would ask each other: "You mean[…]you are still alive? What about the sickness?" This meeting means more to them than just money. They also share ways of how to deal and cope with their diseases' (Bukuluki & Watson, 2012, p. 64).

In Uganda, Gaza, Yemen and Kenya there were widespread indications that regular injections of resources had enhanced the ability of beneficiaries to participate in social and familial activities, with positive effects on social ties and on feelings of self-worth and confidence.

Also in Uganda, where the programme had only recently started in 2011 the findings revealed that older people used the cash transfer to maintain connections and social networks within their communities, for example by visiting friends living further away, and by making contributions to funerals, religious festivals and other social events. A community development worker pointed to the visual manifestation of the effects of cash transfers in breaking the isolation of older people; 'Before, there was not even a path to the older people's homes, because nobody was visiting and they never went out. Now this has changed.' (Bukuluki & Watson, 2012, p. 66). The ability to buy and use items of personal hygiene such as soap and appropriate clothing and shoes was also appreciated. Such purchases were reported to have given beneficiaries the confidence needed to interact with other community members with ease and without shame.

In Gaza, lack of economic resources resulted in individuals and households limiting their attendance at social and familial events. Expressions such as 'money enhances socialisation' were often used by male and female respondents to highlight how cash transfers had enhanced recipients' ability to join or host social activities, such as celebrating weddings or the birth of new-borns. Similarly, beneficiaries of the SWF in Yemen associated poverty with humiliation as a result of the inability to provide for their families and attend social gatherings. Beneficiaries of the SWF reported that the cash transfer had enhanced their dignity, allowing them to cover small household expenses and on occasions to attend social gatherings.

In Kenya, regular cash transfers enabled OVC recipients of the CT-OVC programme to go to school, be better clothed and fed, with positive effects on their self-confidence. Child beneficiaries talked about their future with confidence and pointed out how they wanted to succeed in school and lead a better life. They also spoke of increased acceptance at schools and among their peers, having more friends now than before, which appeared to coincide with when they started receiving the transfer.

The Kenya case study also showed how caregivers who were cash transfer beneficiaries (including elderly widows and others) spontaneously formed self-help groups. One of the activities of these groups was to save and pool cash transfer money, with one member receiving the money in the fund on a rotational basis and then investing it in petty businesses and the purchase of livestock.[9] In addition to the economic benefits that these groups generated, they also provided informal psychosocial support to HIV-positive people and advice to elderly grandmothers on how to care for OVC. Beneficiary Welfare Committees established by the cash transfer programme also contributed to enhancing social capital formation through interactions at regular meetings that focused on issues such as how to best invest the cash transfer or care for OVC.

Drawing on Kabeer's conceptualisation of empowerment as comprising three interrelated dimensions of human capability – resources, agency and achievements – the evidence collected in West Bank and Gaza, Uganda, Yemen and Kenya points to how national cash transfer programmes can contribute to strengthening the resources dimension (both economic and social), with positive effects on the psychological and relational well-being of participants. The example in Kenya shows how the cash transfer programme fostered a form of identity among beneficiaries and bolstered the 'agency' and 'achievement' dimensions of empowerment, with beneficiaries organising themselves and cooperating to pursue collective interests and mutual benefits.

Differential evidence on negative effects. Evidence collected in Yemen, Kenya, West Bank and Gaza points to negative effects of cash transfers on social capital, especially in terms of exacerbating intra-community tensions and generating feelings of unfairness. In these contexts, tensions, both among beneficiaries and between beneficiaries and non-beneficiaries, were widespread and largely linked to targeting-related issues.

In Yemen and in Kenya social transfers were found to have engendered a considerable degree of tension between beneficiaries and non-beneficiaries. This was linked to sentiments of jealousy around the targeting process, which was perceived as leaving out many poor and vulnerable households considered just as needy as those included in the programme.

Similarly, the majority of beneficiaries and community stakeholders interviewed in West Bank and Gaza mentioned feelings of envy, jealousy and resentment among beneficiaries and between bene-ficiaries and non-beneficiaries. Perceived inequities around cash transfer amounts were underpinning such feelings among beneficiaries. Lack of information about programme reforms, objectives, func-tioning, targeting mechanisms and criteria left communities and beneficiaries struggling to understand who was deemed eligible and why, and how poverty levels were ultimately determined. In turn, this created a general climate of confusion and doubt, which was a breeding ground for speculation and suspicion, with perceptions of grievances and intra-community tensions often ensuing.

Tensions were less pronounced in Mozambique and Uganda. This could be partly attributed to the categorical-based targeting approach adopted in those countries, which focused on clearly identifiable vulnerable groups and which possibly limited occasion for claims of exclusion or feelings of injustice on the part of non-beneficiaries. In Uganda, most study respondents agreed that the SCG targeted one of the most extremely vulnerable groups of people and that the targeting was straightforward and fair. As an elderly female beneficiary put it: 'The elderly are the right people receiving this money because we are weak, poor, cannot farm and do business with ease like other categories of people do' (Bukuluki & Watson, 2012, p. 52). In Mozambique, no tensions were reported between beneficiaries and non-beneficiaries, and the absence of such tensions was linked to two main factors. First, there seemed to be a general sense of solidarity in the community, with respondents widely agreeing that the programme should be expanded to include all elderly and disabled people. Secondly, there was a general view that there were more people who needed to be included, rather than there being many beneficiaries who were wrongly included (inclusion errors). Possibly, this was linked to targeted groups of people who were visibly poor and vulnerable. In the words of one beneficiary:

> Relationships between beneficiaries and non-beneficiaries are good because non-beneficiaries who are not yet elderly or do not have disabilities know that their opportunity to receive the benefit has not yet come. Others who are elderly or have a disability but still do not receive the transfer, might not like the situation but have a good attitude toward us because they know that it is not our fault they were not selected, but it is rather those who made the selection who are to blame. (Selvester, Fidalgo, & Taimo, 2012, p. 46)

Implications of the findings. The findings emerging from different country contexts and programmes with different longevity demonstrate a diversity of outcomes with regards to social capital. In most of the cases covered by the TCT project, bonding capital was strengthened, with additional positive spill over effects such as heightened psychological well-being of beneficiaries and a sense of solidarity and inclusiveness. At the same time however, the findings in Yemen, Kenya, West Bank and Gaza also indicate that less welcome outcomes, such as intra-community tensions and feelings of unfairness, can at times occur. Such heterogeneity in outcomes is not surprising given inevitable differences in institutional, political, socio-cultural contexts and in programme design, governance and implementation.

The adoption of a poverty-based targeting approach in countries where large segments of the population are poor *and* where inadequate attention has been paid to participatory components of programmes – including involvement of beneficiaries and communities in all phases of programmes, information sharing on programme functioning, targeting mechanisms and criteria, and the establish-ment and implementation of safe and effective feedback and appeals – may all contribute to erosion rather than enhancement of social capital and ultimately social cohesion. It is therefore important that social transfer programmes are premised on participation and transparency principles – for instance ensuring that communities are informed of the targeting criteria adopted by programmes and of the reasons governing the choice of such criteria.

In addition, and as evidenced in recent World Bank research on the impact of policy-driven efforts to induce participation (Mansuri & Rao, 2013), the potential of participatory engagement may be better harnessed in contexts where programmes are facilitated by a responsive institutional apparatus – both at central and local level – that has internalised the instrumental values of participation and in turn implements programmes accordingly.

Effects on Social Inclusion

Widespread positive effects. Findings from the TCT project indicate the positive contribution of social transfers in fostering the inclusion of marginalised social groups. Some progress towards breaking entrenched patterns of exclusion was linked to the economic support provided through cash transfers and to specific participatory mechanisms embedded in programme design that served to increase the voice of the excluded and their participation in community affairs. In Mozambique, Uganda and Kenya beneficiaries provided similar descriptions of how national cash transfer programmes contributed to greater social inclusion. They emphasised the enhanced social recognition that they experienced and stressed the psychological dimensions of greater inclusion and of dignity in particular.

In Mozambique, beneficiaries living with a disability felt that the injection of resources gave them a certain degree of status in the community, reduced their high level of dependence on family and friends, and afforded them greater dignity and integration. In the words of one beneficiary, 'The transfer means that we have more recognition and credibility in the community' (Selvester et al., 2012, p. 45). Similarly, most beneficiaries in Uganda reported that regular cash transfers had improved their self-esteem and social status by enabling them to act and be considered as active members of their households and communities, rather than as burdens.

The cash transfer programme in Kenya was found to have contributed to greater social acceptance of targeted OVC. Before the start of the programme, such children suffered discrimination and stigma because they were seen as a burden to fostering households and relatives. With the introduction of the programme, the stigma lessened and OVC gained more acceptance both within households and at community level. In particular, their wider acceptance was linked to the material benefits that were accruing to host families, which almost invariably extended from the child to other household members. At the same time the surrounding community also started to increasingly accept OVC and see them as an important investment for the future.

Evidence from Kenya and Uganda highlights how participatory components of programme design and implementation contributed to reducing stigma while boosting acceptance of marginalised groups. In Kenya, the national cash transfer programme sought to actively involve communities in all stages of targeting from the initial selection of beneficiaries to validation of the final beneficiaries' list. The validation process included a community-level public meeting during which the list was presented, discussed, and decisions reached among community members through consensus. There were reports of marginalised people starting to actively participate in these meetings. Elderly widows explained that during public discussions and interactions they were listened to and treated like other members of the community. People living with HIV also felt that they had started to enjoy more participation in community affairs as a result of both their membership in the Beneficiary Welfare Committees formed as part of the design of the programme and their inclusion in public meetings and decision-making processes.

In Uganda, the introduction of the cash transfer brought new importance to the status of 'elder'. Being an older person was increasingly seen as bringing benefits, the voices of older people listened to in community meetings and their views solicited and valued by programme implementers. As a community development officer explained, 'Before the programme, people didn't like to be called "elderly" because it was like an insult; now they are proud of it and actually fighting for it!' (Bukuluki

& Watson, 2012, p. 66). Elderly beneficiaries expressed a sense of heightened dignity through the greater esteem they felt emanating from others as a result.

Isolated negative effects. In comparison to widespread evidence of the positive contribution of social transfers on social inclusion, negative repercussions in terms of engendering greater exclusion and stigma were less pronounced. They were largely limited to the West Bank where the cash transfer programme was associated with social stigma and negative attitudes towards recipients. As a female beneficiary explained, 'They name us beggars. We wish to give up this stigma but we don't have any other choice' (Jones & Shaheen, 2012, p. 63).

Implications of the findings. The findings on the effects of cash transfers on social inclusion are overwhelmingly positive. The potential of social transfers can go beyond the provision of income support and the strengthening of productive capacity to contribute to tackling entrenched social and gendered norms, values and perceptions that in many contexts may prevent marginalised groups from accessing and retaining productive capacity in the first place (Babajanian & Hagen-Zanker, 2012). As such, our findings reinforce a well-known argument: chronic poverty arises not only from material deprivations, but also from the cumulative impact of risk, vulnerability and exclusion. This also resonates with Amartya Sen's reframing of Adam Smith's 'not being able to appear in public without shame' as 'a capability deprivation that takes the form of social exclusion' (Soors, Dkhimi, & Criel, 2013, p. 3).

The greater acceptance of socially excluded groups such as older people in Uganda, people with disabilities in Mozambique, and OVC, people living with HIV and elderly widows in Kenya highlights the potential of cash transfer programmes in contributing to progressive change in societal structures and power relations. In Kenya, communities' active involvement in targeting processes and in beneficiary fora established by the programme has enhanced the ability of excluded groups and individuals to participate in communal decision-making processes, bringing them from the periphery to a more central position in the life of their communities. In Uganda, previously excluded older beneficiaries had greater opportunities to voice their opinions and be listened to.

Effects on Social Transformation

Positive effects of cash transfers evidenced by the TCT research project are predominantly found in relation to 'bonding' social capital and on the acceptance, status and recognition of the excluded within their social milieu. Findings from the case studies do not point to the formation of 'bridging' and 'linking' social capital or to the development of more substantial mobilisation processes by communities and by disadvantaged social groups to work collectively to drive broader processes of social transformation and changes in the status quo.

In Kenya, the establishment of self-help groups and of collective action discussed above remained confined to the village level with little indication of the formation of broader 'bridging' social capital. Nor did interactions between beneficiaries and programme implementers (in spaces such as Beneficiary Welfare Committees) seem to lead to the creation of 'linking' social capital or to more substantial collective undertakings on the part of beneficiaries to achieve changes in the status quo.

The only (limited) indication of a programme contributing to collective action among programme beneficiaries was found in Yemen. Beneficiaries in one district continuously complained to SWF officials about illegal charging of 'commissions' by post office workers responsible for cash delivery and of challenging conditions and poor treatment on payment days. SWF officials listened to beneficiaries' complaints and requested the post office to replace the head of office with someone else in order to minimise abuse. In this case the collective pressure exerted by beneficiaries was real and resulted in some type of change but was ultimately limited to aspects of programme implementation at local level.

In some of the cases, particularly in Uganda where the SCG programme had just recently started up, more time may be needed for such effects to be observed. In other cases, it may be that participatory management and accountability processes, part of a well-functioning programme governance apparatus and responsive implementers, could be further strengthened as a means of stimulating broader social mobilisation, or that overall design and implementation of social transfers needs to be more explicitly embedded in the transformative social protection agenda. This is an area for further policy discussion and research. In general these findings are also indicative of the need to ultimately scale down expectations on the transformative effects of cash injections on social relations. In other words a good degree of realism is needed, accepting that social transformation objectives are inherently ambitious while also being modest about the ability of social transfer programmes to effect change in this regard.

Conclusions, Policy and Research Implications

Fostering greater social cohesion is increasingly considered a critical component and long-term goal of equitable and inclusive social development policies and processes. Several academic and agency reports, including this article, have adopted social cohesion as a broad umbrella concept to guide the analysis and have given special emphasis to its constitutional elements. The main analytical strength of this approach, also useful for policy debates, lies in the prominence given to social relations (through the social capital framework) and to distributional outcomes (through the social inclusion/exclusion framework) at the micro level while also taking into account stressors emanating from higher levels, including institutional, structural and socio-political processes that prevent or hinder cohesion and drive and reproduce poverty.

The qualitative findings that have emerged from the five countries that were the focus of the TCT project have highlighted how cash transfer programmes, as one key instrument of social protection, have helped to strengthen social capital and social inclusion, and in turn may have contributed to progress towards more cohesive societies. In some contexts cash transfers have fostered a sense of social connectedness on the part of beneficiaries and strengthened interactions and ties with the wider community, thus contributing to 'bonding' social capital. They have also generated feelings of mutual support and solidarity, with important repercussions on the psychological well-being of beneficiaries and on dimensions of empowerment. Our evidence further indicates some progress towards breaking entrenched patterns of exclusion thanks to: i) the injection of economic resources which allowed beneficiaries to improve their welfare and ability to more fully participate in social life; and ii) specific participatory mechanisms embedded in programme design and followed through in programme implementation that served to increase the voice of the excluded and their participation in community affairs.

At the same time, evidence from case studies also shows the negative effects that can arise from transfer programmes, especially in terms of fuelling intra-community tensions and generating feelings of unfairness at the community level. When this has occurred, it seemed to be largely linked to targeting-related issues, notwithstanding the variability of local context and pre-existing social structures and dynamics that may have further contributed to the emergence or reinforcement of those sentiments Meanwhile, evidence from the country studies remains more elusive on the effects of cash transfers on the formation of 'bridging' and 'linking' social capital, as well as on the development of more substantial mobilisation processes by communities and disadvantaged social groups to work collectively to drive broader processes of social transformation.

Policy Implications

Our findings highlight a number of key points for consideration by national policy-makers and development partners in support of social transfer programmes that aim to strengthen social relationships at community level and support more cohesive and inclusive societies. It is considered important to take these into consideration to help activating the transformative power of social transfers to contribute to redressing processes of exclusion, poverty and deprivation.

Both the design and implementation of cash transfer programmes should be premised on participatory and transparent targeting criteria and selection processes, accompanied by appropriate mechanisms for grievance and ongoing feedback. The voices, interests and aspirations of communities and beneficiaries should be at the centre of all phases of the programme, from design and implementation, to monitoring and evaluation. To reduce the potential for divisiveness and conflict that is likely to arise from targeting and consequent selective entitlement in contexts where poverty and vulnerabilities are widespread, particular attention must be paid to ensure community participation when poverty-based targeting approaches are implemented. Efforts to ensure participation, accountability and transparency will work best in contexts where central and local authorities are supportive of and meaningfully engaged with a participation agenda.

For cash transfers to realise their potential to engender positive transformation in the institutions, norms, and social relations that create and reproduce unequal and unjust societies, simply targeting marginalised groups such as women, the elderly and the disabled, is not enough. Social transfer programmes should be designed and implemented to include flexible, context-appropriate components and mechanisms that can open up (or build upon existing) spaces and opportunities for the voices, aspirations and interests of socially excluded groups to be heard and valued. For example programme implementers can build on the opportunities that cash transfer distributions, such as distribution days and/or points, create for beneficiaries to interact and socialise. Where appropriate, distribution points can also be developed into spaces for social gatherings, as well as information sharing and interaction between programme staff and beneficiaries. At the same time, distribution points must be carefully planned to take into account the mobility restrictions of older people and people with disabilities, to minimise distance from communities and avoid any adverse effects or stigma that public distribution of benefits might generate.

The evidence discussed in this article illustrates how the positive effects of cash transfer programmes in stimulating social capital and inclusion at the community level are often intertwined with positive psychological outcomes at the individual level, including enhanced feelings of self-esteem, self-confidence and solidarity. Policies should take into account such spillover effects between the social and individual spheres in order to accentuate positive synergies.

Research Implications

This paper has attempted to contribute to the growing body of evidence on the different effects of social transfers on community interactions and dynamics. More structured and in-depth qualitative research is needed on the effects of cash transfers on social cohesion and power dynamics at the community level.

A full, systematic review of available evidence would be useful as a first step in more thoroughly evaluating the emerging evidence base, identifying gaps in knowledge and developing a research agenda. The inclusion of social dimensions within evaluation frameworks for social transfer programmes could also usefully contribute to building a rich body of research and knowledge.

To date, studies and evaluations of the effects and impacts of social transfer programmes have focused primarily on well-being impacts linked to poverty reduction and human capital development goals (particularly health, education and nutrition). A broader conceptual framework taking full account of the multidimensional nature of poverty and vulnerability – including aspects related to social dynamics at community level – could expand the analytical focus in ways that would allow more direct assessment of social capital, inclusion and cohesion effects.[10]

The development of qualitative and quantitative indicators to measure and monitor social impacts of cash transfer programmes, linked to policy goals that are often implicit but not always fully developed in programme aims and design would, perhaps, serve both to render more explicit such policy aims as well as strengthen the evidence base on outcomes.

Lastly, there is a need for clearer empirical understanding on how to better engage with disadvantaged social groups along gender, age, class, ethnicity, and other determinants of exclusion and vulnerability to ensure that cash transfer programmes not only seek to address their material needs but more explicitly aim to open up pathways for redressing their exclusion, enhancing their voices and driving collective processes of social transformation and change.

THE SOCIAL AND POLITICAL POTENTIAL OF CASH TRANSFERS

Disclosure Statement

No potential conflict of interest was reported by the authors.

Notes

1. The TCT project was commissioned by the UK Department for International Development (DFID) and undertaken by the Overseas Development Institute (ODI) in partnership with national research teams. Full country and synthesis reports and other project materials are available at transformingcashtransfers.org
2. Figures refer to total number of research tools conducted across all country studies.
3. Discussions around aspects of social cohesion are found in the work of Emile Durkheim, Max Weber, Pierre Bourdieu, amongst others (Norton & de Haan, 2013).
4. While this article uses social cohesion in a normative way it recognises that there are a number of inherent limitations with this approach, including the possibility that a normative outlook may prevent an objective analysis of the different forms of social cohesion that may be found to exist in a given setting and that social cohesion may not always mean 'a good thing'. As Green et al. (2009, p. 6) argue '[t]oo much cohesion can, arguably, lead to social insularity and backwardness (Banfield, 1958), economic sclerosis (Olson, 1971) or to a failure to address substantive injustices in society'.
5. Mansuri and Rao (2013) juxtapose the notion of 'organic participation' with that of 'induced participation', the latter referring to participation promoted through policies of the state, bilateral and multilateral agencies which typically takes two forms, decentralisation and community-driven development.
6. Social exclusion in de Haan's categorisation (1999) specifically emphasises 'outcomes of deprivation' and 'processes of deprivation'.
7. Social protection programmes may not necessarily be able to address the root causes of deprivation and, depending on the specific goal of the intervention and the country setting (for example fragile or conflict-affected states) may be limited to simply providing emergency assistance (Babajanian & Hagen-Zanker, 2012).
8. A systematic review of conditional and unconditional cash transfer programmes has recently been conducted but only focuses on educational outcomes in developing countries, see (Baird, Ferreira, Özler, & Woolcock, 2014, p. 1–43).
9. The spontaneous establishment of self-help or merry-go-round groups is a common practice in Africa as in other parts of the world.
10. A recent attempt to develop a multi-dimensional evaluation framework of a cash transfer programme in Bangladesh (Robano & Smith, 2014) represents a step forward in this regard, but still very much focuses on individual indicators of well-being rather than social connectedness.

References

Attanasio, O., Fitzsimons, E., Gomez, A., Gutiérrez, M. I., Meghir, C., & Mesnard, A. (2010). Children's schooling and work in the presence of a conditional cash transfer program in rural Colombia. *Economic Development and Cultural Change, 58*, 181–210. doi:10.1086/648188

Babajanian, B. (2012). *Social protection and its contribution to social cohesion and state-building*. Eschborrn, Germany: Deutsche Gesellschaft für Internationale Zusammenarbeit (GIZ) GmbH.

Babajanian, B., & Hagen-Zanker, J. (2012). *Social protection and social exclusion: An analytical framework to assess the links.* ODI Background Note. London: Overseas Development Institute.

Baird, S., Ferreira, F. H. G., Özler, B., & Woolcock, M. (2014). Conditional, unconditional and everything in between: A systematic review of the effects of cash transfer programmes on schooling outcomes. *Journal of Development Effectiveness, 6*(1), 1–43. doi:10.1080/19439342.2014.890362

Banfield, E. G. (1958). *The moral basis of a backward society.* New York, NY: Free Press.

Batliwala, S. (2012). *Changing their world: Concepts and practices of women's movements* (2nd ed.). Toronto: Association for Women's Rights in Development.

Berger-Schmitt, R. (2002). Considering social cohesion in quality of life assessments: Concepts and measurement. *Social Indicators Research, 58*, 403–428. doi:10.1023/A:1015752320935

Bourdieu, P. (1986). The forms of capital. In J. Richardson (Ed.), *Handbook of theory and research for the sociology of education* (pp. 241–258). New York, NY: Greenwood.

Bukuluki, P., & Watson, C. (2012). *Transforming cash transfers: Beneficiary and community perspectives on the Senior Citizen Grant (SCG) in Uganda.* London: Overseas Development Institute.

Chan, J., To, H.-P., & Chan, E. (2006). Reconsidering social cohesion: Developing a definition and analytical framework for empirical research. *Social Indicators Research, 75*, 273–302. doi:10.1007/s11205-005-2118-1

Coleman, J. S. (1988). Social capital in the creation of human capital. *American Journal of Sociology, 94*, S95–S120. doi:10.1086/ajs.1988.94.issue-s1

Daly, M., & Silver, H. (2008). Social exclusion and social capital: A comparison and critique. *Theory and Society, 37*, 537–566. doi:10.1007/s11186-008-9062-4 de Haan, A. (1999). *Social exclusion: Towards an holistic understanding of deprivation*. London: Department for International Development.

Devereux, S., McGregor, A., & Sabates-Wheeler, R. (2011). Introduction: Social protection for social justice. *IDS Bulletin Special Issue: Social Protection for Social Justice, 42*, 1–9. doi:10.1111/j.1759-5436.2011.00265.x

Devereux, S., Roelen, K., Béné, C., Chopra, D., Leavy, J., & McGregor, J. A. (2013). *Evaluating outside the box: An alternative framework for analysing social protection programmes* (IDS Working Paper No. 431. CSP Working Paper No. 010). Brighton: Institute for Development Studies.

Devereux, S., & Sabates-Wheeler, R. (2004). *Transformative social protection* (IDS Working Paper No. 232). Brighton: Institute of Development Studies.

DFID. (2005). *Reducing poverty by tackling social exclusion* (A DFID Policy Paper). London: UK Department for International Development.

Dissanayake, R., Stephenson, Z., & Greenslade, M. (2012). *Evaluating social transfer programmes*. London: Department for International Development, Guidance for DFID country offices.

Easterly, W., Ritzen, J., & Woolcock, M. (2006). Social cohesion, institutions and growth. *Economics and Politics, 18*, 103–120. doi:10.1111/j.1468-0343.2006.00165.x

FAO. (2013). *The economic impacts of cash transfer programmes in sub-Saharan Africa*. Policy Brief. Rome: Food and Agricultural Organization.

Gittell, R., & Vidal, A. (1998). *Community organizing: Building social capital as a development strategy*. Thousand Oaks, CA: Sage Publications.

Gough, I., & Olofsson, G. (Eds.). (1999). *Capitalism and social cohesion: Essays on exclusion and integration*. Basingstoke, UK: Macmillan Press.

Green, A., Janmaat, G., & Han, C. (2009). *Regimes of social cohesion*. London: Centre for Learning and Life Chances in Knowledge Economies and Societies.

Hypher, N. (2011, May 6). *Impact of cash transfers on children – The role of social relations and intra-household dynamics: Findings from a save the children study*. Presented at the ODI Lunchtime Seminar, London: Overseas Development Institute. Retrieved February 28, 2014, from www.odi.org.uk/events/documents/2635-presentation-nicola-hypher.pdf

Jenson, J. (2010). *Defining and measuring social cohesion*. Social Policies in Small States Series Paper. London: Commonwealth Secretariat and United Nations Research Institute for Social Development.

Jones, N., & Shaheen, M. (2012). *Transforming cash transfers: Beneficiary and community perspectives on the Palestinian National Cash Transfer Programme – Part 2: The case of the West Bank*. London: Overseas Development Institute.

Jones, N., & Shahrokh, T. (2013). *Social protection pathways: Shaping social justice outcomes for the most marginalised, now and post-2015*. ODI Background Note. London: Overseas Development Institute.

Kabeer, N. (2010). *Can the MDGs provide a pathway to social justice? The challenge of intersecting inequalities*. New York, NY: United Nations Development Programme.

Leach, M., & Scoones, I. (2007). *Mobilising citizens: Social movements and the politics of knowledge citizenship* (DRC Synthesis Paper. IDS Working Paper No. 276). Brighton: Institute of Development Studies.

Levitas, R., Pantazis, C., Fahmy, E., Gordon, D., Lloyd, E., & Patsios, D. (2007). *The multi-dimensional analysis of social exclusion*. Bristol: Department of Sociology and School for Social Policy, Townsend Centre for the International Study of Poverty and Bristol Institute for Public Affairs, University of Bristol.

MacAuslan, I., & Riemenschneider, N. (2011, April 13–15). *Richer but resented: What do cash transfers do to social relations and does it matter?* Paper presented at conference, 'Social Protection for Social Justice', Brighton: Institute of Development Studies, Centre for Social Protection.

Mansuri, G., & Rao, V. (2013). *Localizing development: Does participation work?* Washington, DC: World Bank.

Miller, C., Tsoka, M., & Reichert, K. (2011). Impacts on children of cash transfers in Malawi. In S. Handa, S. Devereux, & D. Webb (Eds.), *Social protection for Africa's children* (pp. 96–116). London: Routledge.

Narayan, D. (1999). *Bonds and bridges: Social capital and poverty* (Policy Research Paper No. 2167). Washington, DC: World Bank.

Norton, A., & de Haan, A. (2013). *Social cohesion: Theoretical debates and practical applications with respect to jobs*. Background Paper for the World Development Report. Washington, DC: World Bank.

OECD. (2012). *Perspectives on global development 2012. Social cohesion in a shifting world*. Paris: OECD Publishing. Retrieved February 28, 2014, from http://www.keepeek.com/Digital-AssetManagement/oecd/development/perspectives-on-global-development-2012_persp_glob_dev-2012-en#page1

Olson, M. (1971). *The logic of collective action. Public goods and the theory of groups*. Cambridge, MA: Harvard Economic Studies: Harvard University Press.

Putnam, R. D. (1993). *Making democracy work. Civic traditions in modern Italy*. Princeton, NJ: Princeton University Press.

Putnam, R. D. (2000). *Bowling alone. The collapse and revival of American community*. New York, NY: Simon and Schuster.

Ressler, P. (2008). *The social impact of cash transfers: A study of the impact of cash transfers on social networks of kenyan households participating in cash transfer programs* (RENEWAL Working Paper). Washington, DC: International Food Policy and Research Institute (IFPRI)

Robano, V., & Smith, S. C. (2014). *Multidimensional targeting and evaluation: A general framework with an application to a poverty program in Bangladesh* (OPHI Working Paper No. 65). Oxford: Oxford Poverty and Human Development Initiative.

Roelen, K., Edstrom, J., Sabates-Wheeler, R., & Davies, M. (2011). *Child and HIV sensitive social protection in Eastern and Southern Africa: Lessons from the Children and AIDS Regional Initiative (CARI).* Nairobi: UNICEF Eastern and Southern Africa Regional Office.

Samuels, F., Jones, N., & Malachowska, A. (2013). *Holding cash transfers to account: Beneficiary and community perspectives.* London: Overseas Development Institute.

Selvester, K., Fidalgo, L., & Taimo, N. (2012). *Transforming cash transfers: Beneficiary and community perspectives of the basic social subsidy programme in Mozambique.* London: Overseas Development Institute.

Soors, W., Dkhimi, F., & Criel, B. (2013). Lack of access to health care for African indigents: A social exclusion perspective. *International Journal for Equity in Health, 12,* 91. doi:10.1186/1475-9276-12-91

Szreter, S., & Woolcock, M. (2004). Health by association? Social capital, social theory, and the political economy of public health. *International Journal of Epidemiology, 33,* 650–667. doi:10.1093/ije/dyh013

Wietler, K. (2007). *The impact of social cash transfers on informal safety nets in Kalomo District, Zambia: A qualitative study.* Berlin: Ministry of Community Development and Social Services (MCDSS) and German Technical Cooperation (GTZ).

World Bank. (2000). *World development report 2000-01: Attacking poverty.* New York, NY: Oxford University Press.

World Bank. (2013). *Inclusion matters: The foundation for shared prosperity.* Washington, DC: World Bank.

From Social Accountability to a New Social Contract? The Role of NGOs in Protecting and Empowering PLHIV in Uganda

BADRU BUKENYA

Lecturer Department of Social Work and Social Administration, Makerere University Kampala, Kampala, Uganda

ABSTRACT *Social protection and social accountability initiatives are increasingly promoted as mechanisms for securing a new social contract between states and citizens in developing countries. Evidence from Uganda suggests that* social protection programmes with built-in accountability arrangements *led by non-governmental organisations (NGOs) can enable states and citizens, in this case people living with HIV and AIDS, to 'see' each other in different and more positive ways, and as such can provide clues as to how such interventions can help build a social contract at the local level. This finding helps counter critical concerns that NGOs tend to depoliticise state–society relations and undermine accountability.*

Introduction

Those days, before the Mini TASO Project, health workers were so bad and looked at us as sinners. This created self-stigma among us patients. Many of us refused to come out to test or seek other medical services because we felt that health workers had turned us into second class citizens. But with the coming of the MTP you can no longer despise people with HIV/AIDS. TASO taught us how to represent and defend our rights. (Male PLHIV, Kamuli, 1 February 2011)

As staff members at this hospital, our approach and attitudes towards PLHIV clients was not very friendly before the MTP. We used to under look [and] discriminate against PLHIV for the fear that they would infect us with HIV. However after the capacity building by TASO we were able to change our attitudes, we started handling PLHIV as human beings with dignity. This actually improved our relationship with even other patients in the entire hospital. (Female health worker, Kamuli, 21 March 2011)

The role of social protection in reducing the vulnerability of poor and marginal groups has increasingly been framed in terms of the sociopolitical as well as the material gains that such interventions can have. Proponents suggest that social protection interventions can enable the integration of previously marginal groups within communities (Devereux, 2007) and help promote social cohesion more broadly (Hujo, 2009), along with a broader range of 'political feedback' effects including voting habits and regime stability (Barrientos & Pellissery, 2012). More widely, it is claimed that social protection can be a means of extending and improving the 'social contract' between states and citizens (see Hickey and King, this volume), in that it can help render states more legitimate in the eyes of citizens and, where participatory mechanisms are integrated in a more 'transformative' approach (Devereux & Sabates-Wheeler, 2004), it can help enhance the citizenship status and claim-making capacities of local communities.

Similar claims are concurrently being made for the kinds of social accountability mechanisms that are intended to increase citizen voice and power as a means of making service delivery more effective and responsive. For example, Joshi and Houtzager (2012) argue that social accountability should be conceptualised as a means through which state–society relations are transformed in progressive ways, rather than as a technocratic tool. Such an outcome is more likely to occur, they argue, along with other recent work on the politics of social accountability (Booth, 2012), where interventions do not simply empower 'demand-side' actors; they can also challenge and/or support 'supply–side' actors and institutions to adopt more accountable working practices.

It is difficult to assess the validity of these claims, given that the research base concerning the effects of integrating social accountability mechanisms within social protection interventions remains at an early stage. However, recent survey work on the politics of social protection and service delivery does provide some clues: according to a survey undertaken in Uganda and elsewhere by the Secure Livelihoods Research Consortium (SLRC),[1] citizens said that being informed and consulted about such interventions, and the inclusion of accountability mechanisms through which they could raise grievances, were what counted in terms of improving their perception of state legitimacy (Mazurana, Marshak, Opio, & Gordon, 2014). In short, it is the way in which goods and services are delivered that really counts if service delivery is to act as a mechanism for building state–society relations. This research also found that this effect was not dependent on the character of the agency delivering the services in question: citizens did not mind whether it was the state or non-state actors. This is interesting given the presumption in some work on the politics of social accountability that the prominent role of non-state actors in service delivery may undermine state accountability whilst also tending to depoliticise popular agency through a technocratic approach to promoting citizenship participation (see King, 2015 for a review of these debates).

This paper explores these arguments and debates by examining the extent to which intervention by a non-governmental organisation (NGO) in rural Uganda to protect and promote the rights of people living with HIV and AIDS (PLHIV) both empowered those involved as citizens and changed the approach of the state, and in so doing encouraged the emergence of a new social contract. The following section discusses the theoretical links between social protection, service delivery, and the formation of social contracts, and proceeds to introduce the AIDS Support Organisation (TASO) as the NGO case study, its intervention programme, and the research methods employed to investigate the outcomes of its intervention. The two sections that follow assess the extent to which TASO managed to promote higher levels of state capacity and citizenship, respectively, before turning to the wider question of whether social protection programmes with built-in accountability arrangements by NGOs can help to foster a new social contract between states and citizens.

Accountable Forms of Social Protection and the Social Contract: Conceptualising the Links

The role of social protection and social accountability in extending the social contract involves changes on both sides of the equation (Gaventa, 2002; McGee & Gaventa, 2010): generating increased citizenship status, rights, and participation whilst also improving the developmental capacity and commitment of the state to recognise the rights of citizens and deliver goods/services to them (see Hickey and King, this volume).

Social protection is linked to the promotion of citizenship in a number of important ways, starting with the recognition of status that it accords to previously marginal groups. Comparative analysis of the politics of social protection in a range of African and South Asian countries, including the post-Apartheid extension of the social pension to black South Africans, suggests that the expansion of social protection is closely related to the extension of citizenship rights to different categories of erstwhile 'subjects' (Hickey, 2009). Whilst this primarily constitutes an extension of the social rights of citizenship (Leisering & Barrientos, 2013; Marshall, 1963), this form of redistribution and recognition has been identified as encouraging citizens to take up the civil and political rights – and obligations – of citizenship through becoming more active in a range of associational and even political forms of participation, partly to protect or expand benefits but also in a broader sense (Mettler & Soss, 2004; Skocpol, 1992). Campbell's (2003) study of the impact of US Social Security and Medicare programmes on the political activity of senior citizens illuminates this point. Where such interventions include mechanisms through which recipients gain voice and are supported in exercising their agency (for example by capacity building and conscientisation initiatives), these effects can expect to be deepened. Finally, the material resources that social protection offers may also enable recipients to overcome the transaction costs of being involved in civil and political participation (Campbell, 2003).

The argument that delivering social protection, as a form of social policy (De Haan, Jeremy, & Nazneen, 2002), can help enhance state–society relations also draws on a wider set of debates concerning the role of service delivery in generating increased levels of state legitimacy (Batley, McCourt, & McLoughlin, 2012; OECD, 2008). The key mechanisms for this include the delivery of effective services, which signals the will and capacity of the state to act in a responsive manner, and the promotion of participation and accountability, which can enhance citizens' perceptions of the state (Brinkerhoff, Wetterberg, & Dunn, 2012, 276).

What has been less explored, however, is the extent to which non-state actors can play a role in these processes. For some observers, allowing NGOs to take a leading role in social protection and social accountability interventions is likely to undermine the accountability required for more progressive state–society relations to flourish. NGOs may depoliticise the role that citizens and social movements can play in this process as a result of the technocratic forms of participation they tend to employ, particularly when their involvement in service delivery involves their co-optation by the state. According to Wood (1997), when states 'franchise' service provision responsibilities to NGOs, citizens risk losing the capacity to hold providers to account, as NGOs are accountable upwards to the state and their funders rather than downwards to recipients. Swidler and Watkins' (2009) research in Malawi indicates that service delivery NGOs undermined the agency of their communities by teaching them to be subservient to the powerful – government and international – agencies that fund their activities. Others suggest that NGOs can have a negative effect on the development of voice when they establish parallel service delivery structures that act as exit sites for clients dissatisfied with government services (Di John, 2007; Maclean, 2011). However, recent studies suggest that NGOs can foster responsive service delivery skills in government staff (Batley & Rose, 2011) and help to 'forge more productive linkages between communities and public institutions than states are able to establish on their own' (Cammett & MacLean, 2011, 7). It is further suggested that if non-state actors encourage the coproduction of services between communities and the state, this can result both in citizens becoming more engaged and empowered and states becoming more responsive (Mitlin, 2008; Tsai, 2011).

Researching the Politics of Social Accountability in Uganda

This paper explores these debates through a case study of an HIV/AIDS service delivery project implemented by a prominent Ugandan NGO: TASO. The focus on PLHIV is particularly appropriate given the extent to which this category of people have often been treated as second-class citizens in African countries (as elsewhere), and so provides a test case for how far social protection programmes with built-in accountability arrangements can transform relations between the state and marginal groups.

Uganda offers an interesting context within which to explore these issues. Uganda is typically categorised as a semi-authoritarian state, within which processes of democratisation have been heavily compromised by the continued dominance of the ruling party, the National Resistance Movement (NRM). The NRM has secured itself in power since 1986 through its combination of delivering stability and relatively pro-poor forms of growth, the active repression of political opponents and dissenting voices from within civil society, and the use of state resources to deliver services and protection as forms of patronage rather than as of right (Tripp, 2010). Public services such as the national health system are highly visible social institutions, and thus may play an important role in influencing public trust and legitimacy in government. In Uganda, although access to basic services such as education and health increased impressively following election-related policy shifts to reduce costs for users in 1997 and 2001, respectively, the quality of service provision remains very low and the government has yet to make any serious investment in social protection, despite donor pressure to do so. NGOs are warned to 'back off politics' (The New Vision, 2012). Hence the majority confine themselves to service delivery activities (Barr et al., 2005). However, the President was also amongst the first African leaders to promote interventions designed to assist PLHIV, a move that has been credited with the rapid decline in the incidence of HIV/AIDS (Parkhurst, 2005; Putzel, 2004).

To understand causal effects of a particular TASO intervention, named the Mini TASO Project (MTP), this study employed a comparative case analysis of how MTP altered state–citizen relations in two of the districts that it was rolled out in, alongside a control study of a district in which MTP was not present.[2] Our initial investigation discovered that MTP was not rolled out evenly in each district, with key informants identifying Kamuli as a district in which the project had been extended the furthest, compared to others in which implementation was considered by TASO staff to have been 'patchier'. We therefore purposively sought to investigate Kamuli alongside a district in which MTP had been more weakly implemented, namely Masafu, in order to establish if variation in the implementation of MTP had a bearing on performance and outcomes, whilst also including a non-MTP district (Iganga) as a control to offer the full range of possibilities. Retrospective baselines of government capacity to respond to PLHIV were then constructed in Kamuli and Masafu hospitals prior to TASO's MTP intervention, although this was not possible in the Iganga control due to a lack of record-keeping within local government there. In the MTP sites, the study included a temporal element throughout, whereby retrospective questions were asked in order to help identify the situation before and after the MTP intervention, which ran in 2006–2011. The fieldwork was undertaken in November 2010–July 2011 and involved both qualitative and quantitative methods of data collection, namely in-depth interviews (with PLHIV, health workers, district leaders, TASO staff, and other key informants), documentary analysis, observation of service provision, and a small-scale survey of PLHIV service users from the three district hospitals. Here, structured questionnaires were administered to a total of 178 respondents (Kamuli, n = 61; Masafu, n = 71; Iganga, n = 46). As with all such studies, there are methodological limitations to be aware of here, including the fact that the cross-sectional nature of the study does not allow full assessment of impact and sustainability beyond the MTP period, that the retrospective element of the survey is vulnerable to recall bias, and also that the samples for the survey research were too small to allow sophisticated inferential statistical analyses. Wherever possible, steps have been taken to mitigate the effects of these limitations, including the careful triangulation of findings and the use of quantitative data in a descriptive rather than explanatory way.

Towards a New Social Contract in Rural Uganda? The Mini TASO Project

TASO is an indigenous NGO, established in 1987 to 'contribute to a process of preventing HIV, restoring hope and improving the quality of life of persons, families and communities affected by HIV infection and disease' in Uganda (Grebe & Nattrass, 2009). In 2003, TASO crafted the MTP as a capacity-building programme that involved various training programmes for government health workers, financial support to district hospitals, and supporting citizens to demand their rights and engage in coproduction activities with service providers. The name suggested the intention to transform government hospitals into 'TASO-like' agencies which recognised PLHIV as full citizens and ensured that they received the required treatment in an effective and accountable manner (TASO, 2005). Between 2003 and 2010, TASO annually initiated partnerships with two to four district local governments to transform the HIV/AIDS departments in their main hospitals into Mini TASOs. According to TASO documents (TASO, 2005, 2007) and interviewees, MTPs were established through a three-phase programme that involved site mobilisation, capacity building, and service delivery. The MTP thus constitutes both a protective and a transformative form of social protection (Devereux & Sabates-Wheeler, 2004, p. 10), in that it seeks to both increase the provision of the drugs required to ameliorate the effects of HIV/AIDS and to challenge disempowering and discriminatory tendencies that have reduced PLHIV to the status of second-class citizens.

Prior to TASO's intervention in 2006, both Kamuli and Masafu hospitals had introduced antiretroviral therapy (ART) programmes in 2005. Government guidelines stated that before a health facility was accredited to provide ART services, it ought to have capabilities in various areas, including: the presence of basic physical infrastructure for the treatment of PLHIV (for example space for counselling and testing, drug storage facilities); qualified personnel with experience in HIV/AIDS management, and the ability to ensure the provision of follow-up care and support for families and communities with PLHIV (Okero, Aceng, Madraa, Namagala, & Serutoke, 2003).

However, TASO's own evaluation of its intervention sites deemed them to have 'inadequate levels of capacity, resources, community mobilization and community involvement' (TASO, 2007, p. 18). The capacity assessment found that these units had neither the social nor the physical infrastructure for providing ART. Our own research confirmed this: in Masafu, one respondent recalled that health workers started providing HIV/AIDS services 'with hardly any basic understanding of the processes involved in this specialised service area' (Male health worker, Masafu, 14 April 2011). Health workers in Kamuli hospital also claimed that, prior to 2006, they lacked the skills in psychosocial work required to educate and provide counselling services to PLHIV. These observations were further confirmed by the findings of a 2008 Uganda Ministry of Health survey, which reported that 'only one third of facilities prescribing ART and/or medical follow up services have a provider trained in ART prescription or medical services and in counselling for adherence to antiretroviral (ARV) drug therapy' (Ministry of Health and Macro International Inc., 2008, p. 187).

Health workers noted that their inadequate skills in mobilisation, counselling, and ARV administration meant that they recruited fewer patients before MTP (Male health worker, Masafu, 14 April 2011). As shown in Figure 1, Masafu hospital only managed to recruit 27 PLHIV on ART in 2005, whereas this increased fivefold to 135 during the first year of TASO's arrival. Similarly, Kamuli hospital registered a steady increase in PLHIV annual enrolment on ART after getting MTP. The fluctuating figures in Masafu arguably reflect the inconsistent implementation of the MTP there that we noted above.

The interviews and survey findings reveal that, before MTP, relations between health workers and patients were tense and characterised by 'mutual mistrust' in both hospitals (Focus Group Discussion (FGD) with MTP service providers, Masafu, 24 January 2011). Patients claimed that health workers would blame them for being HIV positive and some PLHIV reported incidents of physical harassment by staff (Male PLHIV, Kamuli, 1 February 2011). Acknowledging some shortcomings in retrospect, health workers reflected that their attitude flowed from inadequate awareness of the disease and how to

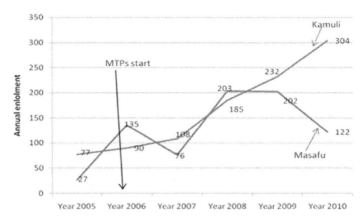

Figure 1. Annual enrolment of PLHIV on ART in Kamuli and Masafu.
Source: *author's calculations based on ART registers*

deal with PLHIV (Interviews with two female health workers, Kamuli, 14 January 2011 and 21 March 2011). In both Kamuli and Masafu, capacity to deal with PLHIV was limited to the central district hospitals, with no outreach programmes for those in remote parts of the district. This reflects the more general lack of 'infrastructural power' in Uganda (Hawkins, 2014), which means that many rural dwellers rarely 'see the state' (Jones, 2009). Given these conditions, it is not surprising that our survey found PLHIV critical of the quality of services available to them prior to MTP. On eight selected indicators about service quality – staff responsiveness, privacy in consultations, opportunity to discuss concerns with health workers, the quality of explanations received, drug availability, waiting time, number of days services were available, and the hours of service – PLHIV in both study sites rated services as below average on six. It is against this background that TASO oriented MTP towards working on the 'supply side' before building citizens' capacity to make demands of the hospital staff.

Did MTP Build State Capacity and Change the Way in Which the State sees PLHIV?

There was consensus among respondents in our MTP districts that the project increased the capacity of government hospitals to deliver HIV/AIDS services. Between 2005 and 2010, the number of PLHIV receiving treatment in Kamuli increased from 334 to 4,152, and from 256 to 2,113 in Masafu. This translates into an annual percentage increase in PLHIV enrolment of 71 per cent and 53 per cent for Kamuli and Masafu, respectively.[3]

MTP provided each participating health facility with UGX 50 million (~GBP 15,000) per annum. This is a significant financial contribution considering the small operational budgets for health facilities in local governments in Uganda. For example, mini hospitals, which offer services to a catchment population of 100,000, receive up to UGX 12 million per annum (Parliamentary Committee on Health, 2012). Around 20 per cent of the MTP budget was reserved for purchasing drugs (Interview with male TASO HQ official, Kampala, 28 January 2011). Before this, health workers would advise patients to buy medicines from private providers, a move that had negative implications for state building, in that it effectively means telling PLHIV to stay away from essentially irrelevant public facilities (Interview with health workers' FGD, Kamuli, 24 January 2011, Kamuli). This finding is corroborated by Nazerali, Oteba, Mwoga, and Zaramba (2006), who observe that, in Uganda, hospital attendance is greatly determined by the availability of drugs. The reliable provision of drugs is also central to citizens' expectations of a functioning health system (Nazerali et al., 2006), with drug availability shaping the perceptions of patients about the trustworthiness of government employees in the health sector (Ssengooba et al., 2007).

As shown in Table 1, whereas 84 per cent of our sample of PLHIV in Kamuli felt that there was poor availability of drugs before TASO arrived, this overall judgement had been reversed by 2011, with roughly the same proportion then claiming that the drugs supply was good. Progress in Masafu was more limited, although still significant, with a switch from 83 per cent registering a negative view regarding the pre-MTP situation to nearly 58 per cent holding the opposite view by the end of the

Table 1. Clients' perception of drug availability

| Facility | Period | Drug availability | | |
		Poor (%)	Fair (%)	Good (%)
Kamuli	Pre-MTP	83.6	14.8	1.6
(n = 61)	2011	4.9	9.8	85.2
Masafu	Pre-MTP	83.1	15.5	1.4
(n = 71)	2011	4.2	38.0	57.7
Iganga	2006	19.6	60.9	19.6
(n = 46)	2011	17.4	67.4	15.2

intervention. In Iganga, our control, the majority of respondents felt that drug supply is just 'fair' in their facility, with marginal changes occurring over a five-year period.

Besides increasing drug supply in targeted sites, TASO's intervention helped public hospitals to respond to two challenges in government hospitals: namely, staffing shortages and inadequate skills among the existing staff. As discussed earlier, the health staff in government facilities lacked technical skills, such as ART administration and psychosocial skills. Efforts by TASO to address these capacity gaps through training programmes were seen by main health workers as enabling them to 'see' PLHIV as citizens in need of special care, in much the same way that TASO did. A senior health worker in Kamuli hospital reflected the sentiments of most of those interviewed at the facility, noting that:

Our attitude towards clients [...] was not very friendly [...] We used to have many PLHIV but we would just under look them. [However,] after the training by TASO we were able to change our attitudes towards PLHIV and [started] handling them in a better way [...] we started moving to the wards to look for our clients, counsel them – to provide them with the psychosocial support, give them information regarding HIV and Positive Living. This actually improved our relationship with the PLHIV. (Female health worker, Kamuli, 21 March 2011)

Generally, health workers claimed that the training and mentoring from TASO reduced their tendency to negatively 'construct' PLHIV as 'sinful' and treat them as second-class citizens (Gilson, 2003; Schneider & Ingram, 2007). Whereas 82 per cent and 80 per cent of the clients in Kamuli and Masafu, respectively, described the responsiveness of TASO in the pre-MTP era as poor, by the time of fieldwork, this judgement had been completely reversed (see below).

TASO's strategy for addressing inadequate staff capacity in the targeted public facilities involved a form of 'coproduction', which Mitlin (2008) defines as citizens and states working together both to extend basic services and as a strategy by and for grassroots groups to secure political influence. 'Expert' service users were mobilised to help the state perform a number of roles required to extend ART provision, from undertaking sensitisation campaigns and mobilising and organising fellow clients during clinic days through to offering health education training, sorting files, packing drugs, and recording the triage details of fellow service users. Health workers acknowledged that this greatly relieved their workload and extended the capacity of their facilities to protect PLHIV from their disease (health workers' FGD, 24 January 2011; observations at MTP clinics, 11–15 April 2011). This form of 'peer-group-led' coproduction is increasingly recognised as a successful strategy for helping public officials to reach socially marginalised groups (Campbell & Cornish, 2010). For example, the use of music, dance, and drama by the peers employed by MTP was proving so effective in mobilising PLHIV that health workers started pairing with drama groups and using the occasions to undertake testing for HIV amongst those attending the shows, and encouraging those testing positive to start accessing medical services. Between 2006 and 2010, the average annual reach of such community awareness campaigns in Kamuli was 4,900 people, while that of Masafu was 1,900; by way of comparison, the majority of Ugandan NGOs reportedly have an average reach of less than 500 people annually (Barr et al., 2005).

MTP targeted another important dimension of state capacity by supporting public facilities to record and store patient details. Although this form of file keeping is characterised by some critics as a form of 'surveillance' that modern bureaucratic states use to governmentalize their subjects (Rose, 1999), coproduction scholars note that marginal groups themselves now undertake their own surveys to ensure that they are rendered legible to the state and thus seen as citizens with valid claims for recognition and redistribution through service delivery (Mitlin, 2008). TASO introduced several data forms to help health workers collect information on PLHIV, and ensured that every Mini TASO hospital had a trained records clerk, records storage facilities such as filing cabinets, and a computer. These interventions had visible impacts: our observations revealed that MTP sites kept far more data on their service delivery activities for PLHIV when compared to Iganga hospital, where the project was not implemented, and in Kamuli there was a 'spillover' effect, whereby the capacities developed by MTP were used to improve records management hospital wide (Male staff, Kamuli, 27 June 2011).

When data showed that the number of clients attending clinics was increasing, MTP administrators increased the number of clinic days from one to four days a week, and a new appointment system was designed to allocate specific types of patients to each day, with Fridays designated for records management. PLHIV leaders observed that this helped to reduce the congestion of patients at the clinic (Female PLHIV, Kamuli, 22 April 2011) and also introduced a structured and more reliable format for state–citizen interactions in Kamuli MTP, a move associated with the development of more 'impersonal' and universalist forms of state provision based on the rights of citizenship rather than personalised negotiations through a patron–client rubric (Corbridge, Williams, Srivastava, & Veron, 2005).

Did MTP Increase Levels of Citizenship Status, Rights, and Participation?

Beyond the advances in the citizenship status and rights of PLHIV discussed above, MTP sought to promote this further in two main ways: namely, the promotion of associational life among PLHIV and the creation of participatory spaces.

MTP Approaches as Participatory Social Accountability

The participatory spaces that TASO introduced at its MTP sites were designed to empower PLHIV to hold service users to account and provide a basis for wider forms of collective action. Various participatory structures were introduced, including clients' representative committees and also client staff meetings, which enabled citizens to be 'invited inside the governmental apparatus itself' to influence programmes that directly affect them (Ackerman, 2004, p. 451). Implementation varied across MTP sites, as Table 2 reveals, with more mechanisms operational in Kamuli than Masafu, although both had significantly more participatory mechanisms than in the Iganga control.

In Kamuli, the general PLHIV meetings took the form of 'citizen juries' (Corbridge, 2005; Goetz & Gaventa, 2001), whereby politicians, government health workers, PLHIV, and sometimes members of the press were brought together in a space through which state officials could receive feedback from citizens and be held to account by them for their actions and inactions. MTP thus offered a means 'for bringing the citizen and the state into [...] unmediated encounter that offers each party an undistorted sighting of the other' (Corbridge et al., 2005, p. 44), providing structures capable not only of more effective service delivery but also increased and improved levels of state citizen interaction, which promotes citizenship and the pro-poor orientation of service providers (Bruns, Filmer, & Patrinos, 2011; Williams, Thampi, Narayana, Nandigama, & Bhattacharyya, 2011). In Kamuli MTP, PLHIV were able to use these mechanisms to influence how the hospital functioned, including the institutionalisation of a bespoke HIV/AIDS department. After several complaints about the inadequate attention given to PLHIV, the medical superintendent attended the PLHIV's committee meeting of 29 May 2010 and informed members that:

> we came to a conclusion to let the Mini TASO become a separate department and be provided with separate staff [...] Since it has become a department, it will run like any other department [...] So if someone does not come to duty, he/she will attract disciplinary action like any other

Table 2. Distribution of dialogue structures in the study sites

Dialogue structure type	Kamuli	Masafu	Iganga
PLHIV/client representative committee	Yes	No	No
Client welfare committee meetings	Yes	No	No
Staff meetings with drama members	Yes	Yes	No
Staff and peer counsellors meetings	Yes	Yes	Yes
General PLHIV meetings	Yes	No	No

person who fails to come to duty in other departments. Any misconduct on a TASO clinic should be handled like any from other departments (Interview with Male health official, Masafu, during the PLHIV's committee meeting, 29 May 2010).

Further complaints from PLHIV caused the medical superintendent to issue a circular warning to all Kamuli hospital staff about their negligence and absenteeism. This finding is consistent with research suggesting that 'bottom up' forms of social accountability can lead to improved levels of oversight which have greater enforceability (Brett, 2003; Goetz & Jenkins, 2001). For some PLHIV, such communications sent a strong signal that their deliberations in participatory spaces were causing the hospital to listen to their concerns, with one PLHIV leader noting that because 'clients' issues are raised in meetings and the medical staff are made to know about clients' concerns, they have changed their ways and in most cases [our concerns] are handled well' (Interview with a male PLHIV, Kamuli, 7 February 2011). However, such mechanisms are clearly far from perfect, with other respondents arguing that:

> When we have meetings with health workers they give us time to give our reports. Sometimes they take on our suggestions [but] other times they do not [...] Sometimes when we speak about certain things the problem becomes worse. (Interview with a male PLHIV, Kamuli, 1 February 2011)

The spaces for interaction between health workers and service users were advantageous in another way. Service users were invited to engage in activities that allowed them to gain insights into the working environment of health workers as well as their roles and expectations. Such opportunities have the potential for enabling the two sides to search collectively for solutions to challenges rather than fight about them (Wild & Wales, 2015). As elaborated in later sections, it may be that the most important outcome of social accountability mechanisms is to enable these forms of dialogue, rather than promoting voice per se (Fox, 2015), with dialogic processes offering a basis for improved forms of state–society relations in support of building a wider social contract.

Promotion of Associational Life

Our findings suggest that PLHIV who benefitted from MTP were more capable and willing to relate to and work with one another than those receiving treatment from standard health facilities. In line with other research on this dynamic (Bebbington, 2008; Moore & Putzel, 1999; Tendler, 1995), our evidence shows that contact with the state stimulated PLHIV to create new or join existing groups, associations, and networks. In Kamuli, 64 per cent of the respondents said that their contact with MTP had encouraged them to join local groups, compared to 56 per cent in Masafu. The rate of group-joining was significantly lower in Iganga, at 24 per cent, where TASO had no intervention, reinforcing the sense that the differential effects across our three districts reflect the extent to which the MTP intervention was actually implemented in each.

The music dance and drama (MDD) groups introduced by MTP encouraged further associational activity amongst participating PLHIV members. In each MTP, membership per group ranged between 15 and 20 PLHIV, with slightly more female participants than men. Group members testified that the group exposed them to new experiences, including the opportunity to travel beyond their own villages or districts, for example to annual regional drama festivals, where several Mini TASOs and TASO service branches competed (TASO, 2008, 2010). Participating in these claimed spaces (Cornwall, 2002) enabled PLHIV to learn from wider experiences of how provision for PLHIV was unfolding in other parts of the country, and, in line with Gaventa and Barret's (2010) overview of participation and accountability initiatives, extend their horizons in broader and empowering ways. For example, PLHIV members talked of how group interactions offered opportunities for them to enhance their ability to speak in public: 'For me I did not know that I would ever stand in front of people to talk about myself. But, through drama, that is exactly what I started doing [...] I even became the chairman of PLHIV in my subcounty of Kitayundwa' explained one respondent (Interview with a male PLHIV, Kamuli, 7 June 2011).

According to Cornwall and Coelho (2006, p. 8), it is through participating in such activities that 'citizens cut their political teeth and acquire skills that can be transferred to other spheres'. Campbell and Cornish (2012, p. 853), drawing on the case of the Sonagachi project for sex workers in India, illustrate how the opportunity to be involved in peer education activities gave sex workers the 'ability to "speak" – at public events, [and] to the media', which in return enabled them to learn 'how to negotiate with police and politicians'. Similar is Williams et al.'s (2011) report of a participatory programme called Kadumbashree in the Indian state of Kerala, where the involvement of formerly marginalised women in neighbourhood groups and state activities enabled them to gain visibility in the public sphere. In the case of MTP, some drama members similarly used their newly acquired confidence and public speaking experience to venture into politics (see below), and thus transcend the 'technocratic' realm of project-level participation for a more political form, and showed how local associations can be effective routes for citizens' empowerment in 'semi democratic' political contexts in the south (Benequista, 2011; Gaventa & Barret, 2010).

The 2011 local elections in Uganda offered a window through which this research could track the political effects of MTP. We found that a greater number of PLHIV contested subcounty council elections in Kamuli in 2011 than in Masafu MTP, where the project was not implemented as thoroughly. We could not identify any contestants in Iganga, and the two PLHIV experts who worked at this facility said that none of the clients had contested (Interview with a male and female expert PLHIV, Iganga hospital, 20 May 2011). Although clearly not conclusive, this evidence tentatively supports claims that service delivery and social protection programmes can be a means for building political skills of citizens (Nyamu-Musembi, 2010).

Discussion: Towards a Deeper Social Contract?

According to the OECD (2008, p. 17), a social contract emerges from a dynamic interaction of four factors: the expectations that a given society has of a given state; the capacity of the state to provide services; the willingness of political elites to direct state resources and their capacity to fulfil social expectations; and the existence of political processes through which the bargain between state and society is struck, reinforced and institutionalised. These are all mediated by the existence of political processes through which the bargain between state and society is struck, reinforced, and institutionalised. To at least some degree, the participatory accountability structures promoted by MTP were engendering some of these processes with a view 'of reaching a state of dynamic equilibrium between the expectations of society and state capacity to meet these expectations' (OECD, 2008, p. 17). Excerpts from the minutes of such meetings revealed that clients and health workers, together with the local political leaders, candidly discussed issues of drugs availability, conduct of particular staff, and government commitment to service delivery. Where MTP was more fully implemented, as in Kamuli, PLHIV developed new and often improved 'sightings' of the state as a result of the changes in health workers' attitudes towards them, the manner in which they were being handled during service provision, and through the different avenues that were established to have direct interactions with health workers and other state agents. From the qualitative interviews, several respondents talked of progressive improvements in their relations with health workers, in particular, and the respective health facilities, in general. One of the PLHIV leaders in Kamuli hospital claimed that:

[MTP] created a link or relationship between health workers and clients, clients with HIV/AIDS. Before TASO came in, there was a big bridge whereby health workers were at the extreme end and we PLHIV on this other end [...] health workers had no good relations with us. However when TASO came, it trained health workers in counselling [...] those health workers, who had no proper communication skills, were able to abandon their old ways (Male PLHIV leader, Kamuli, 21 March 2011)

Table 3. Service users' perceptions on attention of hospital to their concerns

Facility category	Attention by hospital			Total
	Not much	A little bit	A great deal	
Kamuli (n = 60)	10 (16.7%)	13(21.7%)	37 (61.7%)	60 (100%)
Masafu (n = 70)	35 (50%)	7 (10%)	28 (40%)	70 (100%)
Iganga (n = 44)	35 (79.5%)	4 (9.1%)	5 (11.4%)	44 (100%)

Quantitative data, although limited, helps to support these qualitative observations that PLHIV's trust in health workers during service delivery had improved. Our mini survey measured the perceptions of PLHIV about the responsiveness of the hospitals. When respondents were asked how much attention they thought their respective hospitals paid to what people like them think before they decided what to do, Kamuli MTP performed better than other sites (See Table 3).

From Table 3, 62 per cent of the PLHIV in Kamuli and 40 per cent in Masafu reported that, since the MTP intervention, their hospitals were paying 'a great deal of attention' to what they think, while only 11 per cent of the PLHIV in Iganga, where TASO had no intervention, felt the same. A majority of PLHIV (80%) in Iganga thought that their facility did not pay 'much attention' to them, but only 17 per cent and 50 per cent in Kamuli and Masafu, respectively, felt the same. These data suggest that, where the MTP was fully implemented (in Kamuli), state–society interactions became regularised, which made citizens feel that the state was interested in listening to their concerns.

Respondents' evaluation of the hospital and its quality of service became clear when we assessed PLHIV's willingness to pay for the services they received from the respective health facilities. Brinkerhoff et al. (2012) argue that people's confidence in the quality of public agencies is reflected in their willingness to pay for the services delivered there. According to Figure 2, whereas over 96 per cent of respondents in Kamuli and 73 per cent in Masafu expressed willingness to pay, the figure was only 32 per cent in Iganga, providing further evidence that the effects observed here are in line with the level of MTP presence in the different sites, and that the intervention tended to greatly improve levels of confidence and trust in the state amongst PLHIV.

The Problem of Financial Sustainability

The evidence presented so far suggests that social protection projects with built-in accountability mechanisms can indeed help extend social contracts between states and citizens in developing countries, and that NGOs, contrary to some criticisms, can play a positive role in this process. Importantly, however, the MTP was terminated in 2010. Our interviews with senior TASO staff

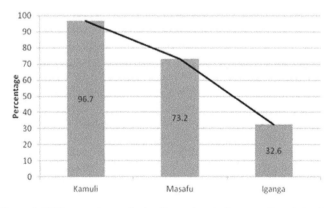

Figure 2. Willingness to pay for health services in the respective study sites.

suggested that the agency struggled to secure further financial backing for MTP from its main international funders because it was channelling funds to government agencies and thus running contrary to the expectation that the Civil Society Fund would primarily benefit Civil Society Organisations (various interviews with current and former TASO employees, Female TASO Central Region official, Kampala, 19 May 2011; Male former employee of TASO, Kampala, 23 April 2011; Male TASO HQ official, Kampala, 13 July 2011). This problem was compounded by the fact that TASO had not undertaken an official evaluation of the MTP despite external recommendations (Scott et al., 2005) and an internal commitment to do so (TASO, 2007), and thus lacked the evidence base required to persuade funders of its success.

This move reflects the dangers of relying on NGOs as the primary agents of progressive change, not because of anything inherent in their institutional character but in relation to the vagaries of NGO financing and because of the limited and time-bound nature of their interventions (Wild & Wales, 2015). Unfortunately, we currently lack the longitudinal evidence required to explore other critical aspects of sustainability, including the extent to which the processes observed here were maintained beyond the lifetime of the MTP intervention.

Conclusion

From the foregoing analysis, it is evident that TASO used the MTP to 'work on both sides of the equation' (Gaventa, 2002); that is, on the one hand, to 'civilise the state' and, on the other, to empower citizens to engage the state to improve service delivery. These effects were consistently deeper and more extensive where MTP had been implemented more fully. 'State civilising' attributes of MTP, such as health workers' shadowing, training, and financial facilitation, enhanced the ability as well as the commitment of government hospitals to deliver increased quantity and quality of HIV/AIDS services. Indeed, the state, especially in areas where MTP was fully rolled out, boosted its legitimacy as a result of meeting citizens' valued needs. On the part of PLHIV citizens, the MTP supplied resources in the form of training, ARV drugs, and actively enlisted their participation in service delivery. These, along with improved levels of service delivery from health workers, enhanced their self-worth. In turn, PLHIV gained confidence to engage in civic and political activities. Social protection programmes with built-in accountability arrangements can therefore provide useful forms of state society linkage, offering opportunities through which marginal groups can start to build a sense of citizenship, creating 'a series of sites where ordinary people might come to see the state in ways they have not done before' (Corbridge, 2007, p. 197). Our findings thus reinforce the growing sense that how programmes are designed and delivered is fundamental to their effectiveness, and that social accountability mechanisms may be less important in terms of enabling citizen 'voice' per se than though bringing stakeholders together from across the state–citizen divide to discuss and understand each other's interests and problems and build relationships of trust (Fox, 2015).

Overall, the experience of MTP supports claims that social protection interventions can potentially offer a route for integrating previously marginal groups within communities (Devereux, 2007), for promoting social cohesion (Hujo, 2009), and for building citizenship. Citizenship building works in a 'snowballing' fashion here, whereby enhanced citizen engagement in one area strengthens the possibilities of successful engagement in other areas. In MTPs, citizen action, whether through contentious action, MDD activities, or engaging in coproduction, left behind key transferable skills that some PLHIV used to engage in other activities, such as direct politics. This finding corroborates the wider sense that 'the journey from silence to a sense of citizenship [occurs] in many small steps' (Benequista, 2011, p. 8).

Lastly, notwithstanding the vagaries of NGO financing and short lifespan of their projects, it is worth noting that such actors can also play a role in helping states to see marginal groups as rights-bearing citizens in need of protection, and so help at least to some extent to reveal a pathway through which more progressive forms of social contracts can be promoted.

Acknowledgements

This paper has benefited enormously from the comments of two anonymous reviewers and Sam Hickey of the University of Manchester.

Disclosure statement

No potential conflict of interest was reported by the author.

Notes

1. SLRC is a multinational study that has undertaken similar analyses in countries like Sri Lanka, Nepal, and South Sudan (details available at http://www.securelivelihoods.org/publications.aspx).
2. In total, MTP was implemented in 13 districts in Uganda
3. Besides dispensing of drugs to PLHIV, however, most of the other HIV/AIDS-related activities here were introduced with MTP and therefore had no baseline with which to be compared.

References

Ackerman, J. (2004). Co-governance for accountability: Beyond "exit" and "voice". *World Development*, *32*, 447–463. doi:10.1016/j.worlddev.2003.06.015

Barr, A., Fafchamp, M., & Owen, T. (2005). The governance of non-governmental organizations in Uganda. *World Development*, *33*, 657–679. doi:10.1016/j.worlddev.2004.09.010

Barrientos, A., & Pellissery, S. (2012). *Delivering effective social assistance: Does politics matter?* (Working Paper No. 9). Manchester: Effective States and Inclusive Development Research Centre.

Batley, R., McCourt, W., & McLoughlin, C. (2012). Editorial: The politics and governance of public services in developing countries. *Public Management Review*, *14*, 131–144. doi:10.1080/14719037.2012.657840

Batley, R., & Rose, P. (2011). Analysing collaboration between non-governmental service providers and governments. *Public Administration and Development*, *31*, 230–239. doi:10.1002/pad.613

Bebbington, A. (2008). Social capital and development studies III: Social capital and the state (seen from Peru). *Progress in Development Studies*, *8*, 271–279. doi:10.1177/146499340800800305

Benequista, N. (2011). Blurring the boundaries. Citizen action across states and societies: A summary of findings from a decade of collaborative research on citizen engagement. In N. Benequista & J. Gaventa (Eds.), *DRC citizenship, participation and accountability*. Brighton: Institute of Development Studies.

Booth, D. (2012). Working with the grain and swimming against the tide. *Public Management Review*, *14*, 163–180. doi:10.1080/14719037.2012.657959

Brett, E. A. (2003). Participation and accountability in development management. *Journal of Development Studies*, *40*(2), 1–29. doi:10.1080/00220380412331293747

Brinkerhoff, D. W., Wetterberg, A., & Dunn, S. (2012). Service delivery and legitimacy in fragile and conflict-affected states. *Public Management Review*, *14*, 273–293. doi:10.1080/14719037.2012.657958

Bruns, B., Filmer, D., & Patrinos, H. A. (Eds.). (2011). *Making schools work: New evidence on accountability reforms*. Washington, DC: The World Bank.

Cammett, M., & MacLean, L. (2011). Introduction: The political consequences of non state social welfare in the global south. *Studies in Comparative International Development*, *46*, 1–21. doi:10.1007/s12116-010-9083-7

Campbell, A. L. (2003). *How policies make citizens: Senior citizen activism and the American welfare state*. New Jersey: Princeton University Press.

Campbell, C., & Cornish, F. (2010). Towards a "fourth generation" of approaches to HIV/AIDS management: Creating contexts for effective community mobilisation. *AIDS Care*, *22*, 1569–1579. doi:10.1080/09540121.2010.525812

Campbell, C., & Cornish, F. (2012). How can community health programmes build enabling environments for transformative communication? Experiences from India and South Africa. *AIDS and Behavior*, *16*(4), 847–857. doi:10.1007/s10461-011-9966-2

Corbridge, S. (2005). *Seeing the state: Governance and governmentality in India*. Cambridge: Cambridge University press.

Corbridge, S., Williams, G., Srivastava, M., & Veron, R. (2005). *Seeing the state: Governance and governmentality in India*. Cambridge: Cambridge University press.

Corbridge, S. (2007). The (Im)possibility of development studies. *Economy and Society*, *36*(2), 179–211. doi:10.1080/03085140701264869

Cornwall, A. (2002). Making spaces, changing places: Situating participation in development. IDS Working Paper no. 170. Brighton: Institute of Development Studies.

Cornwall, A., & Coelho, V. S. P. (2006). *Spaces for change? The politics of citizen participation in new democratic arenas.* London: Zed.

De Haan, A., Jeremy, H., & Nazneen, K. (2002). Social funds: An effective instrument to support local action for poverty reduction? *Journal of International Development, 14*(5), 643–652. doi:10.1002/jid.899

Devereux, S. (2007). Social pensions in Southern Africa in the twentieth century. *Journal of Southern African Studies, 33*(3), 539–560. doi:10.1080/03057070701475542

Devereux, S., & Sabates-Wheeler, R. (2004). Transformative social protection. Working paper series, 232. Brighton: IDS.

Di John, J. (2007). Albert Hirschman's exit-voice framework and its relevance to problems of public education performance in Latin America. *Oxford Development Studies, 35*(3), 295–327. doi:10.1080/13600810701514860

Fox, J. A. (2015). Social accountability: What does the evidence really say? *World Development, 72,* 346–361. doi:10.1016/j.worlddev.2015.03.011

Gaventa, J. (2002). Introduction: Exploring citizenship, participation and accountability. *IDS Bulletin, 33,* 1–14. doi:10.1111/idsb.2002.33.issue-2

Gaventa, J., & Barret, G. (2010) So what difference does it make? Mapping the outcomes of citizen engagement. IDS Working Paper no. 347. Brighton: Institute of Development Studies. 10.1111/j.2040-0209.2010.00347_2.x

Gilson, L. (2003). Trust and the development of health care as a social institution. *Social Science & Medicine, 56*(7), 1453–1468. doi:10.1016/S0277-9536(02)00142-9

Goetz, A. M., & Gaventa, J. (2001). *Bringing citizen voice and client focus into service delivery.* Brighton: Institute of Development Studies the University of Sussex.

Goetz, A. M., & Jenkins, R. (2001). Hybrid forms of accountability: Citizen engagement in institutions of public-sector oversight in India. *Public Management Review, 3*(3), 363–383. doi:10.1080/14616670110051957

Grebe, E., & Nattrass, N. (2009) Leaders, Networks and Coalitions in the AIDS Response: A Comparison between Uganda and South Africa. Research Paper no. 03. Cape Town: The Developmental Leadership Program.

Hawkins, J. R. (2014) Social power and inequalities in Uganda's state formation: A historical approach to understand state instability. 14th EADI General Conference 23-26 June 2014, Bonn.

Hickey, S. (2009). The politics of protecting the poorest: Moving beyond the 'anti-politics machine'? *Political Geography, 28,* 473–483. doi:10.1016/j.polgeo.2009.11.003

Hujo, K. (2009, November 17–19). *Practical strategies to promote social integration: Lessons learned from existing policies and practices.* Background paper for Expert Group Meeting, Accra. UNRISD.

Jones, B. (2009). *Beyond the state in rural Uganda.* London: Edinburgh University Press.

Joshi, A., & Houtzager, P. (2012). Widgets or watchdogs? Conceptual explorations in social accountability. *Public Management Review, 14*(2), 145–162. doi:10.1080/14719037.2012.657837

King, S. (2015). Increasing the power of the poor? NGO-led social accountability initiatives and political capabilities in rural Uganda. *European Journal of Development Research, 27,* 887–902. forthcoming. doi:10.1057/ejdr.2014.74.

Leisering, L., & Barrientos, A. (2013). Social citizenship for the global poor? The worldwide spread of social assistance. *International Journal of Social Welfare, 22,* S50–S67. doi:10.1111/ijsw.2013.22.issue-s1

Maclean, L. M. (2011). State retrenchment and the exercise of citizenship in Africa. *Comparative Political Studies, 44*(9), 1238–1266. doi:10.1177/0010414010374704

Marshall, T. H. (1963). *Class, citizenship, and social development.* New York, NY: Doubleday.

Mazurana, D., Marshak, A., Opio, H. J., & Gordon, R. (2014). *Surveying livelihoods, service delivery and governance: Baseline evidence from Uganda.* Working paper 12. London: Secure Livelihoods Research Consortium.

McGee, R., & Gaventa, J. (2010). Review of impact and effectiveness of transparency and accountability initiatives: Synthesis report. Presented at the Transparency and Accountability Initiative Workshop. Institute of Development Studies, Brighton.

Mettler, S., & Soss, J. (2004). The consequences of public policy for democratic citizenship: Bridging policy studies and mass politics. *Perspectives on Politics, 2*(1), 55–73. doi:10.1017/S1537592704000623

Ministry of Health and Macro International Inc. (2008). *Uganda service provision assessment survey 2007.* Kampala, Uganda: Author.

Mitlin, D. (2008). With and Beyond the state – coproduction as a route to political influence, power and transformation for grassroots organizations. *Environment and Urbanization, 20*(2), 339–360. doi:10.1177/0956247808096117

Moore, M., & Putzel, J. (1999) Thinking strategically about politics and poverty. IDS Working Papers no. 101. Brighton: Institute of Development Studies.

Nazerali, H., Oteba, M. O., Mwoga, J., & Zaramba, S. (2006). Medicines – driving demand for health services in Uganda? In C. K. Tashobya, F. Ssengooba, & V. O. Cruz (Eds.), *Health systems reforms in Uganda: Processes and outputs* (pp. 61–82). Kampala: Uganda Ministry of Health.

The New Vision. (2012, November 17–19). *Back off politics, minister tells NGOs.* Kampala: Vision Publications. Retrieved from http://www.newvision.co.ug/new_vision/news/1302162/politics-minister-tells-ngos

Nyamu-Musembi, C. (2010). Have civil society organisation's political empowerment programmes contributed to a deepening democracy in Kenya? In V. S. P. Coelho & B. Von Lieres (Eds.), *Mobilizing for democracy: Citizen action and the politics of public participation* (pp. 23–47). London: Zed Books.

OECD (2008) Concepts and dilemmas of state building in Fragile situations: From fragility to resilience. *OECD/DAC Discussion paper.* Organisation for Economic Co-operation and Development.

Okero, F. A., Aceng, E., Madraa, E., Namagala, E., & Serutoke, J. (2003). *Scaling up antiretroviral therapy: Experience in Uganda*. Geneva: World Health Organisation.

Parkhurst, J. O. (2005). The response to HIV/AIDS and the construction of national legitimacy: Lessons from Uganda. *Development and Change, 36*(3), 571–590. doi:10.1111/dech.2005.36.issue-3

Parliamentary Committee on Health. (2012). *Report of the parliamentary committee on health on the ministerial policy statement for the health sector for the financial year 2012/2013*. Kampala: Uganda Parliament.

Putzel, J. (2004). The Politics of Action on AIDS: A Case Study of Uganda. *Public Administration and Development, 24*(1), 19–30. doi:10.1002/(ISSN)1099-162X

Rose, N. (1999). *Power of freedom: Reframing political thought*. Cambridge: Cambridge University Press.

Schneider, A. L., & Ingram, H. (2007). Public policy and democratic citizenship: What kinds of citizenship does policy promote? In F. Fischer, G. J. Miller, & M. S. Sidney (Eds.), *Handbook of public policy analysis: Theory, politics, and methods*. Boca Raton, FL: Taylor and Francis group.

Scott, A., Alban, A., Kanstrup, C., Laga, M., Byamugisha, J., Talugende, S., ... Mulemwa, J. (2005). *Mid-term review of the AIDS service organisation (TASO) Uganda*. Kampala: The AIDS Support Organisation (U) LTD.

Skocpol, T. (1992). *Protecting soldiers and mothers: The political origins of social policy in the United States*. Cambridge, MA: Belknap Press.

Ssengooba, F., Rahman, S., Hongoro, C., Rutebemberwa, E., Mustafa, A., Kielmann, T., & Mcpake, B. (2007). Health sector reforms and human resources for health in Uganda and Bangladesh: Mechanisms of effect. *Human Resources for Health, 5*, 3–13. doi:10.1186/1478-4491-5-3

Swidler, A., & Watkins, S. C. (2009). Teach a man to fish: The sustainability doctrine and its social consequences. *World Development, 37*(7), 1182–1196. doi:10.1016/j.worlddev.2008.11.002

TASO. (2005). *The MINI TASO/CBO Strategy*. Kampala: The AIDS Sopport Organisation.

TASO. (2007). *The AIDS support organisation (U) LTD strategic plan 2008–2012*. Kampala: The Aids Support Organisation.

TASO. (2008). *TASO Uganda limited 2007 annual report*. Kampala: The AIDS Support Organisation.

TASO. (2010). *TASO Uganda limited 2009 annual report*. Kampala: The AIDS Support Organisation.

Tendler, J. (1995). *Social Capital and the public sector: The blurred boundaries between private and public*. Paper presented at the Conference of the Economic Development Working Group, Social Capital and Public Affairs Project. American Academy of Arts and Sciences, Cambridge, MA.

Tripp, A. M. (2010). *Museveni's Uganda: Paradoxes of power in a hybrid regime*. London: Rienner publishers.

Tsai, L. (2011). Friends or foes? Nonstate public goods providers and local state authorities in non-democratic and transitional systems. *Studies in Comparative International Development (SCID), 46*(1), 46–69. doi:10.1007/s12116-010-9078-4

Wild, L., & Wales, J. (2015). *CARE's experience with community score cards: What works and why? Synthesis report*. London: Overseas Development Institute.

Williams, G., Thampi, B. V., Narayana, D., Nandigama, S., & Bhattacharyya, D. (2011). Performing participatory citizenship – Politics and power in Kerala's Kudumbashree programme. *Journal of Development Studies, 47*(8), 1261–1280. doi:10.1080/00220388.2010.527949

Wood, G. (1997). States without citizens: The problem of the Franchise state. In D. Hulme & M. Edwards (Eds.), *NGOs, States and Donors: Too close for comfort?* London: MacMillan Press.

Programming for Citizenship: The Conditional Cash Transfer Programme in El Salvador

MICHELLE ADATO*, OSCAR MORALES BARAHONA**
& TERENCE ROOPNARAINE[†]

*Poverty, Health and Nutrition Division, International Food Policy Research Institute, Washington, DC, USA,[1] **Fundación Salvadoreña para el Desarrollo Económico y Social, San Salvador, El Salvador, [†]Independent consultant, Palencia, Spain

ABSTRACT *State-sponsored social protection, while addressing social and economic rights in the concept of citizenship, has rarely engaged systematically with its promotion as a social good. This paper reviews El Salvador's experience with 'programming for citizenship' in its Conditional Cash Transfer (CCT) Programme. Citizenship was promoted through local representative structures, and non-formal education. Outcomes are explained by local political histories, divergent objectives, limited bandwidth in the context of complex programme management, and the structural confines of CCT programme design. Impacts on women's personal empowerment were strongest. El Salvador's experience provides lessons for CCT programmes aiming for transformational outcomes.*

1. Introduction

Since their inception in the mid-1990s, conditional cash transfer programmes (CCTs) have stood out among poverty reduction strategies for their clear and tightly defined set of objectives and well-evidenced logic for how these objectives would be achieved: provide cash transfers that are conditional upon children's school attendance, mothers' and children's attendance at regular health check-ups, and sometimes mothers' participation in training activities. The resulting improvements in children's human capital should enable them to become more productive, better earning adults and break the inter-generational cycle of poverty (Fiszbein et al., 2009; Adato & Hoddinott, 2010). To achieve scale and uniformity in pursuit of these objectives, manage the administrative complexity, and ensure targeting of the poorest among the poor, they are most often designed and run by national governments, with implementation assistance at other levels. This structure, first tested in Mexico's PROGRESA, stood in sharp contrast to a previous generation of poverty reduction programmes, which were controlled by local governments and community-based organisations, and reflected the movement for 'bottom up' development planning that stressed democratic decision-making and local empowerment (Adato & Roopnaraine, 2010a). The streamlined and centralised structure of PROGRESA was, in fact, partially a remedy to the poor targeting, elite capture and clientelism that plagued these earlier programmes (Yaschine, 1999; Yaschine & Orozco, 2010). The proliferation of CCTs across Latin America, however, has seen various forms of more decentralised approaches, finding some spaces for local control or management. These tend to represent a continuum of objectives, from functional/administrative to more transformative/democratic.[2]

The question that this article sets out to explore is how well CCTs can be used to achieve outcomes beyond the more concrete and proximate education and health indicators they primarily target, reaching outward to affect social ends such as more empowered citizens and people, in two main dimensions: CCT programme management and influence, and personal empowerment through new knowledge and social interaction, particularly for women. We examine this question about the possibilities of what we call 'programming for citizenship,' through research we conducted on El Salvador's CCT programme *Red Solidaria* (RS), which began in 2005, and later changed to *Comunidades Solidarias Rurales* in 2009. The article contributes to the literature on CCTs, which is overwhelmingly focused on the proximate human capital impacts, by exploring these potential social and political objectives and impacts. It also builds on the very limited literature examining 'participation' in CCTs by focusing on a programme that is unique in its intentional 'programming for citizenship', and on a small literature on women's empowerment through CCTs.[3]

El Salvador's CCT set a uniquely ambitious agenda with respect to community participation, with objectives and structures to promote 'citizenship' through the CCT. The unusual ambition is stated in the programme's early policy documents from 2007, where *Red Solidaria* describes its citizenship objectives and mechanisms for achieving them:

> By strengthening community organization and participation, we aim to ensure an equitable process among the population and local government, in coordination with governmental institutions. Through non-formal education, families receive training on topics such as gender equality, participation and community organization, prioritization of problems etc., which help them to understand the importance of consolidating organizational structures within the community [...]. (Red Solidaria, 2007)

There were two main channels through which the programme intended to promote citizenship. The first was through the non-formal education noted above provided through monthly trainings to beneficiaries. These were particularly pertinent to women, since it was primarily women who attended, though men were also encouraged to attend. The second was through the programme's organisational architecture: the *Comité Comunitario*, or Community Committee (CC), and the *Comité Municipal*, or Municipal Committee (MC). The Community Committee was to be composed of representatives of the grant recipients of the beneficiary families (usually the mothers) and community leaders. The committee could be part of existing local community-based development organisations, or a new committee could be created. Its practical functions were to support the NGOs contracted to manage the programme at the local level, to constitute a system of representation of beneficiaries, channelling their requests and complaints, and interacting with other institutions of the programme. The Community Committee was also envisioned as part of the 'social comptrollership',[4] a system for monitoring central government, municipal and community projects to increase transparency and accountability. The Municipal Committee (MC) was made up of representatives of the central government, the municipal mayor's office, the implementing NGO, local leaders and community organisations, and beneficiary representatives. The MC assisted in monitoring some aspects of programme implementation, and in resolving programme-related problems that came up in their localities (Red Solidaria, 2007).

The impact evaluation commissioned by the government from 2007 to 2010 was asked to 'assess the impact of *Red Solidaria* on citizenship and social participation'. This question was answered mainly through qualitative studies conducted in 2009 and 2010, examining the performance of the structures and education intended to promote this objective.[5]

The rest of this article is structured as follows: Section 2 provides a theoretical framework for analysing the ways that 'citizenship' can be analysed in the context of CCT programmes, including a review of literature that looks at citizenship in the context of this type of programme or similar. Section 3 provides an overview of El Salvador's CCT programme, while Section 4 describes our research methodology. Section 5 presents our empirical findings, and Section 6 offers conclusions.

2. Citizenship, Participation and CCT Programmes

Citizenship is a contested concept, freighted with multiple dimensions and contrasts: inclusion; identity; status; rights and responsibilities; individual and society; documentation or indocumentation, to name a few of the more salient. In this article, we generally follow Eyben and Ladbury (2006), in defining a citizen as 'someone with rights, aspirations and responsibilities in relation to others in the community and to the state' and citizenship more generally as implying 'a relationship both between citizens themselves and between the state and all those living within its borders' (Eyben & Ladbury, 2006, p. 5). In their study of the relationship between notions of citizenship and cash transfers in South Africa, Plagerson, Harpham, and Kielman (2012) usefully trace the convergence of both social protection and citizenship around the 'interdependence of social, economic and political rights' (p. 970), further noting with Kabeer (2005) that classical liberal concepts of citizenship emphasised civil and political rights, while the extension to social and economic rights was coeval with the development of the welfare state. State-sponsored social protection, in turn, developed as an approach for ensuring the fulfilment of these social and economic rights. A central problematic, however, lies in the fact that state-sponsored social protection initiatives, while certainly addressing the fulfilment of social and economic rights inherent to the *concept* of citizenship, have not on the whole engaged systematically with the *promotion* of citizenship as a social good in and of itself, although as we discuss below, some 'rights and citizenship' approaches and teachings have found their way into social protection programming.

While conditional cash transfer programmes may exhibit some degree of country-by-country variation and contextual adaptation to local realities, a cluster of core features tend to be designed into each new programme; another way of expressing this is simply to note that in a real sense, all CCT programmes carry in their design some of the DNA of Mexico's Progresa/Oportunidades. Such common core features include (but are not limited to): health conditionalities, measured by attendance at pre-natal and post-natal check-ups, growth monitoring, and compliance with early childhood vaccination regimes; an education conditionality, typically measured by enrolment and attendance; the definition of women as signatories to a compact between the household and the state; design and central administration at the national level, with implementation functions at state and local levels; a centralised and 'scientific' beneficiary targeting system using census data to identify eligible households; and the provision of training workshops. Topics typically include nutrition, preventative healthcare, sexual and reproductive health, hygiene and sanitation, and other 'health and wellbeing' themes.

Furthermore, in some contexts, trainings may be either augmented with, or substituted by, formal mechanisms which actively or passively stimulate the development of citizenship and participation: In Peru, a national documentation campaign (National Plan for the Restitution of Identity) was launched in 2005, in parallel with the rollout of the CCT, *Programa Juntos* (PJ). This campaign was particularly relevant in indigenous areas: many of these areas had also been in the forefront of the armed conflict, and a failure to possess a DNI (National Identity Document) card could give rise to suspicion of participation in either terrorism or narcotics trafficking (Correa & Roopnaraine, 2013). Furthermore, obtaining a DNI was considered to be an important enabler for participation in the CCT, given that it facilitated access to the health and education services upon which the conditionality structure was built. As Arroyo (2010) and Reuben and Cuenca (2009) note, non-possession of state identity documents can severely constrain access to services. Correa and Roopnaraine's (2013) study also found that in indigenous Amazonian and Andean communities, possessing a DNI card allowed holders to identify themselves as full Peruvian citizens, visible in the gaze of the state, and no longer ignored, while also conferring privileges such as freedom of movement and legitimacy in dealings with state actors.

The promotion of citizenship through cash transfer programmes has also been conceptualised in different, less ambitious, though not insignificant, ways. For example, in South Africa's unconditional Child Support Grant, Plagerson et al. (2012) examine how operational mechanisms concerned with the day-to-day implementation of the programme may have the effect of encouraging people to think about their relationship with the state. An example of this is the system of 'affidavits': sworn and witnessed documents in which prospective beneficiaries describe their reasons for eligibility to the Government. These were seen by beneficiaries as a channel of communication with the state; the state, in turn was defined in a more personal way for beneficiaries through the provision of cash transfers. The Child Support Grant also represented a form of accountability of the government to the citizens who had voted for it, and built notions of entitlement, particularly for vulnerable children (2012).

In both Nicaragua and Mexico, national CCT programmes incorporated certain design features which promoted participation, and to some degree, a strengthening of the concept of citizenship linked to the empowerment of women and their gradual movement from domestic to public spheres. These programme components centred around the person of the *promotora*, a 'programme-beneficiary liaison' who was usually herself a beneficiary elected by her peers. In Mexico's Progresa (later Oportunidades), the *promotora*, among other things, organised 'her' group of beneficiary women in collective activities and beneficiary meetings where women discussed common experiences and challenges. These, combined with *pláticas* or training seminars, the programme's designation of her as the beneficiary who receives the cash, and the programme's discourse on the importance of women and of girls' education, had a marked effect on women's self-reported improvements in their self-esteem, awareness of women's rights, and confidence in speaking out in public and standing up to their male partners (Adato & Roopnaraine, 2010b). As found in Nicaragua's CCTprogramme, which used a similar design, such activities helped increase consciousness of women's issues such as domestic and public rights and family planning, while also providing women with a space in which to speak publicly (2010b). Brazil's flagship CCT programme, Bolsa Família, offers another example of design implicitly promoting citizenship. In Hunter and Borges Sugiyama's (2014) study, Bolsa beneficiaries in Brazil's severely disadvantaged northeast reported that 'Bolsa had helped them lead more autonomous and dignified lives' (p. 835), that they saw the programme as understandable and fair, and that it increased beneficiaries' sense of both personal agency and social inclusion, necessary for claiming their citizenship rights. Engaging current debates on universal versus targeted, and conditional versus unconditional, social protection models, the authors conclude that social policy designs do not need to be universal or unconditional to have a positive effect on citizenship formation, if rules are clear and seen as reasonable and fair. They also find that 'appropriate program design and discourse is crucial' (p. 831).

Mexico's Oportunidades programme additionally adopted a more explicit promotion of citizenship over the years, with its policy strategy for 2002–2006 emphasising citizenship, participation, and the agency of families. This was conceptualised and operationalised in two dimensions: the first focused on transparency and information dissemination, and an accountability mechanism through the *Sistema de Atención Ciudadana*, where beneficiaries are encouraged to submit problems and appeals, and bi-monthly public forums with programme officials to ask questions and resolve issues (Hevia del al Jara, 2007). Fox (2008) concludes that Oportunidades made substantial efforts to address an important need for upward communications, but that several factors limited its effectiveness, high among them the fact that there was no institutional mechanism to assure beneficiaries a seat at the table or authority to achieve their objectives. He contrasts this with the Mexican anti-poverty programme Disconsa, which does give citizens that seat.

Building on the literature above, and our findings on the intention and practice of programming citizenship though the CCT programme in El Salvador, we propose a framework with five main dimensions of 'promoting citizenship' in CCT programmes: (1) intentionality: that is whether the citizenship objective was intended and explicit in the programme goals, and reinforced by programme leaders; (2) relationship with the state: that is whether membership in the programme has the effect of strengthening citizenship status or perception of that status through documentation or engagement; (3) representative structures: whether functional and accountable; (4) perception of self-efficacy: how beneficiaries perceive their representation and influence, and their interest in participation; (5) personal empowerment: changes in knowledge, confidence, and social participation. We use these dimensions to assess the social/citizenship outcomes of El Salvador's CCT, and analyse why these objectives were met to greater and lesser extents across communities.

3. Methodology

In commissioning an impact evaluation of its CCT, the Government of El Salvador (GoES) required rigorous quantitative and qualitative studies. Mixed method studies had been requested in a number of CCT impact evaluations, to triangulate survey findings, explain them, and provide insights into the socio-cultural drivers of programme impacts as well as less easily quantifiable impacts (see Adato, 2008; Maluccio, Adato, & Skoufias, 2010) One of the key research questions asked by the government was, what was *Red Solidaria*'s impact on citizen participation? This was answered primarily through qualitative methods.

Qualitative research was carried out in six communities across the country. These communities were purposively selected to capture variation across regions, administrative units, NGO management, and service availability. We did not select on the variable of level or structure of local participation – all were intended to be structured in the same way and we did not hypothesise as to what was likely to affect it; rather, our approach was inductive on this variable. Because the research was designed to collect data on many topics, not only citizen participation, the data is more limited than it would have been in a study with this focus alone. It was, however, the subject of modules in all interviews and focus groups. The main strength of the methodology was the depth provided by case studies, where fieldworkers lived in the communities for two months per community, building rapport, interviewing beneficiary and non-beneficiary households, conducting observations in homes and communities, and attending programme-related and other community events.

In the first phase of fieldwork, conducted from March through July 2009, 10 household case studies were conducted per community, for a total of 60 case studies. These were stratified by high and low performance in health and education survey indicators. In total, 195 persons (mothers, fathers, children and other family members) were interviewed using a semi-structured, in-depth method. Additionally, 62 key informant interviews were carried out with health and education personnel, members of Municipal Committees and local leaders, and additional interviews with central government officials. Twenty-two focus group discussions, 28 observations of programme activities and 28 observations of health centres were also conducted. In a second phase of the qualitative research, conducted in 2010, five of the original six communities were re-visited and a new non-programme community added. In this phase, we carried out focus groups with a total of 47 beneficiaries, 43 non-beneficiaries, and 36 key informant interviews.[6]

These samples, while substantial in the context of qualitative work, were far smaller than those employed for the survey work. These differences highlight the contrasts and complementarities of qualitative and quantitative approaches to social research. The latter typically employ large, randomised samples and standardised questionnaires, which contribute to the generalisability of their results, and allow researchers to make reasonably confident statements about causality and attribution between variables. The former – qualitative approaches – almost always focus on smaller, often purposively selected samples and use more open-ended instruments for data collection. This implies some sacrifices in generalisability, but in exchange, qualitative approaches offer substantial strengths and advantages in terms of explanatory power: through building relationships and trust, participant observation, and in-depth interviewing, these methods allow researchers to achieve a deep and nuanced understanding unattainable through survey methods. In the context of the current study, this means that the identification of, for example, causes and drivers of community participation, is based principally on careful and systematic analysis of interview and focus group responses and not derived from statistical analysis of survey results. Such results should therefore be taken as having ethnographic rather than statistical validity.

It is important to note here that the research took place over a period of political transition, where a new government continued the programme with some changes, including the name. The first phase of the research in 2009 was on *Red Solidaria*, while in 2010 it was on *Comunidades Solidarias Rurales*. We returned not primarily to compare the programmes (the follow up was planned long before the election), but rather to observe any changes in the programme over time, a qualitative 'longitudinal' study. The change in government did, however, enable us to look at differences caused by strength-ened 'intentionality' and to some extent the strengthening of structures.

4. The El Salvador CCT Programme

The *Red Solidaria* programme (RS) (2005–2009) was developed by the Government of El Salvador, under the *Alianza Republicana Nacionalista* (ARENA) party to provide social protection to rural families living in extreme poverty. It was targeted first geographically, then by household. Geographical targeting began with the Poverty Map of El Salvador, in which 262 municipalities were classified as severe extreme poverty, high extreme poverty, moderate, and low. From 2005 to 2009, RS was focused on the municipalities with severe or high poverty levels. Families' eligibility for education and health and nutrition transfers in these 100 poorest municipalities took into account remoteness, the presence of children under 15, and/or pregnant women.

The CCT programme conditioned cash transfers on boys and girls school enrolment and attendance from kindergarten to sixth grade; and compliance with growth monitoring and vaccination protocols for children under five, and pre-/post-natal checks for pregnant women. Attendance at monthly trainings was not required but was strongly encouraged. The topics included: the CCT conditionalities; participation and community organisation; gender equality; child rights, child health and nutrition; children at risk (child labour and sexual abuse); domestic violence; sexual and reproductive health, and hygiene and sanitation. RS also had components on Basic Services (including supply side interventions to help meet CCT-related demand) and a component on productive activities. In 2008, the total number of beneficiary families was 83,654 (Secretaría Técnica de la Presidencia de El Salvador, 2013).

In March 2009 a new political party won the national elections, the Farabundo Martí National Liberation Front (FMLN). The FMLN had been a guerrilla organisation formed in 1980, and became a political party through peace accords in 1992. By the time of its election to the presidency in 2009 it had become a moderate leftist party, but still strongly identified with its history rooted in championing the rights and voice of the poor. In June 2009, changes were made to the conception and architecture of social policy in El Salvador. The government set out a Universal Social Protection System called *Comunidades Solidarias Rurales* (CSR) that integrated several programmes, including *Red Solidaria*, and was structured around four axes: The first was Human Capital, which was primarily the same CCT programme, with a few changes, which was continued in the 100 poorest municipalities. It also included a Universal Basic Pension for persons aged 70 and above in a portion of severe extreme poverty and high extreme poverty municipalities. The other components were Basic Services, Income Generation, and Territorial management (local government and community development planning). In 2013, the total number of CSR beneficiary families was 83,315 (Secretaría Técnica de la Presidencia de El Salvador, 2013, p. 86).

RS and CSR were run nationally by Fondo de Inversion Social para el Desarrollo Local (FISDL). At the municipal level a FISDL manager had oversight of programme performance and served as the liaison between the municipalities and FISDL central offices. National or regional NGOs were contracted by FISDL to be the main programme implementing agency at the local level, overseen by the NGO Coordinator. The NGO promoter was the main face of the programme at the community level, assisting beneficiaries with understanding and meeting the conditions and payments.

5. Empirical Findings on Citizenship Promotion in the El Salvador CCT Programme

This section reviews our research findings on the El Salvador CCT programme, against the dimensions of citizenship promotion proposed in Section 2: intentionality; relationship with the state; representative structures; efficacy; and personal empowerment. It focuses primarily on the structures and efficacy, which most of the findings speak to, followed by a later section on personal empowerment that focuses on the training. Although conceptually distinct, in the analysis of our research findings it is difficult to separate these different elements of citizenship. For this reason, we present our findings as case studies rather than analysing them by themes, with the exception of personal empowerment.

As introduced in Section 1, the GoES took a particularly intentional approach to citizenship promotion, reflected in its discourse and programme design. Early policy statements referred not only to programme participation, but also to broader political goals, where programme training would help people to 'understand the importance of consolidating organisational structures within the community' (Red Solidaria, 2007).

In continuing the CCT programme as CSR, the FMLN reinforced this approach, visible in its new rights-based approach to social protection – in this sense seeing social protection as part of the country's 'definition' of citizenship. Government programme documentation describes CSR as:

> the development of a new social policy based on rights and on a universal conception which evolved into the creation of a Universal Social Protection System, which is based on a human rights approach, taking into consideration people's life cycles and characterised by the completeness and diversity of the programmes and interventions comprising it. (Secretaría Técnica de la Presidencia de El Salvador, 2013, p. 83)

Although the elections had been held just before our 2009 fieldwork began, changes in the programme were made later, so it was the 2010 research that captured these developments.[7]

5.1. Strong Structures but Weak Efficacy: the Case of San Juan[8]

San Juan had a strong tradition of local organisation dating back to the 1970s, rooted in the rise of peasant and local church groups, which were active in the conflict of the 1980s and transformed into development committees after the peace accords in 1992. The organisation of the community continued. From our case studies, it appears that such local political history affected organisation of the CC. In this community and another like it, informants explained that high levels of local organisation pre-dated the arrival of the programme and that the programme thus had not contributed significantly to the formation or strengthening of new organisations. Asked whether *Red Solidaria* had promoted local organisations in this community, a beneficiary explained that: 'no, we were already organised'. The main organisation engaging with the CCT here as elsewhere was the *Asociación para el Desarrollo Comunitario* (ADESCO), a structure found throughout El Salvador and other parts of Central America, usually comprised of a group of community members organised to bring in and manage developmental assistance in their villages. Nevertheless, the level of engagement around the CCT was not high. The level of organisation in this community also affected the Municipal Committee, which were said to communicate effectively with beneficiary communities. Interviewees noted that the representatives on the Municipal Committee, after each session, took the initiative of explaining to the community what matters had been addressed.

In 2010, following the CSR transition and '*reactivación*' of community participation, the executive committee at the municipal level was responsible for creating several new sectoral committees, including one for CSR. At the community level, ADESCO was supposed to be responsible for communications with communities and coordination of CCT activities. The promoter who had created the committee raised doubts: 'Afterwards it was decided that a CC would be formed, even though not much would be expected of it [...] it's uncommon that the CC works well in the hamlets, we never expect too much'. As elsewhere, the notion that 'it was decided' from above suggested the weakness in motivation at community level. A CC member explained how the promoter held an emergency meeting with the beneficiaries and announced that she had to 'fulfil a programme requirement and had to set up a committee here'. Because of time constraints, she assigned CC positions to the individuals present at the meeting. However, their presence at the meeting may have suggested they were among the more motivated: another CC member pointed out that the CC is made up of individuals who share an 'interest of working in the community.'

As elsewhere, in this community the CC roles were not clear to the beneficiaries, most of whom had heard of it though some had not. There was a consensus, however, that there was a useful role for a committee to represent beneficiaries and keep them informed. The members of the CC also expressed some lack of clarity about their roles, stating them as managing beneficiary meetings if the promoter was late, and relaying programme information. They did not gather often because they had to wait for the promoter to need them, which wasn't often. This function was considerably narrower and less ambitious than the vision of the FISDL manager in the municipality, who said he hoped that the increased visibility of the CCs would lead to 'more active participation in programme management'. CC members said they would like more engagement and capacity: 'We'd need more orientation, given that we've not got together much; depending on what is available, one starts to take initiative on things which one can do, but so far we don't have much of an idea.' Members were aware, however, that they were meant to represent the beneficiaries.

Another complicating factor was politics, which reduced efficacy. According to a representative of the NGO and member of the Municipal Committee, this was a problem particularly because there were several registered ADESCO organisations in one community, though this risk was present among existing and new committees. He believed that if the committees functioned as envisioned, the programme could change the role of politics in development; however, 'people don't get organised to support the programme but rather to push their development; when a committee is set up to support programme activities, the programme finishes and the committee dissolves – it's not sustainable. We should change the philosophy or logic [...] organising committees shouldn't be for political reasons or to make the programme successful, but to help the communities develop'.

Intentionality was strong, especially in 2010, with a vision for meaningful participation in programme management, as described by FISDL. Structures were also reasonably strong, particularly given the history and role of ADESCO. Engagement with the state does not appear to have been strengthened in this case, probably because existing ADESCOs were already highly engaged, but this, and local politics, appears to have closed space for increased citizenship through programme engagement. Efficacy appears to have been low, with respect to actual roles that the CC played, and beneficiary engagement, in both phases.

5.2. Weak Structures and Low Efficacy: the Cases of El Bálsamo and La Merced

A second explanation for low efficacy stands in contrast to the previous example. La Merced was a community with a low level of organisation historically and currently, and where community members described a prevailing sense of apathy and passivity towards citizen participation and organisation. During the 2009 research, beneficiaries said that they did not have any interest in forming and working actively with the CCs. Some of this was scepticism: there was little faith in community organisations, and committees were characterised by some as dominated by personal interests. Here the CC was constituted and representatives chosen, but never really functioned. According to the NGO promoter: 'The Committee I launched didn't work. [The problem] is that we don't like to participate.'

Community leaders who had participated in Municipal Committee meetings were said to have had no contact with the communities: 'Since this *Red Solidaria* committee was formed [...] I've never seen them come to introduce themselves to the neighbourhood.' One beneficiary observed that the representative on the MC seemed to favour supporters of his political party, rather than beneficiaries.

The paradox is that in these communities where the organisational fabric was historically weaker, there was a gap that a CCT community committee could potentially fill. There was some evidence that the programme did contribute in a limited way to the strengthening of local organisation. One member of the Municipal Committee (MC) perceived that the programme had brought about more community meetings, and another key informant said 'Yes, [the community] is more organised because this programme, which is a blessing from God, has come to teach them to participate in meetings.'

Low intentionality among local officials also helps to explain low participation in this community and others: programme leaders did not sufficiently identify or communicate the function of the CCs and why they were worth constituting and joining. Some responsibility here and elsewhere was put on the NGO promoters, whom a few beneficiaries and community leaders said should have played a more active role in the constitution of the CCs. A leader in a community with similarly low organisation stressed that beneficiaries need to be organised: 'I think, because no-one told them [beneficiaries] to do it [create a CC...] I think that the promoter needs to get them to create a women's organisation.'

This expectation of promoters should be assessed in the context of their broad programme responsibilities, where they were responsible for running day-to-day operations of a complex programme. This complexity also helps to explain why the national government's implementing agency did not focus on promoting participation in the early years of the programme, which in CCTs are administratively the most challenging. Furthermore, given that the roles of the CCs were not very clear, and that some of these roles were similar to those of the promoter and MC, promoters may not have perceived sufficient need to put in the effort required.

Another study community, El Bálsamo, had a CC formed in 2006, but it was not active, and while it had an ADESCO it was less organised than those of other study sites. The CRS initiative led to the *'reactivación'* of the existing CC, including new election or validation of the existing committee representatives, and the NGO was reported to have worked to motivate the community. The experience in this community, however, reveals some of the problems with promoting citizen participation from above, and 'in a hurry', with weak planning processes, and little beneficiary and community motivation. Members were chosen by the promoter based upon *'la cercanía',* their close geographical proximity to the CC meetings, rather than their interest. The CC members recalled that the promoter asked them to be part of a committee, and when they were initially wary of the commitment required, she reassured them that she would only need them for signing documents. CC members described their own uncertainty about their roles: one said the group remained unaware (*'ignorantes'*) about their purpose, while another said he had never before been in this type of group, because 'other people are in charge of the community.' Additional comments revealed a desire for guidance and support to facilitate a greater role: 'They should tell us something then because sometimes there should be a leader who says 'let's do this' or 'this needs to be done' but if [not...] nobody has initiative.'

A beneficiary who served as a member of the CC described the role as limited but significant: 'It is a committee which supports by signing [...] for various reasons, she has to prepare "*Actas*" for whatever problem a child might have, whether it's with the school [...]'. '*Actas*' are documents signed on behalf of beneficiaries who are having problems in fulfilling their CCT programme obligations, or otherwise need to communicate with CRS regarding their status. The FISDL manager in the municipality explained that this was in fact an important role for the CC, facilitating representation of beneficiary issues at the municipal level, and that the '*actas*' are part of that: 'In the municipality, every important change in the family is validated by a letter signed by all the members of the CC.'

Beneficiaries not on the CC were even less clear about the role of the CC. Some were able to describe it, as in one who called it 'an information committee' serving as a liaison between the programme and the community. Some beneficiaries in the focus groups said they had never specifically heard about the CC. Another said 'in my case, I don't really give them too much importance.' Other beneficiaries spoke more generally about the need for a CC to be provide support for 'whatever might happen in the community.' In this case, structure was especially weak in the first phase, and strengthened in the second, but efficacy low in both. Citizen motivation and ownership emerged as important drivers of efficacy. Due in part to the political history of these communities, participation was driven by intentionality at the top and in the latter phase by the middle, but not from the bottom.

5.3. Moderate Structures and Efficacy, and Relationship with the State: Nueva Sevilla

In the research here in 2009, representative structures for the programme were described as weak and unaccountable. The presence of local leaders on the Municipal Committee did not guarantee, a priori, either effective representation or genuine community participation in committee decision-making. Accountability depended, as described above, upon the organisational/participatory characteristics of the communities. Beneficiaries criticised their community representatives on the MC, who had failed to communicate the issues discussed by the committee in a timely manner, including those issues of particular importance to them. Beneficiaries felt that MC members and other municipal authorities should have more contact with the local populations, so as to better understand people's needs.

Efficacy was also perceived to be low because of the structure of the programme, which did not allow for integration of local perspectives in a meaningful way. In this community and others, community leaders and other key informants perceived the programme as rigid and vertical, lacking responsiveness to ideas and proposals coming from beneficiaries and local leaders. Although staff of the implementing NGOs were seen as open and receptive, there was little space for influencing programme decisions. An example was the monthly training for beneficiaries. Although the training topics were far more diverse in El Salvador than in most CCT programmes, beneficiaries and others complained that the training topics were centrally pre-determined, not necessarily what beneficiaries prioritised, and with no room for suggestions: '[...] when we get there, all the papers are ready – they don't say "hey, do you want to do such and such a topic?"' Greater flexibility in the identification and selection of training topics could have promoted more of a sense of ownership among beneficiaries in this one area of particular importance to them.

In 2010, the reactivation process appears to have had a significant effect on this community. Rather than create new community committees, the municipality worked to strengthen the pre-existing committees, particularly the ADESCOs. FISDL and the contracted NGOs located the weakest community organisations that 'sometimes are a bit lost' and invited them to a series of workshops on empowerment, in an effort to help find direction and focus. The initiative first aimed to give these organisations skills to represent and communicate community needs to higher levels of government and to obtain financial assistance. Secondly, it aimed to build more cooperative and effective local leadership. In both communities, ADESCO provided support to the promoter by signing documents for a multitude of beneficiary issues related to programme compliance (the 'actas'). ADESCO led meetings when the promoter had another commitment, and worked with the NGO to organise community-wide events. As one member explained: 'When we need to carry out a broader activity in the community [...] we get together to work together like a family. It is a different institution but focused on the same objective.' Although ADESCO's history and capacity helped in its efficacy, the (CRS-specific) ADESCO members, mostly bene-ficiaries, reported financial and time constraints. One member explained that their socio-economic status prevented them from engaging more at the community level: 'At our level, you've got to work to eat, so practically you do what you can manage [...] one wants more time because there is a lot of need and a lot to improve but they don't train us on that.' Time constraints were exacerbated by the fact that the ADESCO members played various other roles on other community committees.

Despite these limitations, the drive to increase citizenship functions through the CC did result in a more communicative space for engagement between the community, local organisations and the MC, and strengthened existing community organisation and voice vis-à-vis the state. An ADESCO member remarked that community organisations had gained greater legitimacy among government institutions as a result: 'Now there are connections throughout the community, because it's good that way. As though we're becoming more homogeneous in the community, with the government institutions, because before we were excluded.' The NGO promoter reinforced this point, observing that there is 'a bit more communication' between the various institutions, and that both the mayor and the ADESCO CC have been 'more aware' of the work going on in the community. An ADESCO member also observed that this relationship impacted the promoter, who now 'follows the institutions more in looking for information.' The experience in these communities reflects the dimension of citizenship that we characterise as relationship with the state, where the programme facilitated the visibility of citizens in the eyes of the state, and increased direct engagement through programme structures, which in turn facilitated a sense of efficacy among community leaders and beneficiaries.

Despite these strengths, the committee's roles were still vague in the eyes of most beneficiaries, where they could not provide many details on what the CC did, though they did know that it was based on existing community networks. Furthermore, role of the ADESCO in the CCT was limited by its lack of formal authority:

> We, as members and part of the ADESCO, can't do anything [...] and if they need us or approach us as members and directors of the ADESCO and consult us about any problem, what we do is give them the go-ahead and if they need a signature or anything like that, sometimes that is all we

can do at the time – unless this all changes and the committees become completely part of the management of all the ADESCOs in the municipality [...] maybe that would be the solution, but at the moment we can't do that.

This raises an important dimension of structure, which is authority – that is the actual power of the structure to influence decisions. In the case of the CCT, the CC appears to have had an important role in facilitating communications and representing beneficiary interests within the confines of existing programme guidelines, but not a means of influencing those guidelines.

5.4. Strengthening Women's Collective Engagement and Self-Confidence

The last dimension of citizenship explored here is personal empowerment and social engagement, where we found the programme's greatest transformative impact. As with some other CCT programmes in Latin America, this impact was attributed in large part to the monthly training required of or offered to beneficiaries. Beneficiaries and key informants described the empowering impacts of the programme's ambitious monthly training sessions, where women leave the domestic space, learn about the world, and gain confidence to speak out. As one beneficiary from El Manantial observed:

They [other beneficiaries] feel more confident and more secure. Because, above all, they develop and don't feel shy – staying at home isn't the same as going out with a whole bunch of people – which is how we do it now. Before, I felt ashamed but now I see them come laughing and we know each other: we live here, but before we didn't know each other – maybe just by sight but we'd never really spent time together, but now the majority of us have.

A key informant from Los Arcos further explained that: 'it's the trainings – that's where people have woken up.' Through the training topics and the pedagogical techniques that encourage women to speak in public, women interviewed described having greater levels of confidence and self-esteem, and having acquired the potential for better communication, especially with other women. A member of the Municipal Committee of La Merced – notably one of the communities with low participation in other spheres – observed that 'because of those talks and trainings, women now dare to speak out – before, it wasn't like that but now it is – in their nature, in their character, in their charisma – they do it. This is very important.' This assertion was supported by many beneficiary women's testimonies, such as this comment from Nueva Sevilla:

Before, I was so afraid, even to speak to him [her husband], as he was so serious I was almost ashamed, but now, I feel stronger and able to speak to him because of all that they have taught us: that we are also important and that we should feel supported and strong enough to speak to our husbands.

The trainings, through their content and methodology, offered beneficiary women access to new knowledge, some of which, according to NGO representatives, they have gradually put into practice.

Programme elements such as cash transfers under the control of women, together with emphasis placed on education, health and nutrition, as well as the contents of trainings, become resources which parents (usually mothers) can draw upon in order to support their children. The knowledge they received from the trainings and the confidence they gained in speaking has made them more confident and assertive with their spouses. These different elements, when combined, empowered women as they saw improvements in their ability to care for their children and give them a better future. This increased their self-esteem.

In addition to these elements of personal empowerment and empowerment in close relationships (Rowlands, 1998), women engaged in new forms of social participation within their communities. Some of this refers to women's greater degree of social interaction in the public sphere as a result of regular programme activities, at the health services and schools. A public health promoter in La

Merced said that 'here it's the women who go out more, who most support the programmes – they're the ones who take the children to the schools and clinics, and go to the meetings at the school.' In El Manantial, one woman said that she participated more in school meetings and activities, and that through this participation, she met other people, discussed things with them, and felt a sense of community. This suggests that it is not only the trainings offered by the programme, but its emphasis on children's education and the parents' role in this, which has increased social participation in the community.

Social participation is not limited to programme-related activities. In Nueva Sevilla, a beneficiary explained that because of the programme, women went out of their homes more, spoke more, and in the process made contributions to solving community problems 'because sometimes people were embarrassed and hardly ever left the house, but now they go out more, they socialise more and it is possible to spend time calmly discussing the community's problems and finding solutions.' A key informant in Nueva Sevilla similarly said that the programme had generated more participation in the community, even though there was already good local organisation:

> You can see it. They're more alive, more active. Someone who is alone all day at home is unaware of community needs, and because these trainings deal with participation, with helping the community, when there is a meeting I can see that the people pay attention and try to participate, to involve themselves in community work [...]

In several cases it was observed that women decided to play a more active role in community organisations, motivated by experience and skills acquired through the CCT programme. This can be seen in the following excerpt from the field notes kept by a member of the research team in La Merced:

> During one of my visits, the beneficiary was returning from a meeting in which they had selected the new members of the ADESCO; she told me that it was the first time she had been appointed to any of the posts and that what had motivated her was that she had been participating in various other activities in the community, related to different programmes – among them *Red Solidaria* – and that she had lost her fear and was able to express herself better.

6. Conclusion

In principle, promoting citizenship is a reasonable complement to the primary human capital investment dimension of CCT programmes, particularly when we take into account that participation in a CCT programme always involves a compact between the beneficiary and the state – precisely the principals in the covenant of citizenship. It is understandable that governments might want to imbue their main poverty reduction programme with a community-driven approach that reflects their philosophy of development. In practise, however, the priority placed upon human capital promotion in CCT programmes generally works to relegate the enshrining of citizenship to a secondary or collateral concern. It may also be seen – with reason – to potentially undermine human capital impacts through altering programme design or through political influence. The case of El Salvador's CCT programme is exceptional insofar as it sought to foreground the issue of citizenship without compromising the human capital objectives of the programme. Our study provides an examination of how such a programme might be mobilised to address the question of citizenship promotion from a social protection platform, but also insights into the limits or at least challenges to this vision.

El Salvador's CCT programme is among the most ambitious to date with respect to efforts to define and achieve citizenship objectives. In practice, as is more often than not the case in participatory development initiatives, it fell short of its expectations, challenged by a set of endogenous and exogenous factors explored in this article. In the first phase of the programme, when it was *Red Solidaria*, the 'citizenship' objective as strongly stated in programme design documents was not highly prioritised amongst the complicated, and logistic-heavy sets of supply and demand side interventions that characterise CCT programmes in Latin America. Social and historical factors in the communities also confounded intentions, which played out as a lack of interest for different reasons. Stepped up efforts by the new government to promote citizenship through the CCT under CRS, as part of a governing philosophy, helped but also with varied and limited results. Participation appears to have been rushed, driven more from the top than the bottom. This does not mean that there was no role for participation and it was appreciated where it did occur. Beneficiaries often expressed a desire for more representation and some programme officials at the local level continued to see a need for more direct local input into programme decisions. But the programme's essential design did not permit local influence.

The NGO promoters played the main role in organising the CCs and guiding their participation, which meant that CC roles tended to focus mainly on operational assistance, rather than governance that is contributing to decision-making related to programme design or implementation. Assisting with programme operations – such as leading meetings, assisting at paydays, coaching beneficiaries to meet conditions, writing or signing letters to explain why they could not meet them, and other problem-solving – helps beneficiaries and builds capacities of the committee members, and is a form of participation. It does stop short, however, of participation in decision-making and the exercise of authority, or at least a 'seat at the table' that is also part of a vision of citizenship. While the largely centralised structure of CCT programmes rarely includes the latter form, the El Salvador programme is interesting because it did appear to have a broader vision of citizenship as exercised through the programme. The meaning of this citizenship was never fully articulated, however. Programme design documents stated the objectives and structures, but the roles were not well defined and a number of factors undercut that vision.

With respect to the five dimensions we identified as part of the promotion of citizenship through this type of programme, intentionality was strong at the top of the programme, but it did not carry through to the same degree with local programme leadership. Furthermore, in the second phase when that intentionality intensified, it had the effect of creating 'participation in a rush' which did not work well. The programme does appear to have strengthened the relationship of some communities with the state, particularly where there was less pre-existing organisation, but openness to participation. With regard to structure, this should have been strong – the design of the Community Committees and representation on Municipal Committees attempted to ensure representation of communities at two levels. In practice, for many reasons explored, the CCs did not function well. Efficacy is closely linked to the functionality of that structure, and thus was weak, reflected in beneficiaries' limited familiarity with the CCs or their functions, and their perceived lack of effectiveness. This should be caveated with the reports of some key informants who believed that the programme did contribute to community organisation to greater and less extents, especially in the second phase. The MCs generally performed better, and meetings we observed as part of the research were well run and discussed substantive, important programme issues. It may well be the case that MCs benefit from operating at a 'higher' level with greater structural proximity to the state – this interpretation would lend weight to the contention that more ambitious decentralisation agendas in CCT design do not necessarily have advantages, and that in fact, keeping key institutions close to the central state may work best.

Finally, the dimension of citizenship that was best achieved was personal empowerment, particularly of the women beneficiaries through their role as beneficiaries but also primarily through the informal education they received. As found in other Latin American CCTs, a reliable way to increase social participation through the programme is by offering women training and providing them a space to interact socially and develop their self-confidence. This has impacts at the personal and household levels, and to some extent at the community level.

The question of how much else to load onto a CCT programme – which has a primary objective of increasing demand for health, nutrition, and education services – has been debated over the years, as ideas for combining them with credit, productive activities, training, early childhood development, psychosocial support, and other development programmes have been floated and in some cases implemented. Less contemplated and tested are alternative governance structures, or opportunities for including beneficiaries and communities as more active agents. A legitimate question is how much local control or participation is necessary or desirable in a programme that may not work as well with too much tampering with its design and implementation – one which was designed originally (in the case of Mexico) to scientifically target poverty and precisely avoid local elite capture and political manipulation. Furthermore, people may exercise their democratic right *not* to participate, given time constraints, particularly of the poor, and other priorities. Nevertheless, beneficiaries did express their need and desire for better representation, and more responsiveness from programme officials, and they highly valued the training. El Salvador's CCT programme, while not fully realising its vision, provides an experience that other cash transfer programmes interested in achieving more transformational objectives can look to for inspiration, ideas, and lessons.

Acknowledgements

The authors are grateful to the following people: The staff at FISDL and other GoES departments for their assistance in facilitating the evaluation; the research team: Rafael Pleitez, Lissette Calderón, Helga Cuéllar-Marchelli, José Flores, Gladys Meléndez, Tania Meza, Maria Tomasa Tejada, and Liza Vielman; Margarita Beneke de Sanfeliú, Marie Ruel, and Alan De Brauw for management support; Elisabeth Becker and Zhenya Karelina for data coding and analysis; Mauricio Shi, Rodolfo Herrera, Rodrigo Lemus y Oscar Vargas for data management and coding. The time, cooperation and insights from beneficiaries, community leaders, NGOs, and service providers at the local level are gratefully acknowledged. The views expressed in this article are those of the authors alone. Authorship is listed alphabetically.

Disclosure statement

No potential conflict of interest was reported by the authors.

Notes

1. All author affiliations are where the authors were based at the time that the research was conducted. Michelle Adato is currently with the Millennium Challenge Corporation, Washington, DC, but is writing in her personal capacity. Oscar Morales Barahona is currently with the Economics Department, Universidad Centroamericana Jose Simeon Canas (UCA), San Salvador, El Salvador. Terry Roopnaraine is based in Brasilia, Brazil.
2. See Adato and Roopnaraine (2010a) for a review of some of these decentralised features in Latin American programmes.
3. The first CCT literature is vast, but two reviews that cover a broad terrain are Fiszbein et al. (2009) and Adato and Hoddinott (2010). The literature on CCTs, participation, and empowerment is small, and reviewed in Section 3.
4. http://www.redsolidaria.gob.sv/ (Agosto, 2009, p 73)
5. The authors of this article led the qualitative studies of the impact evaluation. For the full evaluation reports, see Adato et al. (2009) and De Brauw et al. (2010).
6. All qualitative data was coded and analysed in NVivo, a qualitative software package.
7. It was at the transitional stage from *Red Solidaria* to *Comunidades Solidarias Rurales* that the findings from the first qualitative study in the impact evaluation, including the low functioning of the Community Committees, were reported to the new government.
8. Note that all community names have been changed to protect the confidentiality of residents and officials.

References

Adato, M. (2008). Combining survey and ethnographic methods to improve evaluation of conditional cash transfer programs. *International Journal of Multiple Research Approaches, 2*(2), 222–236. doi:10.5172/mra.455.2.2.222
Adato, M., & Hoddinott, J. (Eds.). (2010). *Conditional cash transfers in Latin America*. Baltimore, MD: Johns Hopkins University Press.
Adato, M., & Roopnaraine, T. (2010a). Conditional cash transfers, participation, and power. In M. Adato & J. Hoddinott (Eds.), *Conditional cash transfers in Latin America* (pp. 315–347). Baltimore, MD: Johns Hopkins University Press.

Adato, M., & Roopnaraine, T. (2010b). Women's status, gender relations, and conditional cash transfers. In M. Adato & J. Hoddinott (Eds.), *Conditional cash transfers in Latin America* (pp. 284–314). Baltimore, MD: Johns Hopkins University Press.

Adato, M., Roopnaraine, T., Pleitez, R., Morales, O., Calderón, L., Cuéllar-Marchelli, H., & Karelina, Z. (2009). *Informe de satisfacción de los usuarios de la Red* [Report on beneficiary satisfaction with Red Solidaria]. Washington, DC: International Food Policy Research Institute and San Salvador: Fundación Salvadoreña para el Desarrollo Económico y Social.

Arroyo, J. (2010). *Identidad en el Perú: Conflictos interculturales en los servicios de documentación* [Intercultural conflicts in documentation services]. Lima: Fondo Editorial de la Universidad San Martín de Porres y Consorcio de Investigación Económica y Social.

Correa, N., & Roopnaraine, T. (2013). *Pueblos indígenas y programas de transferencias condicionadas: Estudio etnográfico sobre la implementación y los efectos socioculturales del Programa Juntos en seis comunidades andinas y amazónicas del Perú* [Indigenous peoples and conditional cash transfer programmes: An ethnographic study on implementation and sociocultural effects of Programa Juntos in 6 Andean and Amazonian communities of Peru]. Washington, DC: Inter-American Development Bank & International Food Policy Research Institute and Lima: Pontificia Universidad Católica de Perú.

De Brauw, A., Adato, M., Peterman, A., Beneke De Sanfeliú, M., Shi, M., Cuéllar-Marchelli, H., … Becker, E. (2010). *Informe de sostenibilidad del programa* [Report on programme sustainability]. Washington, DC: International Food Policy Research Institute and San Salvador: Fundación Salvadoreña para el Desarrollo Económico y Social.

Eyben, R., & Ladbury, S. (2006). *Building effective states: Taking a citizen's perspective*. Brighton: Development Research Centre on Citizenship, Participation and Accountability, Institute of Development Studies.

Fiszbein, A., Schady, N., Ferreira, F., Grosch, M., Keleher, N., Olinto, P., & Skoufias, E. (2009). *Conditional cash transfers: Reducing present and future poverty*. Washington, DC: World Bank.

Fox, J. (2008). *Accountability politics: Power and voice in rural Mexico*. New York, NY: Oxford University Press.

Hevia del la Jara, F. (2007). El programa Oportunidades y la construccion de ciudadana: Ejercicio y protección de derechos en un programa de transferencias condicionadas en Mexico [The *Oportunidades* programme and the construction of citizenship: exercise and protection of rights in a conditional cash transfer program in Mexico] (Unpublished doctoral dissertation). Centro de Investigación y Estudios Superiores en Antropología Social, Mexico.

Hunter, W., & Borges Sugiyama, N. (2014). Transforming subjects into citizens: Insights from Brazil's Bolsa Família. *Perspectives on Politics, 12*, 829–845. doi:10.1017/S1537592714002151

Kabeer, N. (2005). Introduction. In N. Kabeer (Ed.), *Inclusive citizenship*. London: Zed Books.

Maluccio, J., Adato, M., & Skoufias, E. (2010). Combining quantitative and qualitative research for the evaluation of conditional cash transfer programs in Latin America. In M. Adato & J. Hoddinott (Eds.), *Conditional cash transfers in Latin America* (pp. 26–52). Baltimore, MD: Johns Hopkins University Press.

Plagerson, S., Harpham, T., & Kielman, K. (2012). Cash transfers and citizenship: Evidence from South Africa. *Journal of Development Studies, 48*, 969–982. doi:10.1080/00220388.2012.658371

Red Solidaria. (2007). Programa social de atención a la pobreza [Social care programme for the poor]. Documento Técnico, Secretaría Técnica de la Presidencia y Coordinación del Área Social de la Presidencia [Technical Document, Technical Secretariat of the Presidency and Social Department of the Presidency]. San Salvador: Government of El Salvador.

Reuben, W., & Cuenca, R. (2009). *El Estado de la indocumentación infantil en el Perú: Hallazgos y propuestas de política* [The State of undocumented children in Peru: Findings and policy proposals]. Working Paper. Lima: International Bank for Reconstruction and Development/ World Bank.

Rowlands, J. (1998). A word of the times, but what does it mean? Empowerment in the discourse and practice of development. In A. Afshar (Ed.), *Women and empowerment: Illustrations from the Third World*. New York, NY: St. Martin's Press.

Secretaría Técnica de la Presidencia de El Salvador. (2013). *El Camino del cambio en El Salvador. Legados de 4 Años de gestión* [The path of change in El Salvador. Legacies of four years of management]. San Salvador: Government of El Salvador.

Yaschine, I. (1999). The changing anti-poverty agenda: What can the Mexican case tell us? *IDS Bulletin, 30*(2), 47–60. doi:10.1111/idsb.1999.30.issue-2

Yaschine, I., & Orozco, M. (2010). The evolving anti-poverty agenda in Mexico: The political economy of PROGRESA and Oportunidades. In M. Adato & J. Hoddinott (Eds.), *Conditional cash transfers in Latin America*. Baltimore, MD: Johns Hopkins University Press.

Pathways to Citizen Accountability: Brazil's Bolsa Família

NATASHA BORGES SUGIYAMA

Department of Political Science, University of Wisconsin-Milwaukee, Milwaukee, WI, USA

ABSTRACT *This article examines the pathways – citizen-driven, bottom-up oversight or state-centred administrative controls – that have played the largest role in promoting the accountability of the Bolsa Família programme. The exploratory analysis draws on interviews with local and federal officials as well as beneficiaries of the Bolsa Família in order to identify the ways monitoring and accountability have evolved in practise and on the ground. Field research highlights that citizen- and community-driven participatory mechanisms for ongoing monitoring and accountability are relatively weak. Top-down administrative regulations, such as programmatic transparency and random audits, have largely worked to protect the integrity of the programme. The article concludes by discussing the opportunities for greater community-driven participatory oversight in the future.*

Introduction

The clean delivery of assistance to the poor – where access to services is based on clear eligibility criteria and inclusion is based on principles of citizenship – is part of what constitutes good governance practices. Yet such clean provisioning has proven difficult to accomplish for many middle-income and developing countries. Political interference is a persistent challenge. The political usage of public services by local powerbrokers and politicians, through patronage and clientelism for instance, can render citizens more vulnerable to patron-client relations. Even where well-meaning state actors design social programmes with fairness and equity in mind, their effective implementation can be hindered by low administrative capacity. For the poor who rely on basic social services for their daily survival, the stakes are particularly high.

The development literature has sought to identify mechanisms that promote government accountability. For some scholars and development practitioners, citizens play an important role in holding government accountable for the quality of governance (for example, Peruzzotti & Smulovitz, 2006; World Bank, 2003). 'Users' or 'beneficiaries' of public services in particular, are thought to be important proponents of governmental accountability because they have a vested interest in the equitable and efficient delivery of services. In settings where individual citizens are poorly positioned to monitor governance because of their extreme vulnerability, it is possible that civil society can serve this important function. Scholars have identified numerous ways in which citizen activism can promote accountability. For instance, Fox and Aranda (1996) find that civil society engagement in local development projects in Mexico contributes to positive impacts. In Italy, Putnam (1993) identifies the depth of social capital as important for the promotion of good government performance. Others note that rather than citizen-driven, bottom-up demand for good governance, top-down approaches matter for monitoring and accountability (Brunetti & Weder, 2003; McCubbins & Schwartz, 1984). Politicians, technocrats, and party leaders can institute administrative mechanisms that promote government through transparency and accountability.

For instance, freedom of information laws can render misdeeds more visible to the public. Once the malfeasance becomes apparent, civil society – via protest or the media – can make demands for accountability and reforms.

Brazil's Bolsa Família, the world's largest conditional cash transfer (CCT) programme, provides an opportunity to explore the ways in which government and civil society have promoted accountability. Which pathways – citizen-driven, bottom-up demands or state-centred administrative mechanisms – have played the largest role in promoting accountability of the Bolsa Família? The Brazilian case is particularly useful for examining the capacity of citizens to promote accountability of poverty policy. The Bolsa is well established, having recently achieved 10 years of operation. Brazil is also home to a vibrant civil society. Given the size and scope of the Bolsa Família programme, affecting roughly 14 million families or 55 million individuals (about a quarter of the entire population), it is possible that citizens and the community would engage in 'bottom-up' demands to monitor its operations. At the same time, policymakers with the Ministry of Social Development (MDS) designed a complex federal programme with an eye toward efficiency and accuracy, instituting 'top-down' controls. How have these strategies fared and have beneficiaries and the community at large sought to engage in regularised oversight of the programme?

This article explores the pathways to accountability of the Bolsa Família programme. The analysis draws on interviews with federal technocrats charged with the design and implementation of the programme as well as beneficiaries' experiences and insights. It proceeds as follows: The next section provides a brief overview of the Bolsa Família programme. The third section provides the empirical and theoretical prospects for citizen and community monitoring and state-driven accountability mechanisms. This is followed by an explanation of the research setting for this exploratory analysis. As the cases show, the practise of participatory citizen-led monitoring and accountability of the Bolsa Família is rather weak. Interviews and participant-based research with Bolsa beneficiaries points instead to the relevance of top-down administrative mechanisms that help promote transparency and accountability. The conclusion considers opportunities for greater community-driven participatory oversight in future.

Brief Background on the Bolsa Família Programme

Brazil's Bolsa Família programme is one of the largest and most established conditional cash transfer (CCT) programmes in the world (Fiszbein & Schady, 2009).[1] Started in 2003, the federal programme unified disparate poverty alleviation programmes (Bolsa Escola, Auxilio Gás, and Bolsa Alimentação) into a single CCT. The Bolsa Família aims to alleviate short-term poverty, through the provision of monthly cash grants, and address human development in the long-term, through conditionality requirements. Programme eligibility is based on household income per capita. Applicants, typically mothers, apply to the programme by providing self-reported house-hold income along with identity documentation for themselves and their children. The MDS periodically updates the income eligibility threshold as well as the grant formulas. Households with monthly per capita incomes below US$30 are eligible for a grant. Amounts are based on a formula that takes into consideration household income and family composition, such as size, number of children under 17 years of age, and the pregnancy or nursing status of mothers.[2] Families living in conditions of extreme poverty are eligible for a basic benefit of US$45. The average grant is about US$75 per month; the maximum benefit is US$153 if the family is extremely poor, has three children and two teenagers (Soares, 2011, p. 57). This represents a significant income source for poor Brazilians and benefits roughly 14 million families, about a quarter of the population. To maintain benefits, mothers[3] must fulfil numerous conditionality requirements that are thought to enhance human capacity development. For instance, children should regularly attend school, receive scheduled vaccinations and periodic health check-ups to track their nutrition. Pregnant women are required to obtain prenatal health care and mothers should breastfeed their infants. The MDS frames these conditionalities as consistent with citizens' social rights, which includes access to health care and education provided by the state.

While relatively simple in design, the Bolsa Família programme requires complex institutional and administrative coordination.[4] The programme calls for intergovernmental cooperation between the federal government and over 5500 municipalities. Local authorities are the entryway into the programme. They are responsible for interacting with grant applicants and entering families' data into the Unified Registry (*Cadastro Único*). Conditionality is also tracked locally, with teachers, nurses, and doctors providing the data that is reported back to the federal MDS. Federal authorities at the MDS manage the Unified Registry, select beneficiaries from the applicant pool based on eligibility requirements, and communicate directly with beneficiaries. For instance, the MDS distributes bankcards through which local recipients receive their grants and promotional material that clarifies the programme's operations and requirements. Thus features of its operation aim to effectively target grants, avoid duplication of benefits, and guard against local clientelism. The programme also involves cross-sector cooperation as the programme's conditionality requirements, tied to school attendance and health check-ups, mean the MDS must work collaboratively with the Ministries of Education and Health. In these ways, the Bolsa represents a complex programme that works horizontally, across various sectors, and vertically, through intergovernmental coordination between municipal and national governments.

Mechanisms for social control are embedded in the programme to facilitate civil society oversight and insulate the programme from political interference. For instance, in 2004 the MDS required that cities convene a municipal Bolsa Família council (*conselho*) or committee under Law 10.836.[5] These entities are responsible for planning, monitoring, evaluating, and auditing the programme on an ongoing basis (MDS, n.d., p. 3). To promote good management practices, the federal government developed a federal fiscal transfer for municipal governments called the Index of Decentralised Municipal Management of the Bolsa Família (*Índice de Gestão Descentralizada Municipal do Programa Bolsa Família*, or IGD-M). The IGD-M funding formula acknowledged the importance of social accountability by including two categories related to fiscal transparency and oversight by the Municipal Social Assistance Council (MDS, 2011, p. 5). Aside from councils, policymakers also designed alternative channels for citizens who wish to log complaints, such as a toll-free number to reach the MDS. Finally, the Bolsa is also subject to three agencies that are responsible for formal oversight and control of the programme, including the General Comptroller's Office (*Controladoria-Geral da União*, CGU), the Federal Accounting Tribunal (*Tribunal de Contas da União*, TCU) and the Public Ministry (*Ministério Público*), the latter being an agency open to public complaints.[6] In these ways the Bolsa incorporates multiple channels for accountability and 'social control' (*controle social*).

Empirical and Theoretical Perspectives: Pathways to Accountability

Which pathways – community-driven, 'bottom-up' accountability channels or 'top-down' administrative design features – have played the largest role in promoting accountability of the Bolsa Família programme? This section explores the empirical and theoretical bases for expectations of each.

Prospects for Citizen- and Community-Driven Monitoring of the Bolsa Família

There are several reasons to think that Brazilian citizens may be well positioned to hold government accountable for the proper administration of its CCT. First, federalism in Brazil has provided fruitful grounds for greater citizen involvement. Brazil's three-tiered federal structure expanded political, administrative, and fiscal autonomy of municipal governments. Citizens are used to making political demands on their local representatives and holding them accountable for furthering constitutionally guaranteed social rights (Samuels, 2000). Elections are a key mechanism for citizens to hold officials accountable for corruption and political malfeasance. There is evidence that the Brazilian voter, when provided with information on corruption, is willing to use the ballot box to remove such politicians

(Winters & Weitz-Shapiro, 2013). As the Bolsa Família is administered locally through mayors' offices, in theory, citizens have greater local recourse to hold local officials accountable for the programme.

Second, decentralisation has promoted avenues for direct citizen participation in local decision making through new deliberative institutions.[7] Participatory Budgeting (*Orçamento Participativo*), stands as one of the most well known models for citizen engagement in the allocation of public resources. The first Participatory Budgeting experience emerged in the city of Porto Alegre (Abers, 2000; Baiocchi, 2005) but has since spread to other municipalities (Avritzer, 2009; Wampler, 2007). Importantly, direct citizen engagement is not limited to deliberations over budget expenditures. Local governments have instituted deliberative public management councils (*conselhos*) in sectors such as education, health, and social assistance. The allocation of council seats is typically based on partici-pants' social and administrative roles and includes representatives from civil society, 'users' of services, workers, and municipal representatives. This type of inclusive participatory space facilitates dialogue between governmental operations and civil society. Importantly, municipal officials are often called upon to make their programmatic operations transparent to council members.

While there are normative reasons to promote direct citizen engagement as part of democratic values, scholars also point to instrumental justifications related to improved governmental performance (see for example, Putnam, 1993). With over 20 years of participatory budgeting experience, scholars have been able to identify a number of important democratic and human development outcomes. Baiocchi, Heller, and Silva argue that devolving decision-making authority to local actors serves to increase transparency, taps into local sources of information, improves electoral accountability, and encourages innovation (2011, p. 9). Avritzer (2010) argues that participatory budgeting in the city of Porto Alegre contributed to improvements in living conditions for the urban poor. Similarly, Touchton and Wampler (2014) find that participatory budgeting is associated with increased health spending and lower infant mortality. Cornwall and Shankland (2008) make a similar case for the value of partici-patory deliberative institutions in the health sector and argue that participatory mechanisms through the Unified Health System (*Sistema Único de Saúde*, or SUS) broaden access to health services, provide a framework for 'regulatory partnerships', and help to ensure that the rights and needs of the poor remain central to the SUS.

A third contextual feature of Brazilian politics is that the country is home to a vibrant civil society that has regularly engaged in politics (Encarnación, 2003). During the political opening (*abertura*) in the 1980s under the military regime, social movements played an important role in advocating for democracy and pressing for social rights in the new constitution (Paoli & Da Silva Telles, 1998). For instance, the women's movement (Alvarez, 1990) and sanitarian (*sanitarista*) public health movement (Cohn, 1989; Weyland, 1996) were active in calling for progressive reforms. Many of these move-ments have evolved since democratisation and formed into professional networks and organisations that monitor public policy or work collaboratively with government (Alvarez, 1999). Mass politics appeared to wane after democratisation, but recent history has shown that individuals have not abandoned direct action through mass mobilisation. In June 2013, announced price hikes for public transportation stimulated multiple generalised mass street protests across the country, with a million or more participants taking to the streets to denounce poor government performance, corruption, and overruns on World Cup stadium projects (Romero & Neuman, 2013). Observers characterise recent street protests as leaderless and different from traditional social movements, such as those spurred by labour unions, professional associations, and nongovernmental organisations (see Holston, 2014). Yet, protest activity against government performance may nevertheless reflect a shared belief in the rights of citizens and the obligations of the state to fulfil those rights.

Despite the potential for Brazilian civil society involvement in monitoring public policy, there are important limitations that warrant consideration. First, local governance can present challenges for the practise of accountability. For instance, there is wide variation in the type of participatory institutions available to citizen and civil society organisations across the country. Between 1997 and 2000, only 104 municipalities had participatory budgeting (Baiocchi et al., 2011, p. 4). The quality or effectiveness of these participatory institutions can differ across municipalities. As

Wampler notes in the case of participatory budgeting, how accountability and citizenship rights are extended can depend on mayoral incentives to delegate authority, the particular rules structure used to delegate authority to citizens, and how community organisations and citizens respond to new institutions (2007, p. 4).

A second and not insignificant challenge relates to the incorporation of the poor in monitoring poverty policy. Poverty can have the effect of excluding people from meaningful citizenship. *Social exclusion*, the feeling of being left out and being looked down by others (Narayan, Chambers, Shah, & Petesch, 2000, ch. 7), as well as a lack of *agency*, the feeling of being resigned to life circumstances (Sen, 1999, p. 11), are both associated with poverty and may hinder poor citizens and communities from exercising their right to monitor the Bolsa Família.[8]

Prospects for Administrative Accountability of the Bolsa Família

While civil society oversight of public policy is one possible pathway to governmental accountability, it is not the only one. Public administrators can employ administrative rules or legal protections to ensure that programmes are implemented in a clean fashion. In this vein, technocrats can design public policies to avoid the pitfalls of corruption, clientelism, and other forms of political interference.

Transparency in government operations, especially fiscal transparency, is widely considered to be a prerequisite for good governance and the reduction of corruption (Kolstad & Wiig, 2009; Kopits, 2000). International development institutions such as the World Bank have promoted transparency as a mechanism that allows citizens and markets to hold government accountable for public policies and governmental performance (see World Bank, 2013). Laws that guarantee access to 'freedom of information' are viewed as an important instrument that can reduce corruption (Brunetti & Weder, 2003). As Reinikka and Svensson (2005) show through their policy experiment in Uganda, a newspaper campaign that highlighted local officials' handling of a large education programme diminished the capture of those funds and contributed positively to student enrolment and learning. While Brazil's freedom of information law is nascent (Law 12.527/2011), the Ministry of Social Development built transparency features into the Bolsa Família programme from the onset. One of the most important transparency features may be its public list of beneficiaries on a transparency portal website, allowing any interested party to identify the number of grant-holders per city as well as the names of legally responsible cardholders (Sugiyama & Hunter, 2013). Any interested citizen with questions about the Bolsa Família can also utilise a toll-free number to contact Brasília.

Behind the scenes, federal officials with the MDS also established a number of other oversight and control mechanisms. For instance, the Unified Registry of all applicants includes internal and external crosschecks to determine proper targeting of grants. Crosschecks against applicants' self-reported income, other federal databases (for example, pensions), and 'proxy variables' in the registry (such as consumption), help insure the proper targeting. Importantly, the MDS works with other agencies, including the Public Ministry, to investigate complaints and appeals; the SFC/CGU also conducts annual financial audits and regular bimonthly random-sample quality control reviews; finally the TCU conducts implementation evaluations based on a random sample of the Unified Registry and the Bolsa Família programme (Lindert, Linder, Hobbs, & De La Brière, 2007, p. 23). Thus, federal authorities designed application, audit, and investigative procedures to help guard against the sticky fingers of local politicians. Most of these backstage administrative procedures can be invisible to citizens.

Some administrative mechanisms – particularly transparency and investigative procedures – work especially well when the public engages them to demand governmental accountability. Scholars have identified instances of productive collaboration between government calls for oversight alongside civil society advocacy. In Ceará, Judith Tendler (1997) found that state campaigns urged the public to monitor public services in areas of procurement, health, and drought relief, and Rich and Gómez (2012) argue that national health government officials sought to increase their regulatory capacity by utilising local civic groups as watchdogs.

Research Setting

How has monitoring and accountability of the Bolsa Família unfolded? Rather than test hypotheses on the effectiveness of bottom-up versus top-down mechanisms, this analysis draws on a case study approach to yield insights that are useful for subsequent theory building (Bennett, 2010). This work extends research on the views and experiences of Bolsa Família recipients (Hunter & Sugiyama, 2014; Sugiyama & Hunter, 2013), incorporates interviews with federal bureaucrats with the Ministry of Social Development as well as street-level bureaucrats, and draws on the literature on Brazil's CCT. To understand the experiences of poor beneficiaries, we went to the northeast, a region known for its high concentration of poverty and longstanding practise with clientelism. The study focused on the experiences of three emblematic northeastern cities: Pau Brasil in the state of Bahia, and Camaragibe and Jaboatão dos Gurarapes, both in the state of Pernambuco. The communities varied with respect to important political and demographic contexts, such as size, poverty rates, mayoral partisan affiliations, and history of local political corruption.[9] The research strategy included focus groups with beneficiaries of the Bolsa Família, a survey of the poor, and interviews with street-level bureaucrats.

Focus groups allow us to learn about the experiences of programme participants. This research strategy is especially well suited for Bolsa Família participants who are of a lower social status.[10] Unlike one-on-one interviews, the group discussions are less hierarchical and allow participants to share ideas and reach consensus. Importantly, the free-flowing dialogue can also illuminate areas that are unanticipated by researchers. Our moderators, all Brazilians with advanced social science degrees and experience with the local population, utilised a similar script across all groups but encouraged participants to share personal narratives and elaborate on ideas that were relevant, even if unanticipated. In total, there were 11 focus groups that lasted about an hour each (see Appendix for full list of focus of groups).

We also conducted a 15-minute household face-to-face survey with over a thousand poor residents in each of the three cities. The survey employed a quota sample to include beneficiaries and non-beneficiaries.[11] The focus groups and survey were launched simultaneously in 2009. Interviews provided context for our participants' testimonies and responses. Interviews took place in two stages. In 2009, we met with street-level bureaucrats, including nurses with the Family Health Programme and social workers, who have daily contact with Bolsa Família recipients through their work. We also met with the municipal Bolsa Família administrators in each city. In 2011, we returned to Camaragibe and Jaboatão for follow-up meetings. We also interviewed officials with the federal Ministry of Social Development in Brasília in 2011 and 2014.

Some important caveats are in order. First, data collection was not explicitly designed with the aim of uncovering citizen pathways to accountability of the Bolsa Família. Nevertheless, focus group testimony offers important insights on this topic. Focus groups offer opportunities for participants to share their experiences in their own words and to bring up issues that are unanticipated by researchers. In this way, open-ended questions allow for unscripted responses that can shed light on new subjects, allowing participants to frame their responses in ways that are meaningful to them. Also important, focus groups allow for researchers to analyse the content of what was said, as well as not said. If beneficiaries do not identify an issue as salient when offered an opportunity to do so, this information is also useful. Second, the analyses presented here are not representative of all Bolsa Família recipients or the poor more generally. Despite limitations in representativeness, the research nevertheless provides useful insights into features of programme operations on the ground.

Pathways for Monitoring the Bolsa Família: Possibilities and Challenges

Do community- and citizen-driven efforts to monitor and promote accountability of the Bolsa Família – through electoral means, municipal councils, social movement advocacy, or protest politics – work on the ground?

As Brazil's CCT is a federal programme with local coordination overseen by municipalities, it bears asking which elected representatives voters should hold accountable for its performance. A recent panel study found that 84 per cent of Brazilians identified the federal government as the main funder and manager of the CCT (C. Zucco, personal communication, 2013.). Given the strong identification of the Bolsa Família with President Lula of the Workers' Party (PT), most scholars have focused on the electoral impact of Bolsa voters and presidential elections (see for example Hunter & Power, 2007; Zucco, 2013). The underlying logic is that beneficiaries of the programme would reward Lula at the ballot box for implementing a much-needed programme. Zucco (2009, p. 40) argues that PT mayors were unable to claim credit for implementing the programme in the 2004 elections. But beyond credit claiming, do voters punish mayors – who implement the Bolsa Familia programme on the ground – for the poor management? Importantly, de Janvry, Finan, and Sadoulet (2012) find that first-term mayors with good programme performance were much more likely to get re-elected. In other words, good governance gets rewarded at the ballot box.

The testimony we heard in our focus groups reinforced a connection between beneficiaries and their attitudes toward electoral accountability. When we asked our groups, 'What would you do if a politician tried to take away the Bolsa Família?' voting was the immediate response identified by our participants. The following exchanges are illustrative:

Anon: He wouldn't even come to office!
Anon: He wouldn't get past the front door.
Anon: We'd take him out! (Camaragibe, Female Focus Group 1)

In another group, members had a similar exchange:

Anon: We'd get rid of him first! (Laughter)
Anon: No one would ever vote for him again. Not for mayor, governor, or anything.
Anon: His future would be over, he wouldn't be anything. (Camaragibe, Female Focus Group 2)

In Jaboatão, a participant explained: 'You can be certain that the people would overthrow him' (Jaboatão dos Guararapes, Female Focus Group 2). Across all our groups, participants held the belief that voting mattered and that their strength at the ballot box would mean politicians would not dare eliminate the CCT. A downside to elections for accountability is that the four-year electoral cycle means citizens may wait a long time to express discontent at the ballot box.

Municipal councils, which are deliberative and inclusive of civil society, provide a more immediate opportunity to monitor public policy on a regular basis. To what extent have Bolsa Família councils served as a community-based opportunity for programme monitoring and accountability? As Hall (2008) notes, councils for the predecessor federal *Bolsa Escola* programme were generally weak and unwilling to engage in a policing role (p. 810). Less well known is the performance of municipal Bolsa Família councils. MDS regulations require that cities create opportunities for 'social control' (*controle social*) through either committees or councils. Councils, which would require that 50 per cent of its members are programme beneficiaries, would represent the most inclusive strategy to incorporate the Bolsa participants. When committees are subsumed under an existing municipal council, the share of seats set aside for 'users' of all social assistance programmes is proportionally smaller.[12] The Ministry reports that initially 39 per cent (or 2183) of cities chose to adopt a separate Bolsa Família Council (MDS, n.d., p. 5). A recent government survey, the *Censo SUAS 2012*, revealed that about 98 per cent of cities had placed the Bolsa's 'social control' entity under the auspices of the Social Assistance Council (P. Mollo, author interview, Brasília. 28 May 2014). This development is in large measure driven by reforms to the Unified System for Social Assistance (*Sistema Único de Assistência Social*, SUAS) where reformers have advocated that the participatory responsibilities for the Bolsa Família should fall within their sector's institutional responsibilities and participatory institutions (Mollo, author interview, 2014 interview).

In our study, we saw scant evidence that civil society organisations or Bolsa Família beneficiaries sought councils or committees as vehicles for social control of the programme. In one of our case study cities, local officials explained that their Bolsa Família committee operated under the umbrella of its Social Assistance Council and really did not have a separate character. They acknowledged that a distinct Bolsa Família council would have more opportunities for citizen and civil society representatives to participate in deliberations, but there was no beneficiary or civil society demand for it. Further, administrators had little interest promoting such participation. In all three of our research sites local Bolsa Família administrators reported that councils did not take on a significant role in their programme operations or in creating supplemental activities geared toward Bolsa recipients (A. Adriano, A. author interview, Camaragibe. 8 July 2011; Fernandes, F. author interview, Jaboatão dos Guararapes. 5 July 2011; K. Lopes dos Santos, author interview, Jaboatão dos Guararapes. 6 July 2011; L. A. Perreira, author interview, Pau Brasil, 24 June 2009). For instance, in Jaboatão the local officials presented their accounts to the council, as required by MDS regulations, but the body was not otherwise a participatory space for beneficiaries (Soares, 2011). In this way, committees in the study sites fulfilled the minimum requirements as set forth by the MDS, but did not serve as spaces for dialogue or feedback from beneficiaries.

Our focus group research in these cities yielded some insights on how the poor perceive their role in monitoring the programme. None of our participants reported they served on the councils or committees, much less knew about them. We asked them about obstacles they encountered with the programme and how they solved them. A few participants reported difficulty obtaining their Bolsa Família cards. A few others reported some frustration with the length of time it took them to enter into the programme after applying for benefits. Those that did face difficulty reported they got help from a neighbour or sought self-help strategies. Significantly, no one reported turning to a neighbourhood association, advocacy group, or representative on a municipal council.[13] And while one of our research locations, Camaragibe, is well known for its longstanding experience with Participatory Budgeting (Baiocchi et al., 2011), participants in our study did not identify it as an avenue to report problems or provide feedback. The survey of poor residents in these cities offers some context to explain why beneficiaries did not view community organisations as partners. When asked: 'In the last year, have you participated in a community meeting in your neighbourhood?' Only 25 per cent reported they did so either 'sometimes' or 'frequently.'[14]

To what extent did Bolsa recipients view protest politics as a vehicle to hold politicians accountable for programme management? While none of our focus group participants reported they had engaged in recent protests, several groups identified protests and mobilisations as a reasonable and likely political strategy if they needed to defend the programme. The following exchange was illustrative:

> Moderator: What would you do if the Bolsa Família were cut off?
> Anon: A type of social movement [...] People often go on strike, join movements, protest. I think we could at least try.
> Anon: The people could organise collectively and protest against that government agency (Pau Brasil, Women's Focus Group 2).

This discussion, which took place years before the mass mobilisations in major urban centres in June 2013, serves as foreshadowing of citizens' willingness to protest over governance. Yet, protests are not daily, monthly, or even annual occurrences. Our survey asked: 'In the last year, have you participated in a mobilisation or protest?' Only four per cent of the poor in the communities we surveyed said they had done so 'sometimes' or 'frequently.' This suggests that contentious politics for demanding accountability may be a viable, albeit infrequent, strategy among these communities.

Turning to more 'top-down' bureaucratic approaches, do administrative mechanisms to promote accountability of Bolsa Família work on the ground for the community? Focus group testimony and interviews reveal that administrative accountability mechanisms had tangible effects for citizens.

Freedom of information and transparency of Bolsa Família management are crucial and operate at different levels. From the vantage point of beneficiaries, programme transparency is necessary if the poor are to monitor the programme and stake a claim in its operations. The MDS has made efforts to develop accessible outreach campaigns, including clear literature with simple graphics, which clearly state the eligibility requirements, conditionality, enrolment procedures, and payment information

(MDS, 2006, 2010). Participants in all of our focus groups expressed understanding of how the programme worked, including eligibility requirements and programme conditionalities. For instance, all of our female focus groups reported they followed application procedures to register with the *Cadastro Único* and knew their children had to attend school and get check-ups at health clinics.[15] Participants reported learning about the programme through a number of channels, including television, radio, neighbours, and programme literature. Without basic understanding of how the programme works, it is not possible for citizens to meaningfully engage in monitoring activities to demand government accountability. This is a necessary first step, which the federal government has largely fulfilled. Once beneficiaries understand how the Bolsa Família programme operates, are they likely to take action to ensure its clean delivery? Though none of the participants stated that they had reported an instance of fraud, there was general agreement that they would be willing to do so.

Transparency of programme operations is also important for the broader community. Journalists have taken an active role in monitoring the Bolsa Família and investigating potential problems with the programme, whether with respect to errors of inclusion or exclusion, due to poor targeting or political malfeasance. Their investigative reporting is greatly facilitated by MDS provision of public information, including lists of programme participants. Media coverage of implementation errors was particularly intense in the early phase of the programme (2003–2004). As Lindert and Vincensini (2010) note, there was widespread news coverage of the programme in these early years. As the authors observe, the quality of programme operations and effectiveness matter a great deal for political support (Lindert & Vincensini, 2010, p. 2). 'There was tremendous pressure on this public policy, which was not yet understood as a public policy, and there were big expectations […] [t]hat the results of the programme needed to be good and effective' (Modesto, 2014, p. 88). Federal technocrats understood that for the programme's political survival, they needed to solve technical problems, particularly errors of inclusion and exclusion (L. Modesto, author interview, Brasília. 1 July 2011). A key innovation was the development and use of the Unified Registry (*Cadastro Único*) for managing entry into the programme and catching duplication of benefits (Modesto, 2011 interview, 2014). Once improvements were made, the news coverage and critical tone shifted considerably (Lindert & Vincensini, 2010).

Media coverage of the Bolsa Família not only has feedback effects on public servants, but also on beneficiaries. Our focus group participants reported they were aware of news coverage on the programme. Participants were particularly sensitive to investigations where allegedly ineligible families had enrolled in the programme. This was especially significant in the small community in Pau Brasil, where the individuals are likely to know one another. Importantly, those focus groups reported hearing about investigations by the Public Ministry's office. In the long term, such coverage can be beneficial if it signals the democratic value of fairness, equity, and rule of law. Once the poor can see there are consequences to poor government performance, they may be more confident in the rule of law and democratic processes. Such a transformation would be important as public opinion polls reveal the poor have the lowest rates of support for democracy (Almeida, 2008).

To what extent have the government's calls for public monitoring helped promote accountability of the Bolsa Família programme? We found a clear example of how the provision of information and institutional channels for feedback can encourage programme monitoring by a community organisation. When the leader of a local nongovernmental organisation in Pau Brasil, Friends of Justice (*Amigos da Justiça*), learned that a few destitute families were not recipients of the grants, he began to investigate. Upon learning that there are municipal quotas for Bolsa Família grants, he found a way to download the list of beneficiaries from the Internet. Since Pau Brasil is a small town, he felt he could identify those families that were unlikely to fit the income profile and were taking up the spots that could go to other families. He then lodged complaints with the MDS, Public Ministry, and wrote letters to members of Congress. His complaints had real effects, spurring an investigation by the public prosecutor, the removal of the local Bolsa Família administrator, and local media coverage of mismanagement (Perreira, 2009 interview). Importantly, after his efforts he became a member of the municipal Bolsa Família Council (D. V. dos Santos, author interview, Pau Brasil, 25 June 2009). These events illustrate the importance of transparency of information as well as institutional mechanisms for citizens to lodge complaints. At the same time, it is clear that access to information is insufficient if citizen groups are not poised to use that information to monitor public policy.

Discussion

Why would beneficiaries, citizens, and the community at-large choose to monitor the Bolsa Família programme? The political incentives to monitor the Bolsa have changed over time. Prior to the institutionalisation of the programme in 2003–2004, the federal government faced criticism from political opponents over its design and implementation. Media coverage, including television broadcasts and newspaper reports, initially highlighted administrative difficulties related to the consolidation of pre-existing programmes under Bolsa Família. But as the MDS improved its administrative capacity to effectively target grants and monitor beneficiaries' compliance with conditionality requirements, the tone in coverage shifted notably (Lindert & Vincensini, 2010). At the same time, the political landscape surrounding the programme has also evolved. Public opinion research suggests Brazilians accept the programme and do not blame the poor for their poverty (Castro, Walter, Santana, & Stephanou, 2009). Moreover, presidential candidates who have vied for the presidency against Presidents Lula and Dilma Rousseff of the Workers' Party have pledged support for programme continuity. Thus, the 'high stakes' period to ensure its political survival has subsided. Public policy and politics go hand-in-hand, demonstrating that monitoring and accountability are not politically neutral activities. In this way, the demand for oversight is likely to ebb and flow depending on political sea changes.

Insights from field research also reveal that the incentives and pathways to engage in oversight vary by actors' roles. For beneficiaries of the Bolsa Família, individualised action through voting and protest politics, not participatory action, was the most accessible pathway for holding public officials accountable for governance. For technocrats in Brasília, the motivation to deliver a clean and well-run programme drove them to integrate numerous 'behind the scenes' transparency and auditing controls (Lindert et al., 2007; Modesto, 2011 interview, 2014). Organised civil society, the media and civil society organisations, rather than the poor, were those most likely to utilise those transparency and auditing mechanisms. In many ways, programme design features and their success may affect the demand for oversight by the community at-large. As Melo (2008) reports, local registration of the Bolsa Família undergoes regular audits by the CGU and the Caixa Econômica Federal, the public bank that runs the programme. While there is documentation of fraud in some instances, there has been no case involving widespread corruption (Melo, 2008, p. 183). The presence of a rather clean and well-run social programme may thus explain why we found relatively low levels of community-driven monitoring of the programme. Yet, as I discuss below, there should be a role for meaningful dialogue with and participation by the poor and the community.

Conclusion

This article has sought to examine the pathways – citizen-driven, bottom-up oversight or state-centred administrative controls – that have played the largest role in promoting the accountability of the Bolsa Família. This exploratory analysis draws on interviews with local and federal officials as well as beneficiaries of the Bolsa Família in order to identify the ways monitoring and accountability have evolved in practise and on the ground.

To summarise, field research highlights that citizen- and community-driven participatory mechanisms for ongoing monitoring and accountability are relatively weak. Beneficiaries are more likely to view voting as their best vehicle for holding elected officials accountable. Other non-electoral channels, such as councils and collaborative spaces, are rarely identified as pathways to demand oversight of poverty policy. For the poorest and most vulnerable groups in society, monitoring of public policy is left to the media and civil society organisations. Top-down administrative regulations have largely worked to protect the integrity of the programme. Bureaucratic mechanisms, such as programmatic transparency and random audits, have enabled well-organised interest groups and journalists to investigate and report suspected malfeasance. These are crucial first steps that may lay the groundwork for further engagement of beneficiaries themselves. During our meetings with programme participants, we heard many excellent ideas about how to improve the programme or address unique challenges within their communities. It is a shame that local and federal officials have not structured opportunities to gain this type of valuable insight.

What are the future prospects for greater engagement of the community in ongoing monitoring of the Bolsa Família? Here there are both opportunities and constraints. As Hunter and Sugiyama (2014) note, Bolsa Família participants viewed the programme as a social right. For instance, they utilised a rights-based discourse and expressed the view that access to the programme was a social right. Importantly, this view was consistent between both the female and male groups. This suggests that Brazil's CCT is a marked departure from historic social assistance programmes, which were at best charity and at worst instruments that reinforced patron-client relationships (Sugiyama & Hunter, 2013). Understanding the programme in bureaucratic and rights-based terms may ultimately allow the poor to defend those rights against the state or others who deny them access to it.

Yet, moving from individualised strategic voting to collective action is an obstacle for community-driven, bottom-up monitoring and advocacy. To date, there is no national association of Bolsa Família recipients. Nor have any existing organisations sought to harness Bolsa recipients as a natural political constituency. Such an idea is not far-fetched. Public policies can create 'policy feedback effects' by creating new interest groups that share political goals, capabilities, and resources (Pierson, 1993). Skocpol's influential work on the United States, *Protecting Soldiers and Mothers*, serves as a prime example that details how Civil War pensions spurred veterans to self-consciously organise to demand ever-improving services (1992, p. 59). In the case of poor communities across Brazil, Bolsa beneficiaries may yet develop a similar trajectory. As social citizenship expands and families' most basic needs are met, it is possible to envision a future where Bolsistas could become a formidable political force that demand inclusion in the policymaking process. Only time will tell.

In the meanwhile, can government foster greater community engagement in monitoring of the Bolsa? Here the challenges are notable but not insurmountable. In creating a centralised programme that can withstand local political interference – through a unified registry, municipal quotas, and direct payment mechanisms to families, for example – the MDS centralised the Bolsa as much as possible in a decentralised context (Bichir, 2012). While this has advantages for insulating social policy from variations in local capacity and reducing the risks of local clientelism, it has also had the effect of dampening local dialogue with the poor. For instance, they do not have structured opportunities to provide ongoing social accountability actions that monitor local or federal policy.[16] As the indigent and poor face higher obstacles for collective action, namely lower levels of human and material resources, state-sponsored avenues for participation may be a necessary first step. In this way, top-down mechanisms can serve to facilitate bottom-up demands in the future. Local social control councils for the Bolsa Família are potential avenues for some individuals and community organisations to engage in monitoring and accountability of municipal services. But wider participation would require that federal and local governments energise municipal Bolsa Família councils and devise new mechanisms for state-society engagement.[17] With citizenship development of the poor underway, the potential for such meaningful transformation exists.

Acknowledgements

Thanks go to the Overseas Development Institute, University College London, and UKAid for sponsoring the symposium, 'Transforming Cash Transfers' held 16–17 October 2013, at which an earlier draft of this paper was presented. Wendy Hunter contributed useful insights along the way and graciously shared the data presented here. Special thanks go to Nicola Jones, Maxine Molyneux, and Fiona Samuels for their comments and suggestions.

Disclosure statement

No potential conflict of interest was reported by the author.

Notes

1. Mexico's federal Progresa/Oportunidades is another well-known and well-regarded CCT. Progresa started in 1997 and currently goes toward 6.5 million families, with 100 per cent coverage across all municipalities (SEDESOL website, 2013).
2. For an excellent overview of the Bolsa Família formula and conditionality requirements, see Barrientos (2013, 898).
3. The Bolsa Família prioritises women as household beneficiaries; 93 per cent of Bolsa recipients are female (Costanzi & Fagundes, 2010, p. 267).
4. For an excellent overview of the design and operations of the Bolsa Família programme, see Lindert et al. (2007).
5. The establishment of Bolsa Família councils can be achieved through previously existing social control entities, including social assistance, health, and education councils (MDS, n.d., p. 4).
6. See Olivieri (2010) for more on executive branch monitoring of public policy through internal audit agencies. On other bureaucratic control mechanisms, see Arantes, Loureiro, Couto, and Teixeira (2010).
7. There is a vibrant debate in the literature over participatory mechanisms and whether Participatory Budgeting and public management councils (*conselhos*) are truly 'bottom-up' citizen-initiated versus more 'top-down' initiatives supported by willing mayors or political parties. This analysis focuses on the role of citizens in monitoring governmental performance. Since councils include citizens and civil society representatives in a deliberative body, this analysis frames such engagement as more 'bottom-up', citizen- or community-driven. Citizen engagement in administrative mechanisms is framed as 'top-down' because they are initiated and managed entirely by federal officials.
8. For more on the role of Bolsa Família in developing citizenship for the poor, see Hunter & Sugiyama, 2014.
9. According to census data (IBGE, 2000), these cities faced high levels of poverty. In Camaragibe, 74.5 per cent of the population was poor; in Jaboatão dos Guararapes, 54 per cent; and in Pau Brasil, 52 per cent. Camaragibe (population 136,381) has a long history of left-leaning governments. During our fieldwork, Camaragibe's mayor was João Lemos of the Brazilian Community Party (PCdoB). Jaboatão dos Guararapes (population 630,008), has a prolonged history of clientelistic mayors as was known for public prosecutor's investigations into vote buying. In a marked turn, the electorate voted for Elias Gomes (2008-2012) of the Brazilian Social Democratic Party (PSDB) to lead a reformist centrist government. Pau Brasil (population 12,111) is primarily rural and agrarian; local politics is dominated by personalism rather than partisanship.
10. For more on focus group research see Denzin and Ryan (2007).
11. For more on the logic of quota samples, see Weisberg (2005).
12. Councils are comprised of representatives of civil society, 'users' of services or organisations representing them, social service organisations, and workers in the sector (MDS, 2005). Bolsa recipients would be one of multiple eligible 'users' of social assistance programmes eligible to participate in municipal councils.
13. Interestingly, participants also did not identify political patrons or politicians as helpful.
14. This figure is similar to results on community engagement in São Paulo in Avritzer (2009).
15. Programme knowledge is gendered because nearly all Bolsa Família cardholders are women. The male focus groups reported understanding that the programme was means tested but had less familiarity with specific conditionality requirements required to maintain benefits.
16. Joshi (2008) makes a similar case.
17. Notably, Marilee Grindle's study of municipal governance in Mexico draws a similar conclusion; while civil society in her research sites were poised to make demands for particularistic benefits, ongoing organising accountability almost always required impetus from town hall (2007, 140–141).

References

Abers, R. (2000). *Inventing local democracy: Grassroots politics in Brazil*. Boulder, CO: Lynne Rienner Publishers.
Almeida, A. C. (2008). Core values, education, and democracy: An empirical tour of Roberto Damatta's Brazil. In P. R. Kingstone & T. J. Power (Eds.), *Democratic Brazil revisited* (pp. 233–256). Pittburgh, PA: Pittsburgh University Press.
Alvarez, S. (1990). *Engendering democracy in Brazil*. Princeton, NJ: Princeton University Press.
Alvarez, S. (1999). Advocating feminism: The Latin American feminist NGO 'boom'. *International Feminist Journal of Politics*, *1*, 181–209. doi:10.1080/146167499359880
Arantes, R. B., Loureiro, M. R., Couto, C., & Teixeira, M. A. C. (2010). Controles democráticos sobre a administração pública no Brasil: Legislativo, tribunais de contas, Judiciário e Ministério Público. In M. R. Loureiro, F. L. Abrucio, & R. S. Pacheco (Eds.), *Burocracia e política no Brasil: Desafios para o estado democrático no século XXI* (pp. 109–147). Rio de Janeiro: Editora Fundação Getúlio Vargas.
Avritzer, L. (2009). *Participatory institutions in democratic Brazil*. Washington, DC, and Baltimore, MD: Woodrow Wilson Center Press.

Avritzer, L. (2010). Living under a democracy: Participation and its impact on the living conditions of the poor. *Latin American Research Review, 45*(S), 166–185. doi:10.1353/lar.2010.0044

Baiocchi, G. (2005). *Militants and citizens: The politics of participatory budgeting in Porto Alegre.* Palo Alto, CA: Stanford University Press.

Baiocchi, G., Heller, P., & Silva, M. (2011). *Bootstrapping democracy: Transforming local governance and civil society in Brazil.* Stanford, CA: Stanford University Press.

Barrientos, A. (2013). The rise of social assistance in Brazil. *Development and Change, 44*, 887–910. doi:10.1111/dech.2013.44. issue-4

Bennett, A. (2010). Process tracing and causal inference. In H. E. Brady & D. Collier (Eds.), *Rethinking social inquiry: Diverse tolls, shared standards* (pp. 207–219). Lanham, MD: Rowman and Littlefield.

Bichir, R. M. (2012, August 1–4). *Coordenação federal e implementação local no caso do Programa Bolsa Família.* Paper presented at the 8th Meeting of the Brazilian Political Science Association (Associação Brasileira de Ciência Política (ABCP), Gramado.

Brunetti, A., & Weder, B. (2003). A free press is bad news for corruption. *Journal of Public Economics, 87*, 1801–1824. doi:10.1016/S0047-2727(01)00186-4

Castro, H. C. O., Walter, M. I. M. T., Santana, C. M. B., & Stephanou, M. C. (2009). Percepções sobre o Programa Bolsa Família na sociedade brasileira. *Opinião Publica, 15*, 333–355. doi:10.1590/S0104-62762009000200003

Cohn, A. (1989). Caminhos da reforma sanitaria [Paths of Sanitary Reform]. *Lua Nova, 89*(19), 123–140. doi:10.1590/S0102-64451989000400009

Cornwall, A., & Shankland, A. (2008). Engaging citizens: Lessons from building Brazil's national health system. *Social Science & Medicine, 66*, 2173–2184. doi:10.1016/j.socscimed.2008.01.038

Costanzi, R. N., & Fagundes, F. (2010). Perfil dos beneficiários do Programa Bolsa Família [Profile of the Beneficiaries of the Bolsa Família Programme]. In J. Abrahão De Castro & L. Modesto (Eds.), *Bolsa Família 2003-2010: Avanços e Desafios* [Advances and Challenges], (Vol. *1*, pp. 249–269). Brasília: IPEA.

de Janvry, A., Finan, F., & Sadoulet, E. (2012). Local electoral incentives and decentralized program performance. *Review of Economics and Statistics, 94*, 672–685. doi:10.1162/REST_a_00182

Denzin, N. K., & Ryan, K. E. (2007). Qualitative methodology (Including focus groups). In W. Outhwaite & S. P. Turner (Eds.), *The SAGE handbook of social science methodology* (pp. 578–594). Los Angeles: Sage.

Encarnación, O. G. (2003). *The myth of civil society: Social capital and democratic consolidation in Spain and Brazil.* New York, NY: Palgrave Macmillan.

Fiszbein, A., & Schady, N. (2009). *Conditional cash transfers: Reducing present and future poverty. A World Bank policy research report.* Washington, DC: World Bank.

Fox, J., & Aranda, J. (1996). *Decentralization and rural development in Mexico: Community participation in Oaxaca's municipal funds programme (Monograph Series No. 42).* La Jolla, CA: Center for U.S.-Mexican Studies, University of California-San Diego.

Government of Brazil. (2011). Law Number 12.527, Brasília.

Grindle, M. (2007). *Going local: Decentralization, democratization, and the promise of good governance.* Princeton, NJ: Princeton University Press.

Hall, A. (2008). Brazil's Bolsa Família: A double-edged sword? *Development and Change, 39*, 799–822. doi:10.1111/j.1467-7660.2008.00506.x

Holston, J. (2014). "Come to the Street!": Urban protest, Brazil 2013. *Anthropological Quarterly, 87*, 887–900. doi:10.1353/anq.2014.0047

Hunter, W., & Power, T. (2007). Rewarding Lula: Executive power, social policy, and the Brazilian elections of 2006. *Latin American Politics & Society, 49*(1), 1–30. doi:10.1353/lap.2007.0005

Hunter, W., & Sugiyama, N. B. (2014). Transforming Subjects into Citizens: Insights from Brazil's Bolsa Família. *Perspectives on Politics, 12*, 829–845. doi:10.1017/S1537592714002151

Instituto Brasileiro de Geografia e Estatística (IBGE) (2000). Cidades Database, Brasília.

Joshi, A. (2008). Producing social accountability? The impact of service delivery reforms. *IDS Bulletin, 38*(6), 10–17. doi:10.1111/j.1759-5436.2007.tb00414.x

Kolstad, I., & Wiig, A. (2009). Is transparency the key to reducing corruption in resource-rich countries? *World Development, 37* (3), 521–532. doi:10.1016/j.worlddev.2008.07.002

Kopits, G. (2000, May). *Transparency in government operations.* Paper presented at Transparency and Development in Latin America and the Caribbean.

Lindert, K., Linder, A., Hobbs, J., & De La Brière, B. (2007). *The nuts and bolts of Brazil's Bolsa Família Program: Implementing conditional cash transfers in a decentralized context (Social Protection Discussion Paper No. 0709).* Washington, DC: World Bank.

Lindert, K., & Vincensini, V. (2010). *Social policy, perceptions and the press: An analysis of the media's treatment of conditional cash transfers in Brazil (Social Protection Discussion Paper no. 1008).* Washington, DC: World Bank.

McCubbins, M. D., & Schwartz, T. (1984). Congressional oversight overlooked: Police patrols versus fire alarms. *American Journal of Political Science, 28*, 165–179. doi:10.2307/2110792

Melo, M. A. (2008). Unexpected successes, unanticipated failures: Social policy from Cardoso to Lula. In P. R. Kingstone & T. J. Power (Eds.), *Democratic Brazil revisited.* Pittsburgh, PA: Pittsburgh University Press.

Ministério do Desenvolvimento Social e Combate à Fome (MDS). (2005). *Política Nacional de Assistência Social PNAS/2004* [National Social Assistance Policy PNAS/2004]. Brasília: Author.

Ministério do Desenvolvimento Social e Combate à Fome (MDS). (2010). *Programa Bolsa Família: Agenda da Família* (Bolsa Família Programme: Agenda for the Family). Brasília: Author.

Ministério do Desenvolvimento Social e Combate à Fome (MDS). (2011). *Caderno do IGD-M: Informativo sobre o índice de gestão descentralizada municipal do Programa Bolsa Família* [Notebook on the IGD-M: Information on the index for decentralised municipal governance of the Bolsa Famila Programme]. Brasília: Author.

Ministério do Desenvolvimento Social e Combate à Fome (MDS). (n.d.). *Controle social no Programa Bolsa Família* [Social control in the Bolsa Família Programme]. Brasília: Ministério do Desenvolvimento Social e Combate à Fome, Secertaria Nacional de Renda de Cidadania (SENARC).

Ministério do Desenvolvimento Social e Combate à Fome [Ministry of Social Development and Fight against Hunger]. (2006). *Bolsa Família: Agenda de Compromissos da Família [Bolsa Família: Agenda for Family Commitments]*. Brasília: Author.

Modesto, L. (2014). Entrevista: O papel da gestora na política pública: Revista de políticas públicas e gestão governamental. *Respvblica*, 86–97.

Narayan, D., Chambers, R., Shah, M. K., & Petesch, P. (2000). *Voices of the poor: Crying out for change*. New York, NY: Oxford University Press for the World Bank.

Olivieri, C. (2010). *A lógica política do controle interno - o monitoramento das políticas públicas no presidencialismo brasileiro*. São Paulo: Annablume.

Paoli, M. C., & Da Silva Telles, V. (1998). Social rights: Conflicts and negotiations in contemporary Brazil. In S. E. Alvarez, E. Dagnino, & A. Escobar (Eds.), *Cultures of politics politics of cultures: Re-visioning Latin American social movements* (pp. 64–92). Boulder, CO: Westview Press.

Peruzzotti, E., & Smulovitz, C. (2006). Social accountability: An introduction. In E. Peruzzotti & C. Smulovitz (Eds.), *Enforcing the rule of law: Social accountability in the new Latin American democracies*. Pittsburgh: University of Pittsburgh Press.

Pierson, P. (1993). Review: When effect becomes cause: Policy feedback and political change. *World Politics, 45*, 595–628. doi:10.2307/2950710

Putnam, R. (1993). *Making democracy work: Civic traditions in modern Italy*. Princeton, NJ: Princeton University Press.

Reinikka, R., & Svensson, J. (2005). Fighting corruption to improve schooling: Evidence from a newspaper campaign in Uganda. *Journal of the European Economic Association, 3*, 259–267. doi:10.1162/jeea.2005.3.issue-2-3

Rich, J., & Gómez, E. (2012). Centralizing decentralized governance in Brazil. *Publius: The Journal of Federalism, 42*, 636–661. doi:10.1093/publius/pjs002

Romero, S., & Neuman, W. (2013, June 21). Sweeping protests in Brazil pull in an array of grievances. *New York Times*. Retrieved from http://www.nytimes.com/2013/06/21/world/americas/brazil-protests.html?pagewanted=all

Samuels, D. (2000). Reinventing local government. In P. R. Kingstone & T. J. Power (Eds.), *Democratic Brazil* (pp. 77–98). Pittsburgh: University of Pittsburgh Press.

SEDESOL. (2013). Conoce Oportunidades' [Get to know Oportunidades]. Retrieved from http://www.oportunidades.gob.mx/Portal/wb/Web/oportunidades_a_human_development_program

Sen, A. (1999). *Development as freedom*. New York, NY: Knopf.

Skocpol, T. (1992). *Protecting soldiers and mothers: The political origins of social policy in the United States*. Cambridge, MA: Belknap Press.

Soares, F. V. (2011). Brazil's Bolsa Família: A review. *Economic and Political Weekly, 46*(21), 55–60.

Sugiyama, N. B., & Hunter, W. (2013). Whither Clientelism? Good governance and Brazil's *Bolsa Família* program. *Comparative Politics, 46*, 43–62. doi:10.5129/001041513807709365

Tendler, J. (1997). *Good government in the tropics*. Baltimore, MD: Johns Hopkins University Press.

Touchton, M., & Wampler, B. (2014). Improving social well-being through new democratic institutions. *Comparative Political Studies, 47*, 1442–1469. doi:10.1177/0010414013512601

Wampler, B. (2007). *Participatory budgeting in Brazil: Contestation, cooperation, and accountability*. University Park, PA: Penn State University Press.

Weisberg, H. F. (2005). *The total survey error approach*. Chicago: University of Chicago Press.

Weyland, K. (1996). *Democracy without equity*. University Park, PA: Penn State University Press.

Winters, M. S., & Weitz-Shapiro, R. (2013). Lacking information or condoning corruption: When do voters support corrupt politicians? *Comparative Politics, 45*, 418–436. doi:10.5129/001041513X13815259182857

World Bank. (2013). Anti-corruption and transparency. Retrieved from http://go.worldbank.org/D51GCA82B0

World Development Report. (2003). *Making services work for poor people*. Washington, DC: World Bank and University of Oxford.

Zucco, C. (2009). The president's 'new' constituency: Lula and the pragmatic vote in the 2006 presidential elections. *Journal of Latin American Studies, 40*, 29–49.

Zucco, C. (2013). When payouts pay off: Conditional cash transfers and voting behavior: 2003-2010. *American Journal of Political Science, 57*, 810–822.

Appendix

Focus Groups with Bolsa Beneficiaries

Camaragibe, Pernambuco. Women's Focus Group No. 1, 9 June 2009.
Camaragibe, Pernambuco. Women's Focus Group No. 2, 11 June 2009.
Camaragibe, Pernambuco. Men's Focus Group No. 1, 11 June 2009.
Camaragibe, Pernambuco. Men's Focus Group No. 2, 12 June 2009.
Jaboatão dos Guararapes, Pernambuco. Women's Focus Group No. 1, 13 June 2009.
Jaboatão dos Guararapes, Pernambuco. Women's Focus Group No. 2, 17 June 2009.
Jaboatão dos Guararapes, Pernambuco. Women's Focus Group No. 3, 25 June 2009.
Jaboatão dos Guararapes, Pernambuco. Women's Focus Group No. 4, 26 June 2009.
Pau Brasil, Bahia. Women's Focus Group No. 1, 8 June 2009.
Pau Brasil, Bahia. Women's Focus Group No. 2, 9 June 2009.
Pau Brasil, Bahia. Men's Focus Group No. 1, 8 June 2009.

Transforming Cash Transfers: Citizens' Perspectives on the Politics of Programme Implementation

NICOLA JONES*, BASSAM ABU-HAMAD**, PAOLA PEREZNIETO[†]
& KERRY SYLVESTER[‡]

*Overseas Development Institute, London, UK, **Department of Public Health, Al Quds University, Gaza City, State of Palestine, [†]Independent Consultant, Mexico City, Mexico, [‡]Associação de Nutrição e Segurança Alimentar, Maputo, Mozambique

ABSTRACT *After two decades of cash transfer programming, interest in programme governance and social accountability is growing. Analysts are increasingly realising the importance of issues of politics, power and citizen engagement in shaping programme effectiveness and sustainability. To contribute to a still nascent literature on the politics of programme implementation, this article explores the political economy factors shaping governance and social accountability processes in three established and relatively large-scale unconditional cash transfer programmes in conflict-affected contexts – Mozambique, Palestine and Yemen – drawing on beneficiary and citizen perception data from 2012. We conclude by emphasising the importance of context-specific understandings of demand-side factors.*

1. Introduction

After two decades of experience with cash transfers (CTs) in developing country contexts, there is growing interest in issues relating to programme governance and accountability. Whereas earlier debates focused primarily on issues of targeting and the strengths and weaknesses of programme conditionality (Barrientos, 2013; Fiszbein & Schady, 2009), there is now also an increasing realisation that issues of politics, power and accountability to citizens and to citizen–state relations are of critical importance (Hickey, 2010; Hickey & Mohan, 2008). A growing number of analysts and practitioners alike recognise that poverty and vulnerability are inherently political in nature – in terms of underlying drivers as well as preferred approaches to tackling entrenched poverty and marginalisation (Hickey & Bracking, 2005; Huber, Stephens, & Mustillo, 2008). Fiscal constraints are clearly significant in shaping the contours of national social protection systems, but so too are political attitudes concerning who 'deserves' support and in what form.

Within the emerging body of work on the political economy of social protection, there is a strong emphasis on the politics of adoption of social protection programmes – that is, analysis of the drivers of programme emergence in developing country contexts (UN Research Institute for Social Development [UNRISD], 2010), including in the context of economic crises and subsidy reforms. Research on the politics of implementation is more sparse; our knowledge base on the complex political economy factors shaping programme implementation in different contexts is much more limited.[1] To help address this knowledge gap, this article's overarching objective is to explore the political economy factors shaping programme roll-out in three established and relatively large-scale unconditional CT programmes in conflict-affected contexts (Mozambique, Palestine and Yemen), drawing on beneficiary and citizen perception data collected in 2012.

In order to understand changing power dynamics between the state and its citizens, political economists typically focus their analysis on the balance of power between institutions and incentive structures for different actors in a given policy arena. To situate our findings within this body of thought, we begin in Section 2 with a brief review of theoretical debates on the politics of social protection, especially in terms of social accountability and programme governance in the context of resource-constrained developing countries. Section 3 provides a brief overview of the qualitative research methodology underpinning our beneficiary and community perceptions study in Mozambique, Palestine and Yemen, and provides justification for our comparative case study approach.

Section 4 discusses our findings regarding the strengths and weaknesses of programme governance and accountability mechanisms in the three flagship CT programmes at the heart of our analysis – Mozambique's Basic Social Subsidy Programme (PSSB); the Palestinian National Cash Transfer Programme (PNCTP) and Yemen's Social Welfare Fund (SWF) – and the extent to which these programmes are engaging effectively with beneficiaries and the broader citizenry. We recognise that CT programmes constitute only one strand of broader national social welfare systems, but, given that such programmes (albeit in varying guises) have been in operation in our case study countries since the mid-1990s, this focus allows for a rich exploration of citizens' perceptions of the nature and quality of state–citizen interactions experienced in the context of CT programme implementation over time. Section 5 presents our conclusions and reflects on lessons for programme governance and account-ability in contexts where state-building and the state–citizen contract are nascent at best.

2. Engaging with Theoretical Debates

2.1. The Rise and Evolution of Social Accountability Approaches

Social accountability has emerged as a buzzword among development actors (Ringold, Holla, Koziol, & Srinivasan, 2012), despite there being 'no universally agreed definition of the range of actions that fall within its remit' (Bukenya, Hickey, & King, 2012, p. 10) or, perhaps more importantly, 'little appreciation of what *does not* constitute social accountability' (Joshi & Houtzager, 2012, p. 151). For the purposes of this article, we adopt McNeil and Malena's (2010) definition, which emphasises collaboration rather than confrontation: '"Social accountabil-ity" refers to the wide range of citizen and civil society organization (CSO) actions to hold the state to account, as well as actions on the part of government, media, and other societal actors that promote or facilitate these efforts' (p. 1). Whereas 'vertical mechanisms such as elections and horizontal mechanisms such as institutional checks and balances – have often failed to ensure an effective watch on the use of public authority' and have particularly tended to exclude the poor and other vulnerable populations (Joshi, 2007, p. 13), this more collaborative view of social accountability is in keeping with rights-based understandings of social protection, which empha-sise the potential for such programmes to contribute to a strengthened social contract between state and citizens (Sepulveda & Nyst, 2012). Moreover, because outcomes rather than processes are key to social accountability, it can focus on 'best fit' rather than 'best practice' (Bukenya et al., 2012; Tembo, 2013; Unsworth, 2010). This means it can use lenses that are culturally sensitive and attuned to local political dynamics as well as deploy a wide range of methods to achieve its objectives, including prospective information campaigns and budget analysis as well retrospective social audits and 'contentious actions' (Bukenya et al., 2012, p. 28; Joshi, 2007; Ringold et al., 2012).

This is not, however, to uni-directionally locate social accountability as a demand-led, bottom-up phenomenon. It must be balanced with supply-side space that allows for both collective action and the realisation of reform. Hickey and Mohan (2008) argue 'we need to take a long-term dynamic and mutually constitutive view of state and society interactions' (p.15) and explore how state institutions are organised and in turn influence who engages in collective action and around what types of issues. Joshi's rationale is that it would help shift our understanding of social accountability from a purely technical approach to one better rooted in 'a more politically, historically and sociologically attuned understanding of how change unfolds' (Bukenya et al., 2012). As Joshi and Houtzager (2012) conclude, conceptions of social accountability need to move beyond the 'widget' approach, which emphasises specific tools such as score cards and hotlines, to recognition of its more deeply politicised, iterative role as 'watchdog', in which 'the linkages that local collective actors [have] to national policy networks' are often key to success (p.158).

Reforms of existing programming and the establishment of new programming can offer important entry-points for shifting state–citizen interactions. Whether and how public programmes are designed to encourage social accountability – and whether they ultimately deliver on their design features – depends not only on the primary actors but also the power relations between and within them (Bukenya et al., 2012). Public officials, for example, have a key role to play in terms of delivering on accountability demands as well as 'pushing for accountability reforms and even stimulating social actors to mobilise to make demands on government' (Unsworth, 2010, p. 46). Civil society actors are also important, and must not only work with peer organisations to mobilise their constituents but also negotiate with state actors in highly political environments that value interconnectivity over autonomy and sometimes require them to simply get out of the way (Tembo, 2013).

Two overarching factors shape the relationships within and between these actors (Bukenya et al., 2012): the nature of inequality and exclusion and the character of state–society relations. The former has myriad potential impacts on social accountability. For example, traditionally excluded groups are often disenfranchised from even non-institutional mechanisms by lack of time and other resources, but at other times they create their own institutions (Ringold et al., 2012). Similarly, civil society itself is sometimes plagued by clientelism and rent-seeking (Bukenya et al., 2012), and at other times is seen as the solution to public service systems that are 'driven by the politics of patronage' (Hickey, 2010, p. 20). Tembo (2013) further notes that, where multiple players are engaged in social accountability, without clear guidance and oversight mechanisms, an environment of confusion can prevail. Unless citizens have a clear understanding of institutions and their potential role in exercising social accountability, the costs of implementation and sustainability can be high, and lack of harmonisation of programmes and funding may blur the lines of social accountability, principally between society and the state but also between the state and donors. It is therefore critical to understand how cross-agency collaboration and performance can be better incentivised in any given context.

2.2. Social Accountability and Social Protection Programming

In the social protection field, a focus on state–citizen interactions is often prominent as, if designed strategically, programmes may provide 'a space to transform the social relationships that generate and entrench the poverty and vulnerabilities they are addressing' (Jones & Samuels, 2013, p. 46). Indeed, in the case of Latin American conditional CT programmes, efforts to reshape state–citizen relationships have been explicit. Beneficiaries sign contracts of 'co-responsibility' whereby they, as citizens, commit to availing themselves of basic services aimed at poverty reduction and human capital formation (including education, health and nutrition services and birth registration); the state in turn commits to ensuring adequate provision of these services (Fiszbein et al., 2009).

Although social contracts – 'the set of mutual rights and obligations binding citizens with their polity' (Flanagan et al., 1999, p. 135) – are likely to be attributed to more democratic forms of governance (Di John & Putzel, 2009), 'different forms of social contract will emerge in different contexts' (Bukenya et al., 2012, p. 50). Increasingly, social protection programmes are trying to take such diversity into account and embed a variety of approaches in design that encourage citizens to interact with services, providers and policy-makers. Such approaches also help beneficiaries hold programmes and governments accountable by strengthening community bonds, which can result in a more forceful collective voice, and by building the bridges that can link beneficiaries to the power structures that design and run programmes (Narayan & Pritchett, 1999; Ringold et al., 2012).

This said, despite growing interest in the potential of social protection programming to strengthen state legitimacy, and state-building and citizenship in conflict-affected and post-conflict contexts, the evidence base to date is relatively limited (Carpenter, Slater, & Mallett, 2012). Osofian (2011), for instance, finds that, while there is evidence the Hunger Safety Net Programme in northern Kenya, which included a grievance mechanism and a rights education component, has helped communities hold local government to account, Sierra Leone's Social Safety Net Programme, which was subject to elite capture, exacerbated rather than improved citizens' negative perceptions of the state. Merely receiving services from the state does not mean people feel they are citizens of the state; how the state treats them is a critical factor, 'as even if services are of high quality people can still be alienated by treatment without dignity' (Eyben & Ladbury, 2006, as cited in Carpenter et al., 2012, p. 73).

3. Research Methodology and Country Case Selection

3.1. Research Methodology

Our analysis is based on qualitative and participatory research undertaken in three case study countries – Mozambique, Palestine (both the Gaza Strip and the West Bank) and Yemen – by the Overseas Development Institute (ODI) in partnership with national teams in 2012–2013. While the aim of the primary research was broader than the focus on programme governance and accountability discussed here, all case studies explored linkages between unconditional CTs and beneficiary and citizen perceptions of programme governance and accountability as they affected their own experiences, community dynamics and broader programme efficacy. Research ethics approval processes were adhered to both nationally and internationally as appropriate.[2]

All three studies employed a range of qualitative and participatory instruments, including community mappings; focus group discussions (FGDs) and individual interviews with benefici-aries and non-beneficiaries; key informant interviews (KIIs) at national and sub-national levels; and observational case studies of the programme beneficiary–implementer interface (Table 1). National-level training workshops were held in each country to adapt the research instruments to local context realities and to familiarise the teams with the research conceptual framework, research questions and data collection instruments. The instruments were piloted with local communities and further refined. Sample size was determined by a combination of resource parameters, the importance of triangulating findings across diverse informants using different research tools and the principle of research saturation – that is, reaching a point where additional interviews were garnering no new insights. After obtaining informed consent from research participants, interviews were recorded and subsequently transcribed and translated. The analysis

Table 1. Qualitative research instruments in case study country sites

Instrument	Mozambique		West Bank		Gaza		Yemen	
	Chokwe	Chibuto	Hebron	Jenin	Beit Lahia	Rafah	Hodeidah	Taiz
KIIs (district/community/national level)	19		32		18		16	
FGDs	9		13		12		8	
In-depth interviews	22		23		23		14	
Life histories	13		4		4		9	
Case studies	7		4		4		2	
Community, vulnerability and coping strategies mapping	2		2		2		2	
Institutional mapping and historical timeline	2		2		2		2	
Structured observations (# of observations)	6		6		6		5	

was thematically based, using a common thematic matrix, but with scope for country-specific sub-themes to emerge.

3.2. Country Case Study Selection

We adopted a comparative case study approach (Ragin & Becker, 1992; Yin, 2014), with country-level reports for all three of the unconditional CT case studies serving as the key source of information for this article (Bagash et al., 2012; Abu Hamad & Pavanello, 2012; Jones & Shaheen, 2012; Selvester, Fidalgo, & Tambo, 2012). Our starting point was that, whereas individual case studies can illuminate local complexities, a comparative case study approach can help construct more general understandings which go beyond findings from an individual research site (Yin, 2014) and shed light on why particular programmes or components work or fail to work. Here, we were interested in exploring three different conflict-affected contexts as a means to examine the opportunities for and challenges involved in strengthening state–citizen relations in the context of CT programme implementation.

More specifically, our country case selection rationale was as follows: all three countries have had histories of violent civil conflict and are engaged in nascent state-building endeavours; face high levels of poverty and vulnerability; and have long-established social assistance programmes, including unconditional CTs, which have all undergone and/or are undergoing extensive reforms.

These similarities notwithstanding, the three cases are located across a broad spectrum of political institutional settings. Mozambique enjoys the longest distance from a conflict-affected past but national politics remain highly centralised and elite-dominated. Palestine, and especially Gaza, continues to suffer from punctuated conflicts and ongoing occupation, and thus faces truncated state-building and citizenship options. Yemen has the most fragile governance context of the three, suffering very high levels of insecurity and regional fragmentation, to the extent that normal state functioning in at least parts of the country is precluded.

Taking this discussion further, Table 2 first provides an overview of general political economy factors for each case study country. Drawing on Bukenya et al.'s (2012) two-pronged approach to understanding opportunities and entry-points for strengthening social accountability processes and outcomes, it includes i) the nature of inequality and exclusion and ii) the character of state–society relations. It follows this with a brief overview of the social protection sector more specifically, including the extent to which and how social protection is embedded in legal and policy frameworks, the nature of policy spaces for social protection decision-making, fiscal space for social protection and the monitoring and evaluation culture within the social protection 'sector'.

As Table 2 shows, in terms of inequality and exclusion, the three cases vary somewhat. While the Palestinian Authority (PA) and more recently Hamas in Gaza have managed to maintain comparatively strong human development indicators relative to the country's income level, as well as a relatively low level of inequality (measured by the Gini co-efficient) in part due to longer-term investments in social assistance (World Bank, 2011), both Mozambique and Yemen continue to suffer very high levels of human under-development and regional inequalities. As we discuss in more depth below, the latter pose significant challenges to the inclusive uptake of social accountability spaces and processes.

In terms of the character of state–society relations in the three countries, again we see considerable diversity. There are growing efforts to deepen democracy in Mozambique but elite-dominated politics and the absence of a vibrant opposition mean understandings and practices of citizenship remain incipient. In Yemen, persistent fragility and civil violence is resulting in eroding levels of trust in state institutions, although where programmes such as the Social Development Fund are seen to be working the building blocks of more solid state–citizen relations appear to be in place, at least in parts of the country. In Palestine, citizen satisfaction with national leaders is low, but there is nevertheless a relatively strong rights-based culture, whereby citizens are willing and accustomed to speaking out against injustice. PA leaders are in turn relatively responsive to citizen demands, not least because of the regional volatility following the Arab Spring.

These broader political economy dynamics in turn shape social protection programme design and implementation outcomes. As mentioned above, all three countries have well-established social

Table 2. Overview of political economy dynamics in the three case study countries

	Mozambique	Palestine	Yemen
Nature of inequality and exclusion			
Human development	Very low but improving human development indicators. Relatively high Gini co-efficient (45.7).	Relatively strong human development record of PA; Hamas also service-oriented but stagnating and even declining human development indicators in case of Gaza owing to on-going blockade. Relatively low Gini co-efficient (35.5).	Poor human development indicators, especially malnutrition and high food insecurity. Reasonably low Gini co-efficient (37.7).
Economic context	Least developed country status. High levels of extreme poverty and vulnerability, with high levels of regional inequality. Food, fuel and financial crisis resulted in violent uprisings. Growing liberalisation/privatisation of economy.	Lower-middle-income. Artificially truncated economy and labour market. Economic crisis from mid-2007s in Gaza owing to political division and international blockade. Very high reliance on social assistance in Gaza; much lower in West Bank.	Lower-middle-income. Poorest country in Middle East. Significant problems with international capital flight.
Nature of state–society relations			
Political history	Multi-party elections and post-conflict state-building since 1994 but 15 years on from the Peace Accord political discourse is still marked by hostility and mistrust between Frelimo (victorious in all three elections so far) and Renamo, the major opposition party. Mutual suspicion has reduced opportunity for consensus and collaboration, including on reducing extreme poverty and regional disparities exacerbated by the war	Politics as occupation and periodic conflicts. Divided territories and government with growing divide between West Bank and Gaza following withdrawal of Israel from Gaza in 2007 and on-going international blockade.	Politics of fragility – transition in 2011 averted civil war by removing president but not elites from power and provided framework for longer-term political and economic reforms. However, an evaluation of the Social Development Fund, which provides funding for a broad range of social development projects such as education, health and road building, concluded 'it is contributing to the promotion of solid systems of governance that underscore state building.' (Jennings, 2006, p. 6)

(*continued*)

Table 2. (*Continued*)

	Mozambique	Palestine	Yemen
Social contract	Incipient citizenship; 'choiceless democracy' (Mwandawire, 1999); elite-dominated politics with only limited power-sharing. Deepening democratisation and wider concern for promoting citizens' rights, however, are compromised by political bi-polarity, weakness of opposition and non-state voices and continuing centralised state control over policy decisions and resource allocation.	Strong critique of national governance structures for failing to resolve the broader political crisis – Israeli occupation and internal division among Palestinian territories. However, partly because of relatively high levels of education, a strong local civil society and high levels of engagement by international non-governmental organisations (INGOs) and UN agencies, especially the UN Relief and Works Agency (UNRWA), there is a strong discourse of rights and speaking out against injustice. Because of fragility, the national authorities are also very conscious of being seen to respond to citizen demands.	Gallop poll data show low and eroding levels of trust in state institutions. There is uncertainty about whether the current transition is allowing for greater political access or preserving elite interests.
Role of donors	Heavily donor-dependent as one of poorest countries globally. 2012: ODA provided 14% of gross domestic product (GDP).[a]	Heavily aid-dependent in part because of Israeli blockade following second Intifada and dramatic decline in PA tax base. 2012: ODA provided 16.5% of GDP.	Strong donor presence, but more focused on counter-terrorism than development. 2012: ODA provided 2.3% of GDP.

(*continued*)

Table 2. (*Continued*)

	Mozambique	Palestine	Yemen
Social protection context			
National commitment to social protection	Policy commitment to social protection enshrined in National Strategy for Basic Social Security (April 2010), Regulation for Basic Social Security (December 2009) and Social Protection Law (April 2007). Social assistance seen as part of belated peace dividend; also vital in wake of removal of unsustainable subsidy and rationing programmes following the end of conflict in the 1990s. High level of donor dependence to finance social protection and limited buy-in/resistance from Ministry of Finance. DFID and government of the Netherlands support accounts for 30% of the costs of PSSB.	Concept of social security enjoys a strong foundation within the 2003 Palestinian Basic Law; Articles 22 and 25 emphasise rights to social insurance and social security. Protection from extreme poverty is key source of PA legitimacy – especially as the PA is prevented from fulfilling other 'state' roles because of Israeli occupation. High level of donor dependence to finance social protection, but increasing use of PA budget to cover costs of the CT programme.	SWF originally conceived of through the SWF Law in 1996 as a way to compensate the poor for the removal of subsidies. Relatively low level of national commitment to social protection; strongly championed by donors. High level of donor dependency for spending on social protection.
Policy spaces	Council of ministers. Donor–government–civil society working group meetings/ working group on social action. Cross-sectoral poverty reduction planning.	Cabinet meetings. National Tripartite Social Security Committee under the Palestinian Prime Minister (from 2012). Donor–government sector working group meetings .	National Dialogue designed to resolve political crisis of 2011 – but tensions with entrenched networks of patronage.

Notes: [a] See http://data.worldbank.org/indicator/DT.ODA.ODAT.GN.ZS

assistance programmes, and all three have undergone recent reform processes to strengthen CT programme effectiveness. In Mozambique and Palestine, national leaders actively champion social protection. Mozambique promotes it as a peace dividend: unlike many social assistance programmes in Sub-Saharan Africa, PSSB is already being implemented at scale, with the aim of reaching 90 per cent of all eligible beneficiaries across the country by 2014 (Selvester et al., 2012). Similarly, social protection is viewed as a core part of the PA's mandate, given that many other 'typical' state functions are circumscribed on account of the Israeli occupation. However, both countries are heavily reliant on donor funding to realise these broader commitments.

In Yemen, by contrast, the social protection agenda seems strongly donor-driven: overall reliance on official development assistance (ODA) is relatively low but that used for social protection funding is high. The prominent role of donors therefore complicates lines of accountability somewhat, as we discuss further below.

Within the general political economy context parameters described above, it is critical to underscore that social protection policy and programming developments are not static; it is also therefore important to identify potential agents or forces of change. While civil society is relatively active in both Mozambique and Palestine, coordination challenges, funding constraints and limited scale have meant civil society actors have not been a major force in shaping social protection debates and outcomes (Jones & Samuels, 2013). In Yemen, heightened insecurity means the aforementioned challenges are even greater, including for civil society, which has not had an active voice in social protection debates (Bagash et al., 2012). Instead, geopolitics and donor interests – both in general and vis-à-vis social protection – have played a significant role in recent years. In Palestine, donor funding (primarily from the European Union [EU] and the World Bank) accounts for approximately 50 per cent of the PNCTP budget. This commitment is motivated in large part by the realisation that, without a political settlement with Israel, labour market and mobility constraints cannot be solved and social assistance is essential for large segments of the population, especially in Gaza, where the lack of economic opportunities is extreme. In Yemen, donor support is motivated by, on the one hand, grave concerns about on-going political instability and risks of renewed conflict and, on the other, recognition of the importance of strengthening state legitimacy and state institutions if a sustained peace is to be achieved (Bagash et al., 2012).

4. Citizens' Perceptions of Programme Governance and Accountability: Case Study Findings

We now turn to a discussion of the extent to which social accountability approaches are embedded within the three flagship unconditional CT. Table 3 maps programme details for ease of reference; space constraints mean details on the specific sites in each country can be found in the underlying country reports (Bagash et al., 2012; Abu Hamad & Pavanello, 2012; Jones & Shaheen, 2012; Selvester et al., 2012). In light of Joshi's definition of social accountability guiding our analysis, which emphasises the range of citizen and CSO actions to hold states accountable, as well as government, media and other actors' efforts to encourage such efforts, we focus our discussion on i) communication about the programme by the state and implementers to beneficiaries and the broader public; ii) uptake and quality of spaces for interaction and feedback embedded within the programme; and iii) accessibility, transparency and efficacy of grievance mechanisms. Given the contested nature of social protection, poverty and vulnerability across contexts, however, we begin by looking at needs interpretation and citizens' perceptions of the way CT programmes identify and interpret their needs through programme targeting modalities.

4.1. Citizens' Perceptions of Needs Interpretation and the Role of Social Protection More Broadly

While there is increasing emphasis in international development circles on rights-based approaches to social protection, as highlighted by the International Labour Organization's Social Floor Initiative, the extent to which such an approach has been embraced and operationalised in diverse developing

Table 3. Overview of social transfer programmes in case study countries

	Occupied Palestinian Territories		Yemen	Mozambique
	West Bank	Gaza		
Name, start date	PNCTP; 2010 in West Bank; 2011 in Gaza (although amalgamation of earlier cash transfer programmes funded by EU, World Bank and PA dating from mid-1990s)		SWF; 1996	PSSB; 1992
Transfer amount, frequency	NIS750–1800 ($195–468)		Maximum monthly benefit of YER4,000 ($20) for family of 6 people	MZN130 (approximately $4.5) to MZN380 ($13); increments of MZN50 ($1.8) for each dependant
Target group	Focus on **extremely poor households**; consideration also given to female-headed households, people with disabilities, people with chronic illnesses and older people		Original targeting focused on **vulnerable groups** but since 2008 includes all people living below the poverty line, using proxy means test (PMT), with a plan to gradually phase out those who meet vulnerability targeting but not PMT targeting	Permanently **labour-constrained households** that are extremely poor
Reach	Approximately 120,000 households	Approximately 48,000 families.	Approximately 1,500,000 beneficiaries	261,519 beneficiaries as of 2012, of whom 13,125 were households with people with disabilities

country contexts is more limited. Silva et al.'s (2012) regional review of social protection systems in the Middle East and North African (MENA) region highlighted, for example, that, historically, MENA countries have relied on universal subsidies of basic consumer goods and targeted assistance to specific vulnerable groups (orphans, widows, the disabled), but they are gradually transitioning to a greater emphasis on poverty-targeted social assistance. This has been influenced in part by the post-Arab Spring climate, with strong pressures to create a new social contract between the state and citizenry that is more inclusive while at the same time ensuring redistribution systems are fiscally sustainable.

Such shifts, however, represent macro-level trends rather than necessarily resonating with local community perceptions about programme needs interpretation processes. In the case of Gaza and the West Bank, our study found considerable citizen distrust about the new emphasis on poverty targeting and complaints of 'injustice' and 'unfairness' because of a focus on assets rather than disposable income. The former may have been acquired long ago when labour market opportunities were less challenging, or through relatives. There were also concerns that, by focusing on material poverty rather than citizen entitlements, attention was being displaced from the broader structural and political vulnerabilities facing the Palestinian population. As one young male refugee beneficiary in Rafah, Gaza explained, *'PNCTP is a compensation for the Palestinian people, because they have been uprooted and displaced.'*

In Yemen, respondents in smaller, tighter-knit rural communities perceived the programme targeting process to be fair as it relied on the oversight of traditional community leaders, who are *'best placed to make accurate decisions about their communities'*. By contrast, in larger urban sites the move to poverty-based targeting was widely criticised, as it was applied inconsistently, including to non-deserving party supporters, and largely excluded young people, who it saw as better able to generate an income despite very high rates of youth unemployment. As one 40-year-old non-beneficiary said: *'I was not selected because I am not politically oriented and not a member of any party.'*

In Mozambique, PSSB has strong indigenous roots and, as mentioned above, was not donor-driven but rather has been operating at scale for several decades as part of the ruling party's socialist ethos on the one hand and a desire on the other to shore up political support when its popular subsidy programme had to be discontinued in the late 1990s. PSSB too has recently moved away from a categorical to a poverty-based targeting approach, but, because of limited community awareness of programme mechanics and targeting approaches, respondents had little to say about programme needs interpretation, and were merely waiting to see if they would be selected. Those who were included did not view the PSSB as their right but rather as a 'gift' from the state or God, indicating that notions of citizenship central to social accountability processes will require active fostering and support over time.

4.2. Programme Communication and Information Provision

Social transfer programmes implemented in resource-poor settings often have complex institutional arrangements, including multi-layered targeting and payment procedures that change over time, and are implemented by a wide range of actors (paid and unpaid). Few of these programmes invest in strategic communication approaches to beneficiaries and wider communities, given resource and capacity constraints. However, the web of relationships, rules and procedures involved mean there is ample opportunity for miscommunication – both deliberate and through happenstance. This is especially so in the case of reforms, which all three case study programmes have undergone in recent years.

In Mozambique's PSSB, there were several key areas of divergence between official definitions and community perceptions of potential eligible households, stemming from inadequate information outreach to communities. Officially, the programme targets extremely poor households where all members are permanently labour-constrained, defined as households with women over 55 years and men over 60 years, children below 18 years, people living with severe physical or mental disability or people with chronic illness that renders them unable to work. Our research, however, found that, because PSSB was originally seen as a grant for older indigent people, communities continued to make this assumption; indeed, disabled people who received the transfer reported feeling they were not entitled to the money.

Another key misunderstanding was that the transfer targets individuals rather than households; this results in low uptake of additional money for carers and dependants, as well as mistrust of the system in cases where the transfer is suspended owing to changes in the status of household members that affect their entitlement (such as when a child turns 18 or a member of the family marries an able-bodied adult).

Part of the problem is that there are no written materials clearly explaining the application procedures for potential beneficiaries, including rules and regulations and grievance procedures that could be used during community group meetings and household visits. Although potential benefici-aries may not be able to read official materials, the availability of written materials can safeguard against inaccurate messages. In all communities there are mediation forums that can be used to clarify the rights of beneficiary households, but these are in practice hampered by limited access to informa-tion as well as limited demand from beneficiaries.

Inadequate communication and information dissemination about programme entitlements emerged as a major source of citizen concern in Palestine also. Major reforms of PNCTP in 2010, involving a shift from categorical to poverty-based targeting using a PMT formula (PTMF), were inadequately communicated to key stakeholders, including beneficiaries. As one widow in a FGD in Aroub refugee camp in the West Bank complained, *'Correct information is the people's treasure, but we rarely get it.'* Similarly, a beneficiary woman in Jenin equated the PMTF with *'the secret Coca-Cola formula'.* Moreover, while there were efforts to broadcast information about the changes and registration process through Palestinian National TV, staff from the Ministry of Social Affairs (MoSA), the implementing agency, were inadequately prepared to manage the process. As highlighted through interviews with MoSA staff at governorate level during our research, they still have an incomplete understanding of the details of and rationale behind the PMTF approach, which means they are unable to communicate the reasons for the reforms to either beneficiaries or non-beneficiaries.

As a result, FGDs and individual interviews highlighted multiple concerns relating to indicators, transparency and the formula itself, and expressed a high level of discontent with MoSA. As a middle-aged male non-beneficiary in Beit Lahia, Gaza, angrily noted, *'What really matters when they* [referring to MoSA] *select someone is the colour of the shirt one wears* [referring to green for Hamas and yellow for Fatah supporters].' In the West Bank there were fewer complaints along party lines, but there were similarly high levels of discontent on account of inadequate communication by programme implementers. As one Bedouin woman beneficiary from Anata, Jerusalem, noted, *'Even if we were hanging by a rope they would not help us! They don't tell us anything* [about other services and entitlements] *– only from each other and our neighbours do we learn about our rights.'*

Experiences with Yemen's SWF were not dissimilar. District offices manage SWF daily operations, including registration of potential new beneficiaries. Yet our findings indicate that not only do staff in these offices lack authority to make decisions on beneficiary selection, but also the community leaders who do have more decision-making authority frequently suffer from limited information about important programme details and linkages to other social protection interventions. These information deficits effectively constrain the accountability of implementing agencies and national government to citizens, and are in turn compounded by citizens' lack of information about how the programme operates or its selection criteria. As one female beneficiary from Zabid noted, *'They say it is from the government for the poor people and those who have limited income* [...] *All those who receive it deserve it as they are jobless and poor.'* Accordingly, there is limited capacity to demand accountability from local authorities, particularly as there is a concern among beneficiaries that they might be sanctioned or taken off the list of beneficiaries if they complain, especially in Taiz, an urban and more politicised district.

4.3. Feedback Channels and Spaces for Interaction

In the face of the complex programme implementing environments discussed above, institutionalising regular information provision and feedback channels is an important part of working towards and strengthening the social contract between the state and its citizens. On the supply side, messages about social transfer programmes need to be standardised across all actors; key features of the system need to be explained, in written form and orally. On the demand side, it is important to have spaces for interaction and feedback among beneficiaries, and between beneficiaries and programme implementers. Institutionalised spaces ensure problems or concerns are detected quickly and help providers gauge community responses to reforms or new features.

In Mozambique, community meetings are the most frequently used medium of communication within PSSB, given high levels of illiteracy. When well facilitated and there is space for women to meet separately, respondents noted that they did avail themselves of such opportunities. There is also provisioning for follow-up dialogues with individual beneficiaries using community liaison agents selected by the community to act as brokers between them and the implementing agency, the National Institute of Social Action (INAS). These agents are, in theory, accountable to both the community and INAS; the community can request replacement of the agent if they are not satisfied, and INAS can remove the agent if he or she is judged not to be performing satisfactorily. However, this role is not without problems, given the lack of formal training and the fact that, particularly in rural areas, the person most often selected by the community is also the government's official representative in the area – a voluntary post that inevitably wields considerable local power. The lack of an independent liaison agent and effective checks and balances on power therefore hampers transparency and opportunities to exercise social accountability.

More recently, a Civil Society Platform has been established to provide a forum for civil society actors to voice their ideas and concerns about social protection policies and programming. However, the reach of this participatory monitoring system has to date been limited to a small pilot. Although funding has been secured to expand the approach in a second phase, key informants were of the view that there was little likelihood of countrywide coverage, given cost constraints, unless evidence of clear and significant impact can be documented.

Opportunities for information exchange and feedback between citizens and programme implementers are significantly more constrained in the Palestinian context. The only opportunity for interaction among beneficiaries is on payment days at the banks. In some cases, bank queues provide opportunities for information exchange and networking; in other cases, they give rise to tensions (because of long waiting times) or no interaction at all (that is, some people collect their money without engaging with others). As bank staff are responsible for disbursing payments, the delivery mechanism does not provide an opportunity for beneficiaries to interact directly with programme staff. Instead, since the 2010 programme reforms, the primary interaction between social workers and beneficiaries (or unsuccessful applicants) takes place during short (15–30 minute) home visits when social workers come to assess whether the household is still eligible according to the PMTF poverty criteria. A middle-aged woman beneficiary from Jenin camp noted for instance during the research process that, *'This is the first time that anyone listened to us deeply and in detail. We really appreciate this opportunity.'*

In the West Bank, social workers and beneficiaries alike emphasised there was seldom time to discuss broader vulnerabilities and needs, unless the situation was already very serious (for example child custody contestations or cases of serious child abuse). As a female FGD participant in the Aroub camp, near Hebron, emphasised. *'MoSA officials should come and see themselves and listen to us about our views on the programme.'* Social workers have been effectively removed from the selection process as eligibility is now determined by the PMTF alone, rather than taking into account information obtained during social workers' home visits, to assess the situation of the household as a whole. While this has helped reduce the potential for clientelistic relationships between social workers and beneficiaries, it has also reduced social workers' sense of professional ownership and buy-in. As one social worker from Jenin governorate in the West Bank noted, *'I feel guilty and powerless – I cannot explain why some people are excluded or included. So I can listen to people's problems but I can't really do much. I just gather information but don't have a role in decision-making. It is a very frustrating working environment.'* In other words, despite the existence of a cadre of trained social workers, the very high caseload and the time-consuming nature of the PMT poverty targeting approach mean there is also very little space for social workers to play a more meaningful bridging role between beneficiaries and programme implementers at the governorate level, and even less so at the national level. Given the complexity of the PMTF, social workers reported feeling they had essentially become data collectors, with the bulk of their work now centred on filling out forms rather than providing the specialist psychosocial support they have been trained to do. In the words of one social worker, *'We feel as if we are machines.'*

In Gaza, information flows are weaker still. This is perhaps not surprising, given the strained relationship between MoSA Ramallah and MoSA Gaza (stemming from the political division between the two territories in 2006/07), and the fact that it remains challenging to establish information flows and coordination mechanisms between the two agencies. There is no channel beneficiaries can use to convey their needs and interests to higher decision-making levels, which is reportedly resulting in high levels of stress, frustration and suspicion between beneficiaries and implementers. Many beneficiaries, however, emphasised that they would be eager to have opportunities to come together to express their views about the programme and how it could be improved, as well as to socialise and find support among other beneficiaries. Indeed, when asked about which services they would like to see complementing PNCTP, many of these women said they would value a space where they could meet and openly discuss problems and solutions.

We meet each other only at MoSA, UNRWA and the bank. When we meet we talk about our concerns and situation, but there are no places where we can raise our voices and speak up. It would be great if these places existed. But in these places the people we speak to should also be in a position to help us. They should be people in charge and who can decide and can provide us with the things we really need. (female beneficiary, 45 years old, Rafah, Gaza)

Efforts to institutionalise effective links with community stakeholders in programme governance have also proved challenging, but for different reasons. In the West Bank, social workers are expected to collaborate with local social protection committees to identify potential beneficiaries and screen those who are eligible. However, in practice, instead of holding regular meetings with a full committee, in governorates where the committees are functioning social workers most often call on individual members as an information resource to discuss particular cases. Moreover, social workers did recognise that clientelistic practices, or *wasta*, remain a problem in some instances. Some beneficiaries echoed this viewpoint: *'The protection committee is a big lie. They support those with whom they have interests. I went to them and asked for help but they said nowadays there is no financial assistance. I shouted and said, "You are not fair", but they told me to shut up'* (female beneficiary, 38 years old, Jenin camp, West Bank).

In Gaza, regional social protection committees have not been established, thus household eligibility is determined solely through the PMTF, which is centralised in Ramallah. There are very limited, if any, possibilities for further investigation when an applicant is deemed ineligible. While there is supposed to be a suggestion box in each MoSA office, only a handful of beneficiaries said they had seen them, and, during a structured observation in the MoSA office in Rafah, no complaint box was seen. Among those who said they had seen complaint boxes, some noted they were placed more *'for decoration'* than for collecting and meaningfully acting on beneficiaries' feedback.

In Yemen, formal spaces for information exchange and feedback are similarly weak, and beneficiaries and non-beneficiaries complained about this dearth of spaces. As in Palestine, there are some informal exchanges among beneficiaries on payment day while queuing at the post office to receive the transfer. Generally, though, beneficiaries emphasised that they were not vocal about their concerns or the lack of spaces to express them, as they feared being taken out of the programme. However, some informal approaches are being adopted to fill this gap. Beneficiaries emphasised the important role played in information provision by local community leaders, who were deemed to *'know more about us'* than outsiders, especially in Zabid, where local leaders enjoy considerable legitimacy:

I had not been a leader […] a representatives of SWF came and started talking with other leaders about the need for assistance in their survey to select poor people […] After that the head of the local council addressed me, saying in front of everyone that, "From today onwards, you are one of the leaders." Ever since, I have been assisting many families and guiding them to join SWF. Some of them had never heard about it or dreamt about being a beneficiary. Recently, even the security office asked me to handle some conflicts between people on property, divorce and so on [...] Although working with the poor is so tough in our area given their very large numbers, the feeling of respect by the poor and community members means a lot to me and has been motivating me to keep working with them. (male community leader, Zabid)

4.4. Grievance Channels

In addition to information dissemination and feedback loops, grievance channels provide a third critical mechanism through which citizens can engage in programme governance and accountability processes. Among our case studies we found stark differences in citizen perceptions vis-à-vis the accessibility, transparency and effectiveness of programme grievance mechanisms. In Palestine, programme beneficiaries typically saw their involvement in PNCTP as their right rather than as a gift or charity – especially in Jenin, in the West Bank, where there is a strong rights-based culture fostered by a substantial NGO presence, as these quotes highlight:

This is better than a hand-out. It is my right. (older female beneficiary, Hebron)

You [talking to a bank official] *must pay me this until I'm dead. This is my right. You do not pay it from your pockets.* (older female beneficiary, Jenin, West Bank)

Complaints about PNCTP can be either communicated in writing and posted in local district office complaints boxes or made verbally to social workers or NGOs who in turn record and communicate them to the Ramallah-based Complaints Unit within MoSA. Nevertheless, respondents were relatively negative about the value of utilising grievance and complaints channels, and expressed low levels of confidence in the system, especially in Gaza, where there is a concern that social workers may intercept and manipulate information presented through grievances:

Our complaints are communicated to social workers. We complain, but nothing happens [...] There are no benefits from these complaints. We don't know if our complaints reach the director or the ministry. (middle-aged female, Jenin camp, West Bank)

How can one raise a complaint against the judge? (male, middle-aged ex-beneficiary, Beit Lahia, Gaza)

In addition, the complaints data management system remains uncomputerised, further hindering staff capacity to respond to citizens in a timely and systematic manner. The head of the Complaints Unit (CU) in Ramallah estimated they were able to address just 40–50 per cent of complaints made, given resource and capacity constraints. Nonetheless, CU staff do seem to approach their role from a strong citizens' rights perspective, suggesting that, if technological shortcomings can be addressed, they could play a more proactive role in future:

Our role is not only responding to people's complaints but we find ourselves as advocates for their rights and this is not always positively received by some managers of the different programmes. (Complaints Unit head, Ramallah, West Bank)

In the case of Yemen, SWF officials said they were open to receiving complaints from beneficiaries but there is no official grievance system, and respondents were generally reluctant to complain for fear of being withdrawn from the programme as reporting is not anonymous.

There was political intervention in the past, but after the involvement of the social workers in the process this did not occur so much. But in rural areas there is still a kind of political intervening. (male informal community leader, Zabid)

There were reports, however, of informal action being undertaken to address grievances, suggesting that at least some beneficiaries have a stronger perception of the cash transfer as a right rather than as a gift. One case where pressure brought to bear by beneficiaries was reported to have led to change was in Zabid. Here, following prolonged community and beneficiary complaints about poor treatment during cash distribution at the local post office (where some workers were charging 'commission' to make the payment), the manager of the post office was replaced in an effort to minimise abuse of the system.

Citizen perceptions about grievance channels in Mozambique contrasted sharply with those in the Middle Eastern case studies. Here, the main constraint does not appear to be the design of the PSSB grievance system itself, but rather people's lack of understanding of the underlying principles of social transfer programmes. In theory at least, as discussed in Section 2, social transfer programmes are based on an agreement on the rights and responsibilities of the participating entities – a social contract between the state and citizens, including vis-à-vis the right of vulnerable citizens to receive an appropriate social transfer on a regular basis. In Mozambique, our findings indicated people had no sense of entitlement to the PSSB transfer, and, because they viewed the money as a gift provided by a benevolent state, they felt they should not complain, as to do so would be ungrateful. As one female beneficiary in Chokwe noted, *'Why would I question the type of present I am given?'*

5. Conclusions

Overall, our findings underscore the importance of enhancing our collective understanding of the politics of programme implementation if social protection policy frameworks and programming are to respond better to citizen experiences of poverty, vulnerability and social exclusion and to achieve sustainable changes in beneficiary lives. Our case studies revealed a growing interest in and demand for stronger social accountability mechanisms to be embedded in social protection programming, not least in challenging conflict-affected contexts. While respondents across the three case study countries were all eager to see transfer amounts increased and payments made more regularly (Jones and Samuels, 2013), so too were they consistent in calling for greater beneficiary involvement in programme governance and oversight. In other words, addressing material poverty and vulnerability is undoubtedly of critical importance, but chronically poor and vulnerable people are also demanding to be treated with dignity in the context of social protection programming. For some, this was as simple as having more accessible information about programme provisions, for others there was a strong desire to improve communication channels and to insist on more respectful relationships and the systematic provision of spaces and channels for regular communication between service providers and beneficiaries. Our case study findings also underscored a strong interest in embedding mechanisms within cash transfer programmes so programme implementers can be better held to account, including for abuses of power.

In terms of the lessons about social accountability processes that emerged from our comparative analysis of three conflict-affected but quite divergent political economic settings, our findings underscored the need to focus first on the extent and nature of citizen demand for social accountability. In contexts of 'choiceless democracy' like Mozambique, which also suffer from high levels of inequality and social exclusion, and where understandings of citizenship and a state–citizen social contract are weak, if awareness of citizen entitlements and the right to complain if treated unfairly are not proactively fostered, supply-side provisioning of social accountability feedback loops and grievance mechanisms are unlikely to gain traction at community-level. As Corbridge, Williams, Srivastava, and Véron (2005) have highlighted, however, a sense of citizenship typically evolves from 'seeing the state' – through face-to-face interactions with local state representatives – thus working through non-politicised community agents to increase awareness about eligibility and the scope of entitlements could be an important first step.

By contrast, in contexts like Palestine, where there is already a robust understanding of citizen rights and entitlements fostered by an active civil society and international supporters (INGOs and UN agencies alike), facilitating spaces and channels for citizens to voice and share their views about the programme implementation process would appear to be an appropriate entry-point for strengthening social accountability processes and outcomes. Engagement at this level has the potential not only to secure a greater sense of programme buy-in and legitimacy by participants (a critical resource for programme 'champions' within the state) but also to lead to creative and more effective programming adaptations by securing real-time feedback on what programme components are working well, why and where.

Finally in highly insecure and fragile environments like Yemen, where national government commitment to social protection agendas is not strong and funding for social transfers is heavily donor-dependent, tackling the risk of clientelistic practices and politicised distribution of transfers emerges as a precondition for any social accountability process, given very low levels of citizen trust. It would also appear that social accountability approaches may need to be tailored to sub-national conditions. Where local leaders enjoy legitimacy, working through them to encourage programme information provision and feedback loops could be a possibility. In less cohesive environments, emphasising transparent ways of working with related information provided in widely accessible oral and written formats may be a more fruitful option.

Acknowledgements

The authors are grateful for insightful peer review comments provided by Professor Samuel Hickey and two anonymous peer reviewers on an earlier version of the paper, research assistance by Elizabeth Presler-Marshall and editorial support from Kathryn O'Neil and Roo Griffiths.

Disclosure statement

No potential conflict of interest was reported by the authors.

Funding

They authors wish to acknowledge funding from the UK Department for International Development (DFID) for the field research.

Notes

1. The authors are grateful to Samuel Hickey for this distinction.
2. Each research proposal underwent scrutiny by the ODI Research Ethics Board, which follows the principles laid out in the 2012 UK Economic and Social Research Council Framework for Research Ethics, complemented by ethical approvals obtained from local research ethical clearance committees in the study countries.

References

Abu Hamad, B., & Pavanello, S. (2012). *Transforming cash transfers: Beneficiary and community perspectives on the Palestinian national cash transfer programme. Part 1: The case of the Gaza strip.* London: ODI.
Bagash, T., Pereznieto, P., & Dubai, K. (2012). *Transforming cash transfers: Beneficiary and community perspectives of the social welfare fund in Yemen.* London: ODI.
Barrientos, A. (2013). *Social assistance in developing countries.* Cambridge: Cambridge University Press.

Bukenya, B., Hickey, S., & King, S. (2012). *Understanding the role of context in shaping social accountability interventions: Towards an evidence-based approach.* Manchester: IDPM, University of Manchester.

Carpenter, S., Slater, R., & Mallett, R. (2012). *Social protection and basic services in fragile and conflict-affected situations* (Working Paper 8). London: SLRC.

Corbridge, S., Williams, G., Srivastava, M. K., & Véron, R. (2005). *Seeing the state: Governance and governmentality in India.* Contemporary South Asia, 10. Cambridge: Cambridge University Press.

Di John, J., & Putzel, J. (2009). *Political settlements* (Issues Paper). Birmingham: Governance and Social Development Resource Centre, International Development Department, University of Birmingham.

Eyben, R., & Ladbury, S. (2006). *Building effective states: Taking a citizen's perspective.* Development research centre on citizenship, participation and accountability. Sussex: University of Sussex. Retrieved from http://r4d.dfid.gov.uk/PDF/Outputs/CentreOnCitizenship/drccitizensperspective.pdf

Fiszbein, A., & Schady, N., with Ferreira, F., Grosh, M., Kelleher, N., Olinto, P., & Skoufias, E. (2009). *Conditional cash transfers: Reducing present and future poverty.* Washington, DC: IBRD/World Bank.

Flanagan, C., Jonsson, B., Botcheva, L., Csapo, B., Bowes, J., Macek, P., ... Sheblanova, E. (1999). Adolescents and the "social contract": Developmental roots of citizenship in seven countries. In M. Yates & J. Youniss (Eds.), *Roots of civic identity: International perspectives on community service and activism in youth* (pp. 135–155). Cambridge: Cambridge University Press.

Hickey, S. (2010). *The politics of social protection in Africa: What do we get from a 'social contract' approach?* (Background Paper to the European Report on Development). Florence: Robert Schuman Centre for Advanced Studies.

Hickey, S., & Bracking, S. (2005). Exploring the politics of chronic poverty: From representation to a politics of justice? *World Development, 33*(6), 851–865. doi:10.1016/j.worlddev.2004.09.012

Hickey, S., & Mohan, G. (2008). The politics of establishing pro-poor accountability: What can poverty reduction strategies achieve? *Review of International Political Economy, 15*(2), 234–258. doi:10.1080/09692290701869712

Huber, E., Stephens, J., & Mustillo, T. (2008). Politics and social spending in Latin America. *Journal of Politics, 70*(2), 420–436. doi:10.1017/S0022381608080407

Jennings, M. (2006). *Social fund for development Republic of Yemen, institutional evaluation.* London: DFID.

Jones, N., & Samuels, F., with Malachowska, A. (2013). *Holding cash transfers to account: Beneficiary and community perspectives* (Synthesis Report). London: ODI.

Jones, N., & Shaheen, M. (2012). *Transforming cash transfers: Beneficiary and community perspectives on the Palestinian national cash transfer programme. Part 2: The case of the West Bank.* London: ODI.

Joshi, A. (2007). Producing social accountability? The impact of service delivery reforms. *IDS Bulletin, 38*(6), 10–17. doi:10.1111/idsb.2007.38.issue-6

Joshi, A., & Houtzager, P. (2012). Widgets or watchdogs? Conceptual explorations in social accountability. *Public Management Review, 14*(2), 145–162. doi:10.1080/14719037.2012.657837

McNeil, M., & Malena, C. (Eds.). (2010). *Demanding good governance: Lessons from social accountability initiatives in Africa.* Washington, DC: IBRD/World Bank.

Mwandawire, T. (1999). Crisis management and the making of 'choiceless democracies' in Africa. In R. Joseph (ed.), *The state, conflict and democracy in Africa.* Boulder, CO: Lynne Rienner.

Narayan, D., & Pritchett, L. (1999). Social capital: Evidence and implications. In P. Dasgupta & I. Serageldin (Eds.), *Social capital: A multifaceted perspective* (pp. 269–296). Washington, DC: World Bank.

Osofian, W. (2011, April). *Towards strengthening state–citizen relationship in fragile states and environments: The role of cash transfer programmes.* Conference on Social Protection for Social Justice, Brighton.

Ragin, C., & Becker, H. (Eds.). (1992). *What is a case? Exploring the foundations of social inquiry.* New York, NY: Cambridge University Press.

Ringold, D., Holla, A., Koziol, M., & Srinivasan, S. (2012). *Citizens and service delivery: Assessing the use of social accountability approaches in human development.* Washington, DC: IBRD/World Bank.

Selvester, K., Fidalgo, L., & Tambo, N. (2012). *Transforming cash transfers: Beneficiary and community perspectives of the basic social subsidy programme in Mozambique.* London: ODI.

Sepulveda, M., & Nyst, C. (2012). *The human rights approach to social protection.* Helsinki: Ministry of Foreign Affairs of Finland.

Silva, J., Levin, V., & Morgandi, M. (2012). *Inclusion and resilience: The way forward for social safety nets in the Middle East and North Africa.* Washington, DC: The World Bank.

Tembo, F. (2013). *Rethinking social accountability in Africa: Lessons from the Mwananchi Programme.* London: ODI.

UN Research Institute for Social Development. (2010). *Combating poverty and inequality: Structural change, social policy and politics.* Geneva: Author.

Unsworth, S. (Ed.) (2010). *An upside down view of governance.* Bright61293 on: Centre for the Future State, Institute of Development Studies.

World Bank. (2011). *West Bank and Gaza Coping With Conflict? Poverty and Inclusion in the West Bank and Gaza.* Report no. Washington, DC: Author.

Yin, R. K. (2014). *Case study research: Design and methods* (5th ed.). Los Angeles, CA: Sage.

Understanding Social Accountability: Politics, Power and Building New Social Contracts

SAM HICKEY & SOPHIE KING

Global Development Institute, School of Environment, Education and Development, University of Manchester, Manchester, UK

ABSTRACT   *Calls to deepen levels of social accountability within social protection interventions need to be informed by the now extensive experience of promoting social accountability in developing countries. Drawing on a systematic review of over 90 social accountability interventions, including some involving social protection, this paper shows that politics and context are critical to shaping their success. We argue that the politics of social protection and of social accountability resonate strongly with the broader project of transforming state-society relations in developing countries. This requires a reconceptualisation of social accountability and social protection in terms of the broader development of 'social contracts', and that the current emphasis on promoting bottom-up forms of accountability needs to be balanced by efforts to strengthen and legitimise public authority in developing countries.*

Introduction

Devereux, McGregor, and Wheeler (2011) argue that for social protection to be transformative it must go beyond the management of risk towards tackling the underlying causes of vulnerability. These causes encompass forms of exclusion and disadvantage that are political as well as socio-economic in form. There is therefore growing pressure for social protection interventions to be delivered in ways that enable recipients to exercise agency in holding providers to account for delivering social protection as a right rather than as a hand-out. This move fits with wider calls for both social accountability and social protection to be reconceptualised in terms of a wider project of forging a more just social contract (Hickey, 2011; Joshi & Houtzager, 2012). To help move this agenda forward, our paper summarises findings from an extensive review of research into social accountability initiatives (SAIs) in order to firstly, inform the process of incorporating SAIs within social protection interventions, and secondly, examine the broader implications in terms of establishing more progressive and just forms of state-society relations. It begins with an overview of current debates around social accountability and a discussion of the methodology underpinning the review. The third section presents findings about the kinds of intervention and contextual factors that shape the outcomes achieved by SAIs. This is followed by an analysis of the political considerations critical to understanding and engaging with social accountability in different environments that proposes an analytical framework to help organise thinking and action in this field. The final section discusses the implications of promoting social accountability within social protection interventions as a means to promote more progressive social contracts.

Understanding Social Accountability

Social accountability has come to occupy a central position within inclusive liberal discourse focused on the achievement of 'poverty reduction through good governance', a policy agenda that has also come to include a central role for social protection (World Bank, 2001, 2014). Achieving higher levels of accountability, whereby governments not only deliver goods and services as per their policy promises, but are also responsive to citizens' demands, is considered to contribute to better public service provision while also building a stronger sense of citizenship and promoting empowerment. Social accountability is a contested concept but is most usefully defined here as 'the broad range of actions and mechanisms beyond voting that citizens can use to hold the state to account, as well as actions on the part of government, civil society, media and other societal actors that promote or facilitate these efforts' (Malena & McNeil, 2010, p. 1). There is a consensus that accountability involves both *answerability*, 'making power holders explain and give reasons for their actions', and *enforcement*, 'ensuring that poor or immoral performance is punished in some way' (Hickey & Mohan, 2008, p. 236). Initiatives designed to ensure answerability and enforcement may be demand-side – driven from the bottom-up by non-state actors, or supply-side – encompassing legal and fiscal governmental cheques and balances; and, as we come to argue, may most effectively comprise elements of both.

Under the Post-Washington Consensus, demand-side approaches took centre stage, but more recently these 'social' forms of accountability have come under criticism for being based on a theory of change that does not reflect the political realities of governance and development in most developing countries (Booth, 2012; Brett, 2003). It has also been argued that most SAIs are conceptualised in instrumental and technical, rather than political terms (Joshi & Houtzager, 2012), thereby 'over-emphasising the tools to the detriment of analysis of context', (McGee & Gaventa, 2011, p. 8), despite evidence that their success is highly dependent on the political, social and economic landscape in which SAIs are embedded (McGee & Gaventa, 2011; Menocal & Sharma, 2008). It is therefore particularly important that both thinking and practise around social accountability is strongly informed by the available evidence concerning what works well in particular places, rather than by pre-determined preferences for particular institutional forms and approaches.

This paper draws on a systematic review of the social accountability literature that investigated the key contextual factors shaping the outcomes of SAIs. The review was formulated in part as a challenge to the 'best-practise' approach to designing development interventions, supportive instead of a 'best-fit' approach that is more closely aligned with the realities of different political economy contexts (see Booth, 2012). The review, which followed recommended academic practise (Gough, Thomas, & Oliver, 2013), included 91 research studies, of which 44 were empirical investigations, 18 were synthesis papers, and 29 were generic studies (which covered topics such as decentralisation with clear relevance to the question of how context affects social accountability). Initiatives were judged as either successful, partially successful or as failed according to the evidence and conclusions presented within each study. 'Success' here was considered not merely in terms of the successful delivery of projects and improvement in services generated by the interventions, but also at the broader level of outcomes and impact, with a particular focus on changes in governance institutions and/or citizen empowerment vis-à-vis the state.

The review covered three main types of SAI, namely *transparency* initiatives that seek to increase citizen access to information about state services (for example Public Expenditure Tracking Surveys, citizen score cards, and social audits); *contentious actions*, such as popular demonstration, advocacy and campaigns, and public interest litigation, and also what Hossain (2010) refers to as 'rude' or informal accountability actions including undressing, shouting and spreading rumours; and *participatory governance* initiatives which principally incorporated consultations within poverty reduction strategy papers, participatory budgeting and membership of community management committees.

Selection of research studies followed a thorough bibliographic search of literature pertaining to social accountability, and included research drawing on a range of methodologies such as experimental designs, survey-based studies, and specialised synthesis reviews. In the interest of generating robust and up-to-date findings, only studies with clear methodological rationales published between 2000 and

2012 were included. A qualitative categorical analysis of outcomes, and intervention and context-based factors shaping these outcomes, was conducted with the assistance of Nvivo 9 software, which enabled us to identify specific factors which were associated with success in particular cases, and undertake coding and categorisation accordingly.

This approach encountered two main methodological challenges. First, there are few studies of SAIs in different political-economic environments that focus specifically on the role of context in shaping outcomes. Most evaluative literature has been commissioned by development agencies that tend to emphasise the role of technical tools and institutional mechanisms rather than the role of context. The second challenge concerned the validity of generalising from our approach. Although the methodology outlined here was judged to be fairly rigorous, particularly in terms of the number of studies covered and the mode of analysis employed, it remains problematic within a qualitative methodological approach to seek to abstract categories from different types of study conducted in different types of context, when it is difficult to be confident that any one factor is being defined or understood in the same ways across studies. This would involve undertaking systematic and primary comparative case-study analysis of SAIs in different types of context, something which we argue later should provide the basis for future work in this area.

What Shapes the Success of Social Accountability Initiatives?

This section focuses mainly on the role of contextual factors in shaping SAI outcomes before turning briefly to the role played by intervention-based factors.

Context-Based Factors

A wide range of contextual factors emerged as significant within the literature on SAIs, including the role of different kinds of political institutions, the type and capacity of civil society actors involved in promoting social accountability, and a wide range of different 'relational' factors, whether in the form of state-society relations or relations between groups and citizens. 45 out of the total 91 studies reviewed identified the presence or absence of political will at different levels of governance as a critical factor.[1] For example, one NGO in Madhya Pradesh, *Samaj Pragati Sahyog (SPS)*, which managed to promote higher levels of social accountability, greatly benefited from the support of a senior district official with the authority to impose sanctions upon corrupt junior officials (Chhotray, 2008). Likewise, several studies showed SAIs were undermined by a lack of strong and visible official support, as around the community management committees in the health sector in Bangladesh (Mahmud, 2007), or housing associations in Kenya (Nyamu-Musembi, 2006, p. 137). Corbridge, Williams, Srivastava, and Veron (2005) reveal how bureaucrats and politicians with vested interests in maintaining the status quo actively sabotaged new SAIs. Political will is thus to some extent shaped by the degree to which SAIs offer viable solutions to governance problems that are in alignment with the interests of the political power holders involved.

Well-institutionalised political parties and political opposition can also play key roles within accountability dynamics. Political support from opposition parties can contribute to SAI success as evidenced by better performing community management committees in Midnapore, India, where the communist party was influential in mobilising the poor (Corbridge et al., 2005), and by differential levels of support for participatory budgeting in Latin America closely linked to political party membership (Goldfrank, 2007).

The effects of democratisation on efforts to secure accountability emerge as somewhat ambiguous. Certainly in contexts like Brazil and South Africa, the existence of particular constitutional rights and competent judiciaries have been critical to triggering movements for legislative accountability like those led by the landless workers movement (*MST*) and the Treatment Action Campaign (TAC) (Campbell, Cornish, Gibbs, & Scott, 2010). NGOs such as *SPS* in India also rely on legislative guidelines to fuel citizen mobilisation (Chhotray, 2008), and transparency initiatives have even experienced at least partial success in semi-authoritarian contexts like Uganda (Robinson, 2006). Participatory initiatives are often ineffective, however, in areas where local governments lack resources and bureaucratic competence. Poor facilitation of citizen participation in local governance in eastern India, for example, has been linked to weak incentives for good performance and limited opportunities for career progression (Corbridge et al., 2005).

The capacity of civil society organisations (CSOs), and in particular the depth, extensiveness and character of the relationships amongst CSOs, and between civil and political society, plays a critical role in determining the success of SAIs. The availability of credible and capable civil society allies and a history of effective grassroots mobilisation emerged as particularly strong components within the successful contentious actions reviewed. TAC in South Africa, for example, gained strength from activist experiences of the historic struggle against apartheid and from the strategic bridging relation-ships available with academics, churches, international activist organisations and trade unions with significant political influence (Campbell et al., 2010). The inverse of this is that high levels of competitiveness between CSOs, often linked to a highly donor dependent operating environment, can contribute to failure, as this tends to fragment collective action. Environments with high levels of clientelism may also be poor incubators of coalitional action (Goldfrank, 2007), given that the vertical character of patron-client relations tends to undermine the emergence of horizontal forms of collective action (Mitlin, 2013).

High levels of inequality between citizens can limit the success of SAIs. Low levels of income and education have a direct effect on citizen capabilities for participation – particularly in formal partici-patory spaces. Campbell et al. (2010) suggest that initiatives can attempt to mitigate these effects by incorporating the provision of citizen education and capacity-building into interventions. Studies of demand-side mobilisation in Bangladesh (Kabeer, Mahmud, & Castro, 2010), and also, more recently, in Uganda (King, 2015), suggest that securing the participation of poorer citizens in initiatives for social justice may do better when linked directly to potential livelihood and economic gains. Finally, socially subordinate groups sometimes rely on informal methods for extracting accountability, and the review suggested that these strategies are often pursued in contexts where governance is weak and civil society lacks the capacity or inclination to hold civil servants to account (Hossain, 2010).

The character of state-citizen relations is also important as this relational field directly shapes capacity for, and commitment to, activism for social justice among citizens and civil society actors. Inequality and exclusion can be the impetus for collective action – in the case of the *MST* landless movement in Brazil for example. It can also undermine drives for participation and inclusion. Studies show that village education committees in eastern India are dominated by local teachers, upper-caste landlords and their kinsmen, and that the social exclusion endured by lower castes contributes to their much lower levels of political awareness and involvement (Corbridge et al., 2005). Where political and economic power are intertwined, local citizens may fear to express their views openly, for example, villagers participating in social audits in India have feared reprisals from local officials (Shankar, 2010).

Intervention-Based Factors

35 out of the 91 studies reviewed found the credibility of lead actors to be critical to success and this was particularly significant within transparency initiatives and contentious actions. Transparency advocates needed to show capability in extracting, managing and disseminating reliable data. Key credibility considerations for participatory governance initiatives in 12 out of the 19 studies reviewed were that institutions and processes 'had teeth' in terms of being able to impose sanctions for poor performance or corruption. 36 studies found that higher levels of state-civil society collaboration within accountability mechanisms translated into greater success. Where CSOs were left out of initiatives like poverty reduction strategy paper processes or transparency initiatives, the kinds of accountability achieved were weak. Even within contentious actions, which might be expected to involve adversarial state/activist relationships, receptivity to civil society advocacy among political actors, and effective interfaces for engagement, were important to success. The persistence of

mobilisation over time also contributed to effective influence, suggesting it may be important to consider social accountability as the outcome of longer-term and iterative processes of bargaining between social and state actors (Joshi & Houtzager, 2012), rather than one-off interventions.

Improving the access of citizens to high quality, relevant information was critical to both transparency and participatory governance initiatives. Key considerations were whether information was supportive of attention-grabbing public messages; the degree to which information offered citizens clear and practical data that they could make sense of and use; and in relation to participatory governance mechanisms, whether opportunities were widely and appropriately publicised. Another important success factor in 13 studies was the degree to which an issue resonated strongly with citizens – education, livelihoods, access to land and access to life-saving medicines have all catalysed strong reactions from citizens across the three regions covered by the review. Finally, synthesis studies and research into transparency initiatives and contentious actions in particular, stressed the importance of taking an integrated approach to promoting social accountability that combined both demand- and supply-side factors; or from the demand-side, employing multiple interlinking strategies such as litigation, community mobilisation, and media campaigns.

Summary

That context and politics matter to development outcomes is nothing new. This review demonstrates specifically, however, that the pursuit of downwards accountability is advanced by the presence of state actors interested in building alliances with civil society, of coalition-minded civil organisations and citizens that display interest in participating in governance mechanisms, and of design features that reduce the asymmetric distribution of status and resources among participants. Bottom-up accountability interventions generally achieve greater success where they are able to forge synergies with top-down and/or horizontal accountability mechanisms. Success is particularly closely linked to levels of political will amongst state functionaries, especially those in elected positions able to hold service providers to account. The choice of public goods around which accountability is sought is also important, suggesting that a stronger 'social contract' exists around some public goods than others, based on the historically informed expectations of actors on both sides of the governance equation.

Analysing Social Accountability in Context

There is a strong convergence between the findings reported above and the growing focus on the politics of development over the past 10 years, particularly work that focuses on the forms of politics and power which underlie and shape the performance of institutions (such as Leftwich, 2005; North, Walliss, & Weingast, 2009) and on the importance of state-society relations (Unsworth & Moore, 2010). Importantly, this convergence challenges many of the underlying assumptions that have tended to characterise most mainstream thinking and practise on social accountability (and 'good governance' more broadly) over the past decade (World Bank, 2004), within which 'the common feature is assumed to be the mobilisation of citizen demand for accountability' (Booth, 2012, p. 69), and suggests the need for reconceptualising this work within a more contextually and politically attuned theory of change. This section therefore takes a political lens to organising the findings of the review into an analytical framework that can inform attempts to understand accountability dynamics. The first part of the discussion identifies four dimensions for this framework and briefly relates these to other generic studies of SAIs; the second part unpacks each of these dimensions, and their interrelationships, in greater depth.

The Contextual Dimensions Shaping Social Accountability

Although the particular configuration of contextual factors that matter most in shaping SAIs differs from place to place, and also over time, the evidence examined for the above review suggests that the most critical features can be categorised into four overarching dimensions. These comprise the two institutional spheres of civil and political society and their interactions, as located within the broader fields of power relations between states and societies and within society. Figure 1 offers a provisional suggestion as to how these dimensions might be mapped in relation to each other and also identifies the key factors within each of them, with a particular focus on capacities, commitment and the interrelationships between key actors and spheres. In a holistic sense, the diagram represents the politics of social accountability in terms of the broader social contract between states and citizens around the protection of rights and the provision of resources.

At first glance, our key findings on how context matters for accountability outcomes are broadly in accord with those reported in a number of other recent synthesis studies. O'Neill, Foresti, and Hudson (2007) identify political contexts, existing power relations, the enabling environment, the nature of the state and its institutions, and the social contract between state and citizens as key variables shaping SAI outcomes. Both Menocal and Sharma (2008) and Agarwal and Van Wicklin (2011) note the significance of capacity and commitment on both sides of the state-society equation. Several of the studies reviewed by McGee and Gaventa (2011) also note the significance of supply-led factors in ensuring SAI success, particularly in terms of legitimate state authorities imposing sanctions on public officials. In most cases, civil society activism without reforms on the other side of the equation will fail to yield sustained results. However, and by their own admission (as noted by McGee & Gaventa, 2011), these studies lacked the systematic basis of this one, and few have gone on to show either how these different factors can be conceptualised in relation to each other, or through breaking these down into more specific forms (Figure 1).

Political society. Political society is critical to SAI success, particularly regarding the political will of state functionaries and the role played by political institutions (such as political parties) that appear from the evidence of our studies to mediate the effects of democratisation. Political society is viewed here, following Corbridge et al. (2005, p. 189) discussion of Chatterjee's (2004) work, as the arena

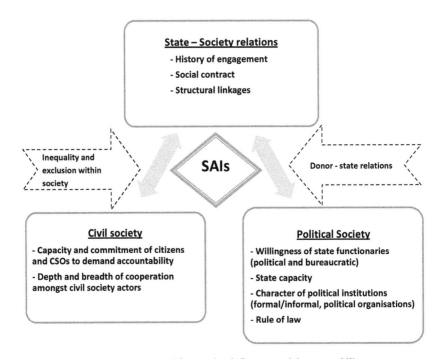

Figure 1. Contextual factors that influence social accountability.

within which people perceive and encounter the state on an everyday basis and which creates and maintains different patterns of political rule that shape the scope for 'citizenship empowerment'. It is constituted by a loose community of recognised political parties, local political brokers and councillors, public servants, a set of institutions, actors and cultural norms that provide the key links between 'government' and 'the public'. For Chatterjee, it is the identity and quality of the actors who mediate power in political society that matter most in shaping the lived experience of citizenship, even if civil society actors can help mediate these encounters in favour of greater accountability towards citizens. We focus here on the three elements of political society that emerge as most important for the effective operation of social accountability, namely commitment, capacity and the nature of key political institutions.

The **commitment** of key actors to promoting social accountability, both in terms of bureaucrats and elected officials has emerged as central here and in other meta-reviews (McGee & Gaventa, 2011). Houtzager and Joshi, (2007, p. 6) emphasise the critical role played by public sector officials in not only delivering on accountability demands, but also pushing for accountability reforms, and even stimulating social actors to mobilise for claims-making. Our studies tend to emphasise the role played by elected representatives who are both susceptible to popular pressures and also in a position to shape the behaviour of public officials through sanctions and other forms of supply-led accountability. This points to the need to think about ways of linking social accountability interventions with forms of political accountability, particularly through making links to supply-led enforcement mechanisms and involving elected officials in the design of demand-side initiatives.

There have been a number of calls to unpack the notion of political will, but few analyses have managed to go beyond a standard disaggregation of political actors into different types such as elected representatives or public sector professionals as we have done here. Others have argued that it is more useful to move beyond the language of political will or commitment to examine the 'incentives' that structure and guide elite behaviour (Booth, 2012). This focus on elite interests and incentives links to a new wave of thinking around what shapes not only the commitment of elites to development but also the capacity of states to deliver, which focuses on the character of the 'political settlement' (Khan, 2010; North et al., 2009). The 'political settlement refers to the balance or distribution of power between contending social groups and social classes, on which any state is based' (Di John & Putzel, 2009, p. 4). The key implication here is that the commitment of elites to development, and the capacity of the state to deliver, will be strongly shaped by the terms of the political settlement and the incentives that this places before them to act in favour of certain interests over others. Ruling coalitions need to maintain certain types of relationship both horizontally (with other elite factions) and vertically (with organised social groupings) in order to preserve regime stability and survival, and this creates strong incentives to act in particular ways.

This approach also offers a more nuanced and relational reading of the **capacity** of public and elected officials to act in the public interest, around accountability issues but also more broadly. The developmental capacities of the state need to be defined not only in terms of its organisational competence (levels of human resource and bureaucratic capacity for example), but also its capacity to forge and maintain synergistic relations with different social actors (Vom Hau, 2012). Whereas the key relationships that matter for economic growth are those between state and capital (Evans, 1995), the successful promotion of human capabilities is more strongly associated with states characterised by cooperative and synergistic relations between political and civil society (Evans, 2010). This analytical approach might be further advanced by extending the focus on 'incentives' away from an instrumental reading to one that also takes account of the role that 'ideas' (around notions of public service for example) play in shaping elite behaviour (Hickey, 2013).

A focus on the specific forms of politics and power relations shaping SAIs may be more useful than grappling with broad concepts like democratisation. What seems to matter here are the forms of state-society relations within which accountability resides, and also, the **types of political institutions** that mediate the relationship between democratic procedures, like elections and public policy processes. For example, Brautigam's (2004) review of participatory budgeting notes that democracy or even popular participation per se is less significant in achieving government responsiveness to pro-poor concerns than the role of well institutionalised and programmatic political parties. This suggests a need to introduce a clearer focus within current thinking on social accountability concerning the ways in which participatory and representative forms of democracy can be woven together to achieve greater success. The preceding discussion suggests that a particular focus on the social and ideological character of particular political organisations, and greater collaboration between social accountability advocates or activists and elected officials and political parties, might further improve identification and design of interventions.

Overall, the evidence suggests that the capacity and commitment of actors within political society to undertake effective forms of governance reform are closely shaped by the incentives with which they are presented, and the room for manoeuvre available to them within the broader field of power relations. This focus on power relations is central to our analysis here, and is explored further below.

Civil society. The success of SAIs relies heavily on the capacity of CSOs to mobilise citizens and to network effectively, both within civil and political society. CSOs are unable to achieve much by acting alone, and their capacity to develop alliances with those pursuing similar projects is critical to accumulating the power required to achieve change. The type of civil society that emerges as significant from this review is a much more politicised and relational realm than the the de Tocquevillian vision of an associational realm that operates in a distinct sphere from the state (Hyden, 1997), and which has generally been promoted within international development theory and practise over the past two decades. Here, 'civil society' is not free from the logic of how power and politics operate in developing countries, but a space within which citizens and CSOs often find it very hard to find room for manoeuvre for their projects within the broader politics of patronage, ethnicity and exclusion. Agency within civil society is closely shaped by the underlying field of power relations, involving forms of inequality and exclusion along economic, social and cultural lines. Importantly, the capacity of CSOs to be effective in this realm has less to do with their autonomy from the state than with the relationships and networks that they are able to forge with other actors in both civil and political society over time (also Lavalle, Acharya, & Houtzager, 2005). This version of civil society is best captured within a Gramscian reading of civil society, which recognises the power relations that shape civil society and the historical fact that progressive struggles are nearly always constituted by actors from both sides of the state-society divide (Bebbington, Hickey, & Mitlin, 2008; Fox, 2004), an issue we return to below. This should direct advocates of social accountability away from assessing the 'strength' of civil society alone, and towards identifying and assessing the nature of the relationships and networks across state and society and supporting their strengthening in more progressive directions.

The available literature is less useful in breaking down which elements of civil society are particularly important in shaping social accountability and the drivers behind such agents. However, what appears to matter most is the capacity and commitment of citizens and CSOs to mobilise and act, both individually and collectively, around social accountability demands, particularly those involving contentious actions and direct participation. In terms of CSO capacity, 'mobilisation, coalition-building, negotiation, and advocacy' (Agarwal & Van Wicklin, 2011, p. 7) are critical. The origins of these capacities are not made clear in the particular studies, although at the collective level, it seems likely that these are built up over time through successive rounds of bargaining with the state (Houtzager & Joshi, 2007), often over a prolonged period. An example is the *MKSS*' right to information campaign in India, which started in the early 1990s, gained partial success in 2000 when the Indian state of Rajasthan passed the right to information act (Ramkuma, 2008), but continued for another five years before the nation-wide Right to Information Act (RTI) was passed (Aiyar, 2010; Ramkuma, 2008).

Inequality and exclusion. The field of power relations that shapes social interactions and popular agency within society plays a crosscutting role in shaping the success of SAIs. This is particularly apparent in terms of the barriers that prevent people from undertaking initiatives that demand high levels of participation. At the individual level, education and income emerged as particularly significant in participatory governance studies, reflecting the wider sense in which citizenship-based activities are strongly circumscribed by the level of agency that different individuals are able to exert within particular contexts. For critics, this represents a failure to take structural constraints seriously, and recognise the ways in which marginal and vulnerable individuals and groups in particular struggle to transcend these.

State-society relations: towards a new social contract?   State-society relations have increasingly been recognised as critical to the politics of development, and SAIs constitute attempts to institutionalise more democratic and developmental forms of such relations, while also being closely shaped by their existing character. For Di John and Putzel (2009), social accountability is more likely to emerge when the political settlement, which is predominantly based on an agreement between elites on what the rules of the game are and how they should operate, becomes more inclusive of broader social groups. At this stage it becomes possible to discuss state-society relations in terms of a 'social contract', which refers both to the legitimacy of political rule, including the capacity of citizens to hold rulers to account, and also the pursuit of social justice as a fundamental principle of government (de Waal, 1996).[2] The notion of a social contract thus offers a highly relevant framework for the politics of social accountability and social protection. Social accountability and social protection can each be understood as both flowing from, and helping to support, more democratic and socially just forms of social contract, as has been argued in relation to both participatory budgeting in Latin America (Goldfrank, 2007) and cash transfers in Brazil (Alston, Melo, Mueller, & Pereira, 2013).

It is important to contextualise this notion of social contracts which derives from Western history and theories of state formation and change. Much literature on social accountability imagines a social world consisting of autonomous, well-informed and active citizens who are able to make demands of capable and responsive public officials (Hickey, 2011). In many developing contexts, state-society relations are heavily personalised or informal, and underpinned by a logic of patronage which is glaringly at odds with these Western theories of governance and change (Booth, 2012). Different forms of social contract will emerge in different contexts, depending in part on the balance and interaction between democratic and more clientelist forms of politics. For example, contracts can emerge within the context of semi-authoritarian regimes, usually on the basis of presidential patronage and/or a ruling party with an ideological commitment and/or strong incentives to offer certain public goods. In either context, elections can provide a window of opportunity for politicising certain demands and beginning to forge new public agreements around them. This may mark the start (or part) of longer-term bargaining around this particular issue or public good, or could locate the provision of public goods insecurely in the field of asymmetrical reciprocity that defines patron-client politics in some contexts. For example, de Waal's (1996) analysis of social contracts around food security in Africa and India shows that the strongest such contracts have been derived from processes of popular mobilisation at key moments of state formation, which then became institutionalised within constitutional commitments and protected by political institutions such as programmatic parties and parliaments more broadly. This also suggests that more research is required into the possibility that informal mechanisms may provide 'good enough' forms of accountability in certain contexts.

The broad notion of a 'social contract' can be broken down further by examining the agreements or settlements that exist around different sectors, or what others call the 'structural linkages' that bind states and citizens to each other (Skocpol, 1992). This is critical, as what is expected by citizens and what states are prepared to commit to delivering, varies according to the particular goods and services under discussion, their level of popular and political importance, and the history of state-society bargaining around them (Houtzager & Joshi, 2007). Assessing the possibilities for both locating SAIs within existing social contracts, and deepening them as a result, could therefore start from an analysis of how the rights of citizens to different resources and public goods have been differentially distributed over time and on what basis. Evidence that a social contract is operational in relation to a particular public good for at least some citizens may be derived in part from an examination of constitutional rights and provisions, as with the Right to Information campaign in India. However, it would be more strongly evidenced by the presence of an active process of popular pressure and state-society bargaining around this good (de Waal, 1996). Recent calls to 'go with the grain' of governance in developing countries (Booth, 2012) suggest that it might be wise for external actors to promote SAIs where such a degree of commitment already exists, rather than to seek out the creation of new social contracts around public goods that are not recognised within current bargains. It is important not to underestimate the contentious character of state-society relations however. A social contract approach may be able to shed considerable light onto the actual forms of power and politics that matter in securing accountability, but no easy routes have yet been devised to operationalising a social contract approach within development policy and practise (Hickey, 2011).

Implications: Social Accountability and Transformative Social Protection

Beyond emphasising the extent to which social accountability interventions are profoundly shaped by the contexts within which they are located, this review has illuminated the particular forms of politics and power relations that matter most in shaping the success of such interventions. Several implications flow from this for thinking through how to conceptualise and promote social accountability moving forward, including within the realm of social protection. This final section draws out three main dimensions of this agenda at the level of analysis, design and also research. The first concerns the need to rethink social accountability in distinctly political, as opposed to technocratic, terms; the second involves revisiting the design of SAIs to render them more attuned to both the kind of evidence presented here and the contexts within which they are required; and the third relates to the need for a much stronger evidence base on how contextual factors shape social accountability interventions and outcomes.

Politicising the Theory and Practise of Social Accountability: Towards a Social Contract Approach

Achieving improved levels of social accountability is a profoundly political challenge, not least because such initiatives often seek to challenge powerful vested interests in the status quo (McGee & Gaventa, 2011). Our findings strongly suggest that sustained and effective SAIs require a re-ordering of how politics operates, particularly in terms of the broader social contract between states and citizens. This conclusion resonates with other attempts to shift the theory and practise of social accountability away from a technocratic approach in a more political direction, including Fox (2007) and Joshi and Houtzager's (2012) distinction between 'watchdogs' and 'widgets'. In seeking to reframe social accountability in more political terms, Joshi and Houtzager draw on the 'polity approach', which Houtzager (2003) had earlier adapted from Skopcol's (1992) seminal work on the politics of welfare reform and social policy. Similar to our focus on social contracts here, the polity approach focuses on 'the ways in which state and societal actors are constituted, become politically significant, and interact across the public-private divide' (Houtzager, 2003, p. 13). A polity approach shows how politics is mutually constituted by state-society relations, and draws attention to four kinds of processes: (1) the processes of reform of state institutions; (2) the impacts of state institutions on collective actors interested in specific policy arenas; (3) the 'fit' between collective actors with specific goals and the points of access and leverage afforded by political institutions; and (4) path dependence of policies and social action' (Skocpol, 1992, p. 41). This involves reconceptualising social account-ability as an 'ongoing political engagement by social actors with the state as part of a long-term pattern of interaction shaped both by historical forces and the current context' (Joshi & Houtzager, 2012, p. 146). Adjusting the lens in this way has important implications for policy and practise, some of which this paper turns to now, with specific reference to social protection.

Design Issues: A Politically-Attuned Approach to SAIs

Adopting a political rather than technical approach to social accountability means thinking less in terms of the 'widgets' that constitute the particular inputs of social accountability initiatives and more in terms of the 'watchdog' nature of social accountability actors. This is particularly appropriate given that 'the watchdog approach is more rooted in the organic politics of particular contexts' (Joshi & Houtzager, 2012, p. 158). In practical terms, this is now being recognised through an emphasis on developing the political capacities of CSOs and citizens to demand accountability, including through mobilisation and coalition building (Agarwal & Van Wicklin, 2011, p. 7; Menocal & Sharma, 2008). However, the policy and operational focus clearly needs to go far beyond civil society. As Devarajan, Khemani, and Walton (2011, p. 7) have identified: 'civil society's effectiveness will almost always depend on incentives and in particular the activation of sanctioning mechanisms, within the state. These may take the form of internal bureaucratic structures within implementing agencies, or formally independent institutions of accountability within the state, including the legislature, judiciary, auditing departments etc.'

There are few grounds here for suggesting that SAIs are a panacea for improved levels of governance and development, and much to suggest that their success is closely determined by context and their interaction with other accountability mechanisms, most notably supply-led forms. As argued by Menocal and Sharma (2008, p. ix), support for 'voice-based approaches', 'may prove problematic in terms of increasing voice without a parallel effort to build the effectiveness and capacity of state institutions to address growing demands and expectations'. In particular, our paper concurs with the more general sense in which 'much of what we call accountability reflects only the weaker category, answerability. While citizen-led or public initiatives often involve "soft" peer or reputational pressure, they rarely involve strong enforceability' (McGee & Gaventa, 2011, p. 11).

The incentives to which state functionaries respond are as likely to require 'demand-' as well as 'supply-led' sources of power, particularly in contexts where democracy and the rule of law remain contested. This is where the disciplinary power required to ensure that accountability interventions achieve both enforcement and sanctions resides; and where more contextualised understandings of how such incentives operate are required. Several case-studies help make this point, from the role of presidential commitment around UPE in Uganda (Hubbard, 2007) through to the critical role played by mayors and other elected officials in ensuring bureaucratic buy-in to social accountability in Bangladesh (Mahmud, 2007), India (Chhotray, 2008) and Kenya (Nyamu-Musembi, 2006). Taken alongside our finding that increased levels of state capacity enhance the success rate of social accountability, this insight further emphasises the need to re-balance the emphasis on demand-side approaches (World Bank, 2004) with a focus on also strengthening public authority. This resonates with the argument that achieving social accountability requires both the expertise and hierarchical discipline associated with top-down governance approaches as well as the legitimation and empower-ment that can result from bottom-up approaches (Brett, 2003). Going further, Booth (2012) argues that social accountability is better conceived of as a 'collective action problem' rather than one of deficits in solely supply or demand. Reconceived in this way, the promotion of greater accountability requires generating incentives for actors across the state-society divide to collaborate by 'creating space for local problem-solving and facilitating collective action' (Booth, 2012, p. 72). This reflects the earlier argument by Fox (2007) that institutionalised forms of accountability require coalitions between reformers in the state and participatory actors from civil society.

This has some important implications with regards to the promotion of more effective and accountable forms of social protection in developing countries, including with regards to the tendency for social protection to be promoted by external rather than domestic political actors. External actors often seek to deliver social protection through non-state mechanisms with accountability to be ensured via community-based involvement in the distribution and monitoring of goods. As noted above, however, the poorest and most vulnerable people who are the main target of social protection interventions are those worst-placed to generate the agency required to mobilise and hold public institutions to account. Popular agency requires able-bodiedness, an ability to articulate interests in accessible and affordable spaces of governance, and room for manoeuvre within social relationships, all things which are least available to the poorest (Cleaver, 2005). Furthermore, the modal form through which social protection mechanisms such as cash transfers are delivered may actually under-mine the emergence of collective forms of agency, given both the nature of the good that is delivered and its targeting of individuals. Such private goods do not necessarily require the forms of collective public action which can be witnessed around demands for public goods such as education or the kinds of private goods that involve some degree of collective consumption as with housing and associated infrastructural requirements (Mitlin, 2006). That said, some important clues to squaring this apparent circle can be found in some instances of social protection where programme design has a stronger built-in focus on agency and rights. For example, the Vulnerable Groups Development Programme in Bangladesh requires that local people mobilise to receive the transfers in ways that promote empowerment of the poor rural women who constitute its main recipients (Hossain, 2007). Perhaps more promising still here, are public works programmes which have catalysed high levels of collective bargaining, particularly when inscribed as a constitutional right as with the Maharastra Employment Guarantee Scheme (Moore & Jadhav, 2006) and now the Mahatma Gandhi National Rural Employment Guarantee Scheme (Joshi, 2010). Finally, a further implication may be that for social protection interventions to become more accountable and sustainable, there is a need to cast them as universal entitlements rather than means-tested benefits in order to align poor and non-poor groups around a shared sense of vulnerability (Nelson, 2003). This raises the possibility of non-poor groups bringing their often-higher levels of agency to bear in terms of both maintaining social protection interventions and ensuring that they deliver.

Citizens and their organisations have not commonly been associated with promoting social protection in developing countries (Hickey, 2009). It therefore seems more likely that citizen-led forms of accountability will emerge as citizens come to see the goods that are distributed to them through various social protection instruments as entitlements rather than as a form of patronage. It may well be that the growing and continued presence of social protection itself becomes the main driver of higher levels of accountability as recipients become used to receiving transfers and start to see them as entitlements for the long-run rather than temporally limited hand-outs associated more with a politics of patronage than rights. The formation of such 'policy constituencies' around social protection is evident at low levels in some countries already, as with the long-standing if minimalist Public Welfare Assistance Scheme in Zambia (Harland, 2014). It was also apparent in earlier historical moments in sub-Saharan African countries where a social contract around food security appeared to be developing until a mixture of political conflict and disruptive forms of humanitarian aid intervened (de Waal, 1996). This in turn has implications for the delivery of social protection and raises questions concerning the tendency to sidestep government delivery mechanisms for fear of leakage. Such moves have the potential to undermine the development of a social contract whereby social protection can become a 'structural linkage' binding states and citizens and a medium for wider forms of bargaining. From this social contract perspective, it makes sense to ensure that governments are closely involved in the distribution of social transfers and well placed to reap the political benefits such as increased legitimacy. It is rare to secure win-wins in development policy and practise when it comes to politically and technically optimal solutions to service delivery. This paper suggests that 'politically optimal' solutions, which are 'good enough' from a technocratic governance perspective (Grindle, 2007) and which also serve political interests and goals in the short and longer-term may offer the best route forward.

The Challenge for Research and Evaluation

A key finding of our investigation was that the evidence-base on what shapes SAI effectiveness is sorely lacking, particularly regarding the role of contextual factors, and most notably around how social accountability mechanisms are shaped by power and politics. This is particularly true of social accountability mechanisms within social protection interventions, where the evidence base is especially weak. A key challenge moving forward is therefore to devise a stronger evidence base about SAIs from which to draw out a clearer understanding of the interactions between context and design. This offers further grounds for the now standard call for institutionalising political analysis, or what some call higher levels of 'political intelligence', within donor agencies and programming procedures (Menocal & Sharma, 2008, p. v). More specifically, and in line with the move away from 'best-practise' to 'best-fit' type approaches, there is a need to find ways of ensuring that this involves a closer mapping of interventions onto the particular context, so that as far as possible social account-ability interventions are designed and rolled out in line with '(a) supporting existing domestic initiatives and pressures for change, and (b) in ways that are consistent with the initial state of the polity' (Devarajan et al., 2011, p. 32). Given that politics differs significantly across countries, this 'suggests a procedural case for linking external support with diagnosis of the institutional functioning of a country, sector, region or wherever the focus of desired action is' (Devarajan et al., 2011, p. 32).

To achieve this, however, there is a need to radically alter the ways in which SAIs are currently designed, monitored and evaluated, including in the context of social protection interventions. Few of the dozens of social accountability studies that we reviewed paid any in-depth attention to the role of context and politics in shaping their success. This requires that the diagnostics performed to each stage of the process, from baseline studies, through monitoring to evaluation need to include a strong focus on the political and contextual factors that enable and constrain such interventions in particular places. As McGee and Gaventa (2011, p. 3) note, 'a learning approach to evaluation and final impact assessment would give power and politics a central place in monitoring and evaluation systems'. Part of the challenge here is to identify particular *types* of context, within which there are different possibilities for the effective implementation and success of different types of SAIs in social protec-tion. There is some evidence of movement in this direction, as with the distinction that some make between two different types of context: one where there is a legal framework and political system that permits access to information, and civil society has capacity and the government is willing to engage; as against one where 'the legal framework and political will to allow civil society participation is weak or non-existent' (Agarwal & Van Wicklin, 2011, p. 12). An alternative approach, suggested by recent work on 'political settlements', is to distinguish between polities in terms of how political power is organised on the one hand, and the level of institutional capacity and 'impersonality' of the state on the other (Levy, 2014). In terms of methodology, some promising alternatives are now being promoted to the highly popular quasi-experimental approach to programme evaluation in this field, which are better able to capture the complex interactions between social and political dynamics and interventions in specific contexts, including a 'theory-based' approach to impact evaluation (McGee & Gaventa, 2011, p. 26).[3] This report has gone further to argue more specifically that the current weight of evidence on how context matters for SAIs can be best appreciated from a polity-based theory of change (Joshi & Houtzager, 2012) which views social accountability as part of an historical process through which state and non-state actors forge social contracts around particular public goods over time. Again, such a reframing offers the first step towards a fuller appreciation of the role of political context in shaping social accountability.

This paper has used a systematic review of current evidence on social accountability interventions to provide a theoretically- and empirically-informed basis on which to integrate such interventions within the field of social protection. Further work along the lines presented in this special edition is required to explore the extent to which SAIs face the same types of problems when promoted as part of social protection policies and programmes. However, some of the findings from this paper are particularly relevant and should provide some pointers as to how that work can move forward, both in theory and in practise. For example, our finding, along with many others, that the recent tendency to emphasise bottom-up forms of accountability as the pre-eminent strategy for achieving more responsive, empow-ering and effective forms of provision are misplaced. Achieving bottom-up forms of social account-ability within social protection schemes targeted at poor and marginal people is likely to be particularly problematic, given that the capacity of citizens to engage in social accountability initiatives, and to hold public officials to account, is closely shaped and differentiated by power relations involving inequality and exclusion along multiple lines. Those most in need of social protection are thus the least able to exercise the agency required to demand accountability. There are also concerns that the nature of many social protection interventions will tend to further undermine popular agency via both individuating distribution mechanisms used such as cash transfers and the fact that social protection tends to offer private rather than public goods, and therefore do not necessarily require collective forms of action and bargaining to gain and maintain them. Gaining further insights into and seeking to unravel these conundrums will not be easy, although clues can be gained from some instances where social protection initiatives are designed in ways that both require and help to support demand-making by vulnerable groups. The politics of social protection and of social accountability both resonate strongly with the broader project of transforming state-society relations in developing countries, and as such, there remains a powerful logic to pursuing their combined contribution to the deepening of social contracts in progressive directions.

Acknowledgements

This paper, and the project on which it is based, would not have been possible without the contributions of Dr Badru Bukenya, previously a PhD student at IDPM, University of Manchester, and now a lecturer at Makerere University. Badru was responsible for the data analysis component of this work and helped co-author the longer report from which this paper is drawn. His significant contributions are gratefully acknowledged here. The authors would also like to record their thanks to two anonymous reviewers for their insightful comments and to Maxine Molyneux for her encouragement and editorial expertise.

Disclosure statement

No potential conflict of interest was reported by the authors.

Notes

1. Political commitment is a tricky concept to define, and for the sake of argument we define it narrowly here as 'the extent of committed support among key decision makers for a particular policy solution to a particular problem' (Post, Raile, & Raile, 2010, p. 569). However, and as will become clear later in the paper, this policy-focused approach needs to be firmly located within the broader political context within which key decision-makers operate.
2. See Hickey (2011) for a review of the conceptual basis of social contract thinking in international development, with particular reference to social protection.
3. The same authors also call for 'an appreciation of complexity thinking and methods such as qualitative case studies, in-depth interviews, ethnographic studies or participatory methods' (McGee & Gaventa, 2011, p. 26).

References

Agarwal, S., & Van Wicklin, W. A. (2011). *How, when and why to use demand-side governance approaches in projects* (Social Development How-to-Notes). Washington, DC: World Bank.

Aiyar, Y. (2010). Invited spaces, invited participation: Effects of greater participation on accountability in service delivery. *India Review*, 9(2), 204–229. doi:10.1080/14736489.2010.483370

Alston, L. J., Melo, M. A., Mueller, B., & Pereira, C. (2013). Changing social contracts: Beliefs and dissipative inclusion in Brazil. *Journal of Comparative Economics*, 41(1), 48–65. doi:10.1016/j.jce.2013.01.006

Bebbington, A. J., Hickey, S., & Mitlin, D. C. (2008). Introduction: Can NGOs make a difference? The challenge of development alternatives. In A. J. Bebbington, S. Hickey, & D. C. Mitlin (Eds), *Can NGOs make a difference? The challenge of development alternatives* (pp. 3–37). London: Zed Books.

Booth, D. (2012). *Development as a collective action problem: Addressing the real challenges of African governance* (Synthesis Report of the Africa Power and Politics Programme). London: Overseas Development Institute. Retrieved March 11, 2014, from http://www.institutions-africa.org/filestream/20121024-appp-synthesis-report-development-as-a-collective-action-problem

Brautigam, D. (2004). The people's budget? Politics, participation and pro-poor policy. *Development Policy Review*, 22(6), 653–668. doi:10.1111/j.1467-7679.2004.00270.x

Brett, E. A. (2003). Participation and accountability in development management. *The Journal of Development Studies*, 40(2), 1–29. doi:10.1080/00220380412331293747

Campbell, C., Cornish, F., Gibbs, A., & Scott, K. (2010). Heeding the push from below: How do social movements persuade the rich to listen to the poor? *Journal of Health Psychology*, 15(7), 962–971. doi:10.1177/1359105310372815

Chatterjee, P. (2004). *The politics of the governed: Reflections on popular politics in most of the world*. New York: Columbia University Press.

Chhotray, V. (2008). Political entrepreneurs or development agents: An NGO's tale of resistance and acquiescence in Madhya Pradesh, India. In A. J. Bebbington, S. Hickey, & D. C. Mitlin (Eds.), *Can NGOs make a difference? The challenge of development alternatives* (pp. 261–278). London: Zed Books.

Cleaver, F. (2005). Rethinking agency, rights and natural resource management. In S. Hickey & D. Mitlin (Eds.), *Rights-based approaches to development: Exploring the potential and pitfalls* (pp. 127–144). Boulder: Kumarian Press.

Corbridge, S., Williams, G., Srivastava, M., & Veron, R. (2005). *Seeing the state: Governance and governmentality in India*. Cambridge: Cambridge University press.

Devarajan, S., Khemani, S., & Walton, M. (2011). *Civil society, public action and accountability in Africa*. Washington, DC: World Bank.

Devereux, S., McGregor, A., & Wheeler, R. S. (2011). Introduction: Social protection for social justice. *IDS Bulletin*, *42*(6), 1–9. doi:10.1111/idsb.2011.42.issue-6

Di John, J., & Putzel, J. (2009). *Political Settlements: Issues Paper*. Governance and Social Development Resource Centre, University of Birmingham.

Evans, P. (1995). *Embedded autonomy: States and industrial transformation*. Princeton, NJ: Princeton University Press.

Evans, P. (2010). *The challenge of 21st century development: building capability-enhancing states*. New York, NY: United Nations Development Programme.

Fox, J. (2004). Empowerment and institutional change: Mapping 'virtuous circles' of state-society interaction. In R. Alsop (Ed.), *Power, rights and poverty: Concepts and connections* (pp. 68–92). Washington, DC: World Bank/DFID.

Fox, J. (2007). *Accountability politics: Power and voice in Rural Mexico*. Oxford: Oxford University Press.

Goldfrank, B. (2007). Lessons from Latin America's experience with participatory budgeting. In A. Shah (Ed.), *Participatory budgeting* (pp. 91–126). Washington, DC: World Bank.

Gough, D., Thomas, J., & Oliver, S. (2013). *Learning from research: Systematic reviews for informing policy decisions*. London: Institute of Education, University College London.

Grindle, M. (2007). Good enough governance revisited. *Development Policy Review*, *25*(5), 553–574.

Harland, C. (2014). Can the expansion of social protection bring about social transformation in African countries? The case of Zambia. *European Journal of Development Research*, *26*, 370–386. doi:10.1057/ejdr.2014.8

Hickey, S. (2009). The politics of protecting the poorest: Moving beyond the 'antipolitics machine'? *Political Geography*, *28*(8), 473–483.

Hickey, S. (2011). The politics of social protection: What do we get from a 'social contract' approach? *Canadian Journal of Development Studies*, *32*(4), 426–438. doi:10.1080/02255189.2011.647447

Hickey, S. (2013). *Thinking about the politics of inclusive development: Towards a relational approach* (ESID Working Paper 1). Manchester: Effective States and Inclusive Development Research Centre.

Hickey, S., & Mohan, G. (2008). The politics of establishing pro-poor accountability: What can poverty reduction strategies achieve? *Review of International Political Economy*, *15*(2), 234–258. doi:10.1080/09692290701869712

Hossain, N. (2007). *The politics of what works: The case of the vulnerable group development programme in Bangladesh*. (CPRC Working Paper 92). Manchester: Institute for Development Policy and Management.

Hossain, N. (2010). Rude accountability: Informal pressures on frontline bureaucrats in Bangladesh. *Development and Change*, *41*(5), 907–928. doi:10.1111/dech.2010.41.issue-5

Houtzager, P. (2003). Introduction: From polycentrism to the polity. In P. Houtzager & M. Moore (Eds.), *Changing paths: International development and the new politics of inclusion* (pp. 1–31). Ann Arbor: University of Michigan Press.

Houtzager, P., & Joshi, A. (2007). Introduction: Contours of a research project and early findings. *IDS Bulletin*, *38*(6), 1–9. doi:10.1111/idsb.2007.38.issue-6

Hubbard, P. (2007). *Putting the power of transparency in context: Information's role in reducing corruption in Uganda's education sector*. Washington: Center for Global Development.

Hyden, G. (1997). Civil society, social capital, and development: Dissection of a complicated discourse. *Studies in Comparative International Development*, *31*(1), 3–30.

Joshi, A. (2010). *Review of impact and effectiveness of transparency and accountability initiatives: Annex 1 service delivery*. Brighton: Institute of Development Studies.

Joshi, A., & Houtzager, P. (2012). Widgets or watchdogs? *Public Management Review*, *14*(2), 145–162. doi:10.1080/14719037.2012.657837

Kabeer, N., Mahmud, S., & Castro, J. G. I. (2010). *NGOs' strategies and the challenge of development and democracy in Bangladesh*. (IDS Working Paper No.343). Brighton: Institute of Development Studies.

Khan, M. (2010). *Political settlements and the governance of growth-enhancing institutions*. London: School of Oriental and African Studies.

King, S. (2015). Political capabilities for democratisation in Uganda: Good governance or popular organisation building? *Third World Quarterly*, *36*(4), 741–757. doi:10.1080/01436597.2015.1024436

Lavalle, A. G., Acharya, A., & Houtzager, P. P. (2005). Beyond comparative anecdotalism: Lessons on civil society and participation from São Paulo, Brazil. *World Development*, *33*(6), 951–964. doi:10.1016/j.worlddev.2004.09.022

Leftwich, A. (2005). Politics in command: Development studies and the rediscovery of social science. *New Political Economy*, *10*(4), 573–607. doi:10.1080/13563460500344542

Levy, B. (2014). *Working with the grain: Integrating governance and growth in development strategies*. Oxford: Oxford University Press.

Mahmud, S. (2007). Spaces for participation in health systems in rural Bangladesh: The experience of stakeholder community groups. In A. Cornwall & V. S. P. Coelho (Eds.), *Rights, resources and the politics of accountability.* London: Zed Books.

Malena, C., & McNeil, M. (2010). Social accountability in Africa: An introduction. In C. Malena & M. McNeil (Eds.), *Demanding good governance: Lessons from social accountability initiatives in Africa* (pp. 1–28). Washington, DC: World Bank.

McGee, R., & Gaventa, J. (2011). *Shifting power? Assessing the impact of transparency and accountability initiatives.* (IDS Working Paper 383). Brighton: Institute of Development Studies.

Menocal, A. R., & Sharma, B. (2008). *Joint evaluation of citizens' voice and accountability* (Synthesis Report). London: Overseas Development Institute/DFID.

Mitlin, D. (2006). *The role of collective action and urban social movements in reducing chronic urban poverty.* (CPRC Working Paper No. 64). London and Manchester: Chronic Poverty Research Centre.

Mitlin, D. (2013). *Politics, informality and clientelism – exploring a pro-poor urban politics.* (ESID Working Paper 34). Manchester: Effective States and Inclusive Development Research Centre.

Moore, M., & Jadhav, V. (2006). The politics and bureaucratics of rural public works: Maharashtra's employment guaranteed scheme. *Journal of Development Studies, 42*(8), 1271–1300. doi:10.1080/00220380600930598

Nelson, J. (2003). Grounds for alliance? Overlapping interests of the poor and not so poor. In P. Houtzager & M. Moore (Eds.), *Changing paths: International development and the politics of inclusion* (pp. 119–138). Ann Arbor: University of Michigan Press.

North, D. C., Walliss, J. J., & Weingast, B. R. (2009). *Violence and social orders: A conceptual framework for interpreting recorded human history.* Cambridge: Cambridge University Press.

Nyamu-Musembi, C. (2006). From protest to proactive action: Building institutional accountability through struggles for the right to housing. In P. Newell & J. Wheeler (Eds.), *Rights, resources and the politics of accountability.* London: Zed Books.

O'Neill, T., Foresti, M., & Hudson, A. (2007). *Evaluation of citizens' voice and accountability: Review of the literature and donor approaches.* London: DFID.

Post, L. A., Raile, A. N. W., & Raile, E. D. (2010). Defining political will. *Politics & Policy, 38*(4), 653–676. doi:10.1111/polp.2010.38.issue-4

Ramkuma, V. (2008). *Our money, our responsibility: A citizens' guide to monitoring government expenditures* (The International Budget Project). Washington, DC: World Bank.

Robinson, M. (2006, June 21–25). *Budget analysis and policy advocacy: The role of nongovernmental public action.* Paper for a panel on 'Negotiating Change and Striving for Justice: The Role of NGPA Actors', 6th CIVICUS World Assembly, Glasgow.

Shankar, S. (2010). *Can social audits count?* (ACARC Working Paper 09). Canberra: Australia South Asia Research Centre. Retrieved February 28, 2014, from https://crawford.anu.edu.au/ acde/ asarc/pdf/papers/2010/WP2010_09.pdf

Skocpol, T. (1992). *Protecting soldiers and mothers.* Cambridge, MA: Belknap Press.

Unsworth, S., & Moore, M. (2010). *An upside down view of governance.* Brighton: Centre for the Future State - Institute of Development Studies.

Vom Hau, M. (2012). *State capacity and inclusive development: new challenges and directions.* (ESID Working Paper 2). Manchester: Effective States and Inclusive Development Research Centre.

de Waal, A. (1996). Social contract and deterring famine: First thoughts. *Disasters, 20*(3), 194–205. doi:10.1111/disa.1996.20.issue-3

World Bank. (2001). *World development report 2000/1: poverty* (World Development Reports). Washington, DC: World Bank.

World Bank. (2004). *World development report 2004: Making services work for poor people* (World Development Reports). Washington, DC: World Bank.

World Bank. (2014). *World development report 2014: Risk and opportunity.* (World Development Reports). Washington, DC: World Bank.

Index

For Product Safety Concerns and Information please contact our EU
representative GPSR@taylorandfrancis.com
Taylor & Francis Verlag GmbH, Kaufingerstraße 24, 80331 München, Germany

www.ingramcontent.com/pod-product-compliance
Ingram Content Group UK Ltd.
Pitfield, Milton Keynes, MK11 3LW, UK
UKHW051831180425
457613UK00022B/1201